Jon Kremer

Bournem[illegible] Go! Go!

Jon Kremer

First published in 2012 by Natula Publications
Natula Ltd. www.natula.co.uk

ISBN 9781897887950

A CIP catalogue record of this book is available from the British Library.

Printed and bound by 4edge Ltd, Hockley, Essex.

For

Abi - *You make my heart sing, you make everything groovy*

And

Daniel – *My Past, Present and Future*

In memory of Mum and Dad

Blanche Kremer (1921 – 2006) and Monty Kremer (1920 – 1995)

You were right: Love is all you need

Contents

Al Stewart and Jon Kremer
rock 'n' roll high above Branksome Park 1964

Foreword

Somewhere in Bournemouth, a long time ago
There once was a second-hand shop
That was filled with guitars, and records and gear
For teens who were ready to bop

And so I went in, and said that I wished
To try out a reverb device
And then plugging in an electric guitar
Gave a tentative twang once or twice

But anyone passing the store on that day
Might have uttered a startled curse
If ever there was an immaculate noise
Then this would be it - in reverse

It emitted a sound from deep underground
An indignant bellow and roar
Combined with a squeal and a rattle and yelp
And still it seemed eager for more

And though I was no longer playing, it showed
A disinclination to stop
'Till finally it gave up the ghost with a hiss
And a boom and a click and a pop

Now, round about then I'd begun to regret
My impulsive desire to try it
So I said after careful and diligent thought
I did not, at this time, want to buy it

Well, this shop was run by a jovial man
And the jovial man had a son
Who was riding the wake of a rock 'n' roll dream
And who said "Call me Jonny, or Jon"

So we talked about all of the records we loved
Never noticing time tick away
And the conversation we started back then
Is still going on to this day

And we went to the clubs, and we heard all the bands
There were 80 in Bournemouth alone
And ran into some Beatles, a Crystal, a Fripp,
Some Manfreds, and later a Stone

I don't think we thought about very much else
You could say we were somewhat obsessed
Do people still think about music that way?
They should; it turned out for the best

I almost forgot about being that young
'Till this book arrived letting me know so
Now clearly it's time to stop talking in rhyme, because
Here it is!...Bournemouth a go go.

Al Stewart
Los Angeles, August 2012

Intro

'Nostalgia is a thing of the past' they say – like, 'It's déjà vu all over again'. Putting amusing truisms to one side, our memories, both shared and personal, are after all is said and done, the essence of the individual self, living always in the present, hoping for our future, while remembering what has gone before.

Ah, what has 'gone before'? Andrew Loog Oldham suggested, perhaps not originally, but accurately: "There are three sides to every story – yours, mine and the truth!"

My music based Bournemouth recollections contained in this book may spark a connection to your mind, full of thoughts of times past: particularly if you are of, or close to, my generation, these words might create a shared walk along the pathways of that so close, yet so far, yesterday.

Some people keep diaries, though not many in that Edwardian sense of diary keeping. But we all, to one degree or another, possess a Boswell to the Dr. Johnson that is our lives: music. Music, songs, records, sounds from radios, stereos, iPods, live shows and TV. This ongoing personal soundtrack appears to work in an almost magically direct, Proustian way, to enable a quality of feeling for bygone days that nothing else can.

The speed of thought, once started by the rhythms and rhymes we hear, transport each and everyone in a 'time machine' to moments, sometimes magic, sometimes not, that are more 'real' and intense, than dusty, diary words can produce.

The 'Jonny Remembers' trip this book hopes to provide, will not follow the chronological, railway line way of historical writing – but rather the random 'lucky dip' way that conversation can allow.

Although these musical memories are reaching you via the 'old school' technology of the printed word and not the very immediate, interaction of the digital world, the aim is that they will join with yours, to produce a few glances over our collective shoulders, to the Bournemouth of the mid-late 20th century.

Why Should We Not?

'Why Should We Not?' This rather un-grammatically posed question begins the recording career of Manfred Mann, and given their connection to the south coast town that is central to this memoir, may serve well as our beginning.

Bournemouth? Why should we have a book based on Rock 'n' Pop reminiscences of a town that would surely not spring to mind in the way Memphis, Nashville, New Orleans or The Beatles' Liverpool might. Or Mozart's Vienna come to that: although the possibility of revisiting this musical heritage has frequently been provided by the Bournemouth Symphony Orchestra.

In fact this very question finds an echo in the opening lines of Alexis Korner's sleeve note for Zoot Money's first LP: "Come to Bournemouth – home of the southern blues; that doesn't sound quite right," he suggested with tongue firmly, if affectionately, in cheek. Introducing *It Should've Been Me*, the Big Roll Band's Columbia Records debut in 1965, he goes on to say that this is the unlikely birthplace of Zoot Money.

It would also have been possible to reference Bournemouth and surrounding area as the 60's home and/or starting point for Al Stewart, Andy Summers, Robert Fripp, Greg Lake and Gordon Haskell, as an indication of the local names that were to reach a worldwide audience in the years ahead. Or even Tony Blackburn, the first voice to be heard on BBC Radio 1.

From this handful of names spring music, songs, records and stories, sufficient to justify answering the initial enquiry with: yes – we should.

So let's begin as we began with Manfred Mann. As suggested in the intro, these words are not intended to be an A-Z of every Bournemouth beat band, gig, venue and record; but reminiscences of moments such as this one, back in the spring of 1963.

As the evolution of 60's beat groups throughout the western world has frequently shown, a prerequisite to an eventual Fame 'n' Fortune journey, however brief or bountiful, includes initially time spent underground. Underground because more often than not, the hot, crowded, smoke filled clubs they performed in were in cellars, basements, or the like. Liverpool's Mathew Street had its Cavern and Bournemouth's Holdenhurst Road: Le Disque a Go Go.

Situated at No.9, underneath a fruit and veg shop, Le Disque opened in early 1963 under the astute management of Alan Azern and his partner Tony Silvestro. It had been previously known as the Downstairs Club, run by Jerry Stooks as a jazz club.

This perfectly timed transformation coincided with a countrywide move from jazz venues to R 'n' B clubs. The policy of Le Disque was to present live music purveyed by not only local groups, but those usually available only to patrons of London's Marquee and Flamingo clubs. Alan's success in achieving this aim was to prove a key element in the early mid 60's Bournemouth scene. First, and perhaps foremost, of the many non local groups his club booked, was an embryonic Manfred Mann. Known then as the Mann-Hugg Blues Brothers. In fact the small 'What's On', *Bournemouth Echo* ad, which alerted me to their existence, added to this already rather long band name: featuring Paul Jones.

Scanning the *Echo*, as a Broadstone dwelling 16 year old that late April evening, I was looking to find something to make the trip into town worthwhile. In those pre-driving licence, still bussing it, teenage days, the No.10, Hants and Dorset double-decker, was at least 30 minutes of travel to consider. Spotting this ad, alongside one for Zoot Money's Sands Combo, I reached for the phone and dialled the Wimborne number of my then, as now, close friend Al Stewart.

Already involved with the local group scene as lead guitar with the Trappers, Al swiftly agreed to meet up for the first of our many forays into the realm of Le Disque.

Al and I had first met the previous autumn, of which more (much more!) later. This day's rendezvous was the then relatively new, town centre bus station, situated close by the Lower Pleasure Gardens. Now long gone following a fire, which required a complete rebuild that never came, it evolved firstly into a temporary car park and then what would appear to be a permanent one.

A short walk to the Square, then of course pre-pedestrianisation, a busy roundabout, complete with the charming option of trolley bus transport. Now a decision to be made. Should we lazily hop on a trolley bus for the short haul to the Lansdowne, or take a stroll up Old Christchurch Road? I must admit our usual default position on this would frequently have been the 2d (old pence) bus ride. On this dry, clear skied evening, however we opted to walk and talk. Our chit-chat had already progressed over the past few months to that relaxed level where you are fairly sure your friend will have something interesting to say, and also be pleased to hear your thoughts. Someone overhearing us would probably have heard lots of laughter and talk of records, groups, guitars and girls.

We would certainly have expressed our mutual curiosity regarding both these Blues Brothers and the club. Although frequenting the Pavilion ballroom's *Big Beat Night* on a succession of recent Tuesday evenings, to be regaled by Zoot Money and Tony Blackburn, this would be our initiation into the world of the cellar clubs. And with music provided by a genuine, London based R 'n' B band.

With the full blown UK R 'n' B boom still on the horizon, Bournemouth in keeping with the rest of this green and sceptred isle was still in thrall to early Merseymania. In fact even this was balancing on the cusp from the previous era of Cliff/Shads etc. Zoot Money, to be fair, with his fondness for all things Ray Charles, seemed slightly ahead of this musical curve.

A few hours earlier would have seen us detouring into one or more of Bournemouth's various record shops. Or to be accurate: shops within shops. In the early 60s Top 20 record buying took place for the most part in department stores or record outlets aligned with music shops. For example in the town centre our Lansdowne walk would have taken us past W.H. Smiths, J.J. Allens, Beales and nearby Minns Music, all purveyors of 45s and LPs. Perhaps the most significant in many ways was to be found on a corner opposite Horseshoe Common: Bourne Radio.

But as at that time of the day, they were all closed, we stopped for a coffee in the El Cabala. This was situated on Old Christchurch Road, just before Bourne Radio and opposite the Calypso and 81 Club.

Coffee bars: one of those nationwide flashpoints of change, alongside Rock 'n' Roll, Teddy Boys and Commercial TV that erupted on the mid 50's demarcation line between the black and white before and the Technicolor time to come. These espresso centrals in that pre-corporate Starbuckian era were actually, at least for teenagers, the cool place to be. Originally they had been deemed an 'eight day wonder', a craze, like Hula Hoops or Davy Crocket hats. By now they had survived to be an accepted part of the townscape. One of course, Paul Lincoln's famous 2i's coffee bar, in Soho's Old Compton Street, had been the launch pad for UK Rock 'n' Roll: its basement hosting the career debuts of Tommy Steele, Cliff Richard, Johnny Kidd, Hank B. Marvin and Jet Harris plus employing Peter Grant as a bouncer; later to be known as the semi-notorious manager for Led Zeppelin.

As we talked and drank atop a pair of the El Cabala's chromed bar stools, music was provided courtesy of a small Juke Box, mounted on the wall behind us. For a sixpenny piece you could soundtrack life to be just as you wanted it to be.

"Guess what," invited Al, "Tony's suggested the Trappers should back him at the Pavilion. He thinks we can solve his problem." Ah yes: Tony Blackburn's 'problem'. This essentially, but not exclusively, was down to money. At the time, Tony the teenage son of a Lower Parkstone based doctor, was engaged in business studies by day, at Bournemouth College and attempting to fulfil his desire to be the South Coast's Cliff Richard, by night. Rumour had it that he regularly travelled back and forth to London, to attend the Maurice Berman School of Pop Singing. Yes, it did exist! Helen Shapiro being one of the 'school's' illustrious alumni.

The Pavilion's house band was that of Jan Ralfini, who also ran Tuesday's *Big Beat Night*, featuring Z. Money and T. Blackburn. The problem, as we understood it to be, was Tony received £5 a night, out of which he was required to pay his group The Sabres. This would lead several of the local semi-pro musicians, certainly those au fait with Musician Union rates, to decline the gig. Not so the Trappers!

Recently formed by bass guitarist Pete Ballam from Poole, they featured, alongside Al on lead, Geoff Westwood on rhythm guitar and their very own 'Ringo', Barry on drums. Coincidently another Tony, Tony Barrett was soon to become the group's vocalist.

"I think we'll do it," continued Al. "At least I'll be playing the Pavilion and not just part of the audience."

This shortly came to pass with mixed moments, including Al breaking a couple of his guitar strings and Tony Blackburn suggesting that, perhaps Al and the Trappers' drummer, Barry, were a little loud! Included in the numbers performed that night were Bobby Vee's 'Night Has a Thousand Eyes', Skeeter Davis' 'End of the World' and Gerry and the Pacemakers 'How Do You Do It'.

Another Tuesday, as Al and I imbibed something stronger than coffee, a lager and lime (an unfortunate concoction popular at the time) in the Pavilion's Hampshire Lounge bar, Tony Blackburn approached with a request for the Trapper's lead guitarist. For some reason he was short of a guitarist for at least part of that night: would Al stand in? My ever (musically) confident friend replied yes.

The three of us then made our way to the band room, a small area directly behind the ballroom's stage. Here I watched as the two of them quickly rehearsed a few songs from the Sabre's current set. One of which I recall was Chris Montez's 'Let's Dance'. The odd broken string aside it all went rather well.

The highlight was an interpretation of the Presley hit 'One Night', replete with a gold lamé jacketed Mr. Blackburn lying on his back near the front of the stage in mock ecstasy, to the squealing approval of a handful of girls. This last point I must confess left me with a certain sense of envy of Bournemouth's Cliff at that moment. As indeed I was to experience, watching in the days before turning 17 and my first car, his progression from mini to E-Type, via an MGB.

Before we leave the El Cabala and this conversation, it's worth mentioning Al singing of his Pavilion beat group days, in the title track of the *Melody Maker* 1969 Folk Album of the Year, his 2nd LP, *Love Chronicles*:

> *In the halcyon days of my late adolescence my goal seemed clearly in sight*
> *Playing electric guitar in a beat group, we set the ballrooms alight*
> *Acting it up for the died blonde receptionists who told us we were alright*
> *An ego trip for a teenage superstar on thirty shillings a night*

As we continued on our way up the hill towards Holdenhurst Road, Paul Jones plus Blues Brothers, having somehow managed to manoeuvre Manfred's Hammond organ down the steep Le Disque stairs, to reach a tiny stage, were already in full *mojo working* swing.

Entering the club we first encountered Alan Azern taking the entrance money quickly followed by his bouncer, Frank, who seemed to us to possess shoulders almost as wide as the narrow corridor which led, right then left, to a flight of stairs. Opposite these a door opened on to the rear of the building and a car parking area, accessible from Lansdowne Road, where the group had left their van. Before reaching the bottom of the stairs an aural wave of alto sax/harmonica led 12-bar blues surrounded our ears, followed closely by the sight of twenty to thirty people gathered around a small stage directly ahead. Perhaps you were one of them? A few couples were dancing in a pre-mod variation on the shake – but more were watching a line up that wasn't even close to the standard pop/beat group template of two electric guitars, bass guitar and drums. Moving through the dancers for a better view we exchanged glances: this band didn't possess a single guitar!

At that moment Mike Vickers, who was soon to become the Manfreds' guitarist was playing alto sax, alongside him Dave Richmond on double bass, just behind them on drums: Mike Hugg. Manfred Lubowitz was seated behind his Hammond, his back to a wall, sideways on to the right of the stage. Centre front, harmonica in hand stood vocalist Paul Jones.

A Hoochie Coochie Man or two later, we edged back through the audience towards the rear of the Disque, to find a small coffee bar and a few seats. We glimpsed in the club's smoky half light some familiar faces: one belonging to Chris 'Fergie' Ferguson, a Zoot Money drummer, one day to record with Bournemouth band the Nite People. The half-shouted conversations quickly reached a simple, but accurate, conclusion i.e. the Mann-Hugg Blues Brothers were a) terrific and b) going places.

The latter was proven a mere 12 months down the line as Manfred Mann, courtesy of Ellie Greenwich's 'Do Wah Diddy Diddy' reached No.1 in both the UK and America.

Before this leap from obscurity to pop fame could be achieved several steps had to be taken: first, of course, a recording contact. It happened around this time when under the management direction of Ken Pitt, later to be David Bowie's manager. After a few auditions for Decca, Pye and EMI they signed with EMI's HMV label.

Concurrent with this was step number two: a name change. Obviously something shorter, catchier and more commercial was required. Although not an immediately popular choice with the group, their designated producer, John Burgess's suggestion of using a slight variation on Manfred's stage/journalism name of Manfred Manne was accepted.

The year before, Manfred Lubowitz, not long after arriving in England following his departure from South Africa in part due to his distaste for apartheid, had been contributing to *Jazz News*, using the name Manfred Manne. The Lubowitz had been replaced with Manne in homage to American jazz drummer Shelly Manne.

Continuing the evolution from jazz-blues club band to Top Ten beat group, the noticeable lack of a guitar would have to be rectified. Here the multitalented, Southampton born, Mike Vickers stepped forward, having been persuaded to set aside his first choice instruments: alto sax and flute.

The first time he performed in Bournemouth with his newly acquired semi-acoustic Gibson, his unsurprisingly tentative playing was commented on by two well meaning, but slightly critical, teenagers near the front of the stage. Overhearing this, Manfred leant into his mike and sardonically announced that "The remarks of the two 'Professional Gentleman' to my left were not helpful!" Al and I didn't know if we should be pleased or embarrassed – knowing our egos we were probably pleased!

Early the following year the transformation to a *Ready Steady Go!* friendly image was completed when jazz enthusiast Dave Richmond left the group, by mutual agreement, to be replaced by electric bass guitar playing Tom McGuiness.

During the months following that initial visit I returned frequently to be entertained in Bournemouth's premier live music venue: often with Al, sometimes accompanied by girls; or more often meeting them in Le Disque. Al's group the Trappers were soon to play the first of many dates at the club. And Manfred Mann established a weekly Bournemouth residency throughout 1963, drawing ever larger crowds until the few dozen early enthusiasts had grown to hundreds, almost causing the walls of this relatively small club to expand!

The centre of attention for many Manfred Mann enthusiasts in those early days was the man Manfred himself. The natural focus should have been, and was soon to become, the vocalist; but as several of the numbers in their repertoire were instrumentals like Cannonball Adderley's 'Sack O'Woe' and their own 'Why Should We Not', Paul Jones was frequently performing as one of the musicians. This allowed cool, keyboard playing Manfred to dominate.

And very cool for 1963 indeed was Manfred: with a hint of Jacques Loussier's beard, Hank Marvin's black horn-rims and a laconic hipster's speech patterns. One example which impressed 16 years old me occurred in Holdenhurst Road's Metropole bar. Le Disque in common with many live music clubs of the day did not hold a licence to serve alcohol, therefore during breaks in the sessions both band members and more than a few of their audience would decamp to the Metropole directly opposite. As the weeks passed by I would frequently find myself in conversation with one or other of the Manfreds. On this occasion chatting with Manfred and a couple of girls, he repeatedly referred to one of them as 'man' – something I'd previously only heard successfully said to a woman in American movies!

One of these mid-session breaks caused Al much amusement, as he observed my failed attempt to persuade an attractive dark haired girl called Freddie to join me for a drink over the way. "Thanks, but no," she politely declined. Moments later her response to Paul Jones's casual invitation: "Coming over to the Metropole?" was an enthusiastic, "Oh yes!" To be fair this was after all, the soon to be *Top of the Pops* starring guy, who only the year before had turned down his friend Brian Jones's offer to sing with his newly formed Rollin' Stones group – and I was, of course, only me.

The Stones had originally been given the 'g-less' adjective: Rollin', in honour of the Muddy Waters blues song 'Rollin' Stone'. As I've mentioned the Manfreds did perform, along with a handful of their contemporaries on the fledgling R 'n' B scene, several songs created by 1950's blues artists; but they were also heavily into jazzy instrumentals, a highlight in their Bournemouth days being 'Why Should We Not'. This evocative, percussive, Mann-Hugg original was to be their first single for HMV, c/w an instrumental version of 'Frère Jacques': 'Brother Jack'.

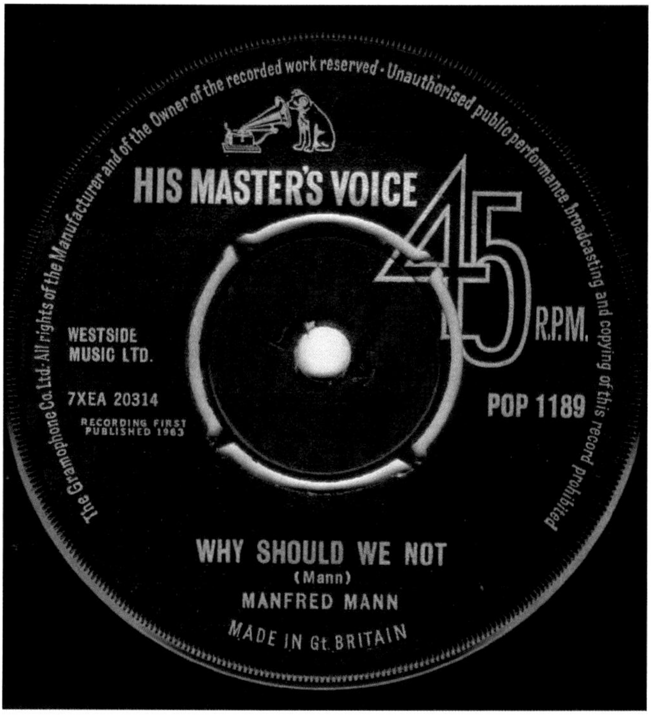

Manfred Mann's first single 1963

Now where as I, and perhaps you, loved this record, only a very small number of 'pop-pickers' actually bought it. My copy was purchased from Bourne Radio and of course I still have it. But, and it's quite a big but, how did they ever believe a cool instrumental would launch an unknown group into the charts? After all Top Ten jazzy instrumental records were always a rarity, and in recent years, excluding the lightweight ersatz New Orleans efforts of Bilk and Ball, were limited to 1961's remarkable Brubeck Quartet's 'Take Five'. In fact 1961, following on from 1960's golden year of electric guitar hits, was a high-water mark for instrumental records in the UK Top 30 provided by, among others, the Shadows, Duane Eddy, the Fireballs, the Ramrods, and Rhet Stoller.

Knowing the band and their producer had decided on 'Why Should We Not' for the first single, Al and I, with what was to become an increasingly needed armour of bravado, decided to approach them with our 'idea' on how to improve this Hit Parade doomed record into something with at least a chance. Al who had been writing songs and poetry, alongside twanging a guitar, as a defence against boarding school life, concocted a set of lyrics for 'Why Should We Not'.

As the next Disque opportunity presented itself we gave Manfred, the man, the dubious benefit of our 'idea'. Al handed him a piece of note paper: Manfred with slight hesitance accepted it, perused it, and returned it with – "No thanks, I think we'll keep it instrumental." Not a surprise really when I recall the opening line: *'Why should we not, while the flames of passion run hot'.*

As we all know by the time electric guitarist Al had developed into singer-songwriter Al, the quality of his lyrics had improved exponentially. Fast forward to the mid 70s and we find Manfred (+ Earthband) was to eventually record an Al Stewart song: 'Nostradamus'.

Their second tilt at the charts came a few months later; this attempt with lyrics: 'Cock-A-Hoop' c/w 'Now You're Needing Me'. The A-side had a vocal that in a slightly risqué – slightly humorous refrain outlined the possibilities available to the opposite sex when the group were in town: *'Look out you chicks and grown up hens it's in your town / it's called Manfred Mann and it runs around!'*

Manfred Mann with two of the Crystals at an all night Le Disque a Go Go party

Still no chart action. That would have to wait for the third single: '5-4-3-2-1'. Released in January 1964, resulting from a commission to write a new intro for Rediffusion's in-crowd TV show *Ready Steady Go!* This time they hit the mod pop-art target perfectly. The combination of weekly television exposure and a very catchy countdown theme made it a Top 10 cert.

This also meant the moment had now been reached to say au revoir to the club scene and hello 'package tours'. The last Le Disque date was covered by the *Bournemouth Times* and included a photo of the band with a few others, including myself. Standing next to me was Tony Arnold, well known on the local music scene and one day to open Arny's Shack, a recording studio in Lower Parkstone. It was here, in September 1981, the by then world famous Bournemouth guitar maestros, Andy Summers and Robert Fripp, recorded part of their *I Advance Masked* LP.

Keenly anticipating the sight of my first newsprint photo, I opened the following week's issue of the *Bournemouth Times* only to find an O.K. picture of the Manfreds and T. Arnold, with me caught in an un-posed, flashlight moment that resembled an image slightly reminiscent of Edvard Munch's picture The Scream. Ah well – not one for the photo album.

Before leaving this tale of Manfred Mann's Bournemouth beginnings, there was a coda. In February 1964 they returned, this time to play the Winter Gardens, with The Crystals and The Rockin' Berries. After the gig Alan Azern hosted an all night party at his club. I was there, as was Al, Zoot Money, Alex Harvey and best of all, from my point of view, a couple of Phil Spector's Crystals.

Around 4.00 a.m. after watching the Manfreds jamming with Alex Harvey and Zoot Money, and enjoying a quantity of free beer, Al and I somehow managed to get back to The Branksome Park flat, that my parents and I had moved to just before Christmas 1963. Al finally making it to his Canford Bottom, Wimborne, home around 3 o'clock that afternoon

"Now would be a good time!" exclaimed Avon when calling for instant teleportation in *Blake's 7*. Perhaps now might be a good time to take a sideways step and for me to tell how I came to a Bournemouth-based life infused with the fun and fantasy delivered by plastic records, charismatic performers and guitars, songs, sun and sea.

Backbeat

I was born in 1947, at the height of the post WW2 baby boom, in a pre-Wombles' Wimbledon. The extra high 'Bulge Years' birth rate following the end of the war in the late 1940s, resulted in a correspondingly high demographic as my generation (along with P. Townshend's) reached teenagedom in the 1960s.

My 'real' beginning could fairly be said to be 5 years earlier, courtesy of a musical moment.

Jealousy is not an emotion to recommend: however 'Jealousy' the Jacob Gade composed tango is something else again. As the Hammersmith Palais band played this tune, in the late autumn of 1942, a young Hampshire Regiment Sgt. asked a slightly younger lady civil servant if she would care to dance. As they danced along with hundreds of other couples enjoying a brief respite from war-time London, my future parents made that rare and instant spark that lasts forever – fortunately for me!

A date swiftly followed to see the box office hit movie *Eagle Squadron*. Soon after this they decided in a 'carpe diem' moment, not uncommon in those dangerous days, to marry. Initially their whirlwind romance was to reach that special occasion on Valentines Day 1943. However General Montgomery had other plans, resulting in my dad-to-be heading for North Africa and the 8th Army before the end of 1942. Given the uncertainty of the ongoing conflict many couples would probably have postponed the wedding: Blanche and Monty chose to bring it forward!

They married on the 3rd of December 1942. With no time for a honeymoon, the new bride's husband departed. They were not to meet again for over three years.

Having communicated via letters and photos, at last, sometime after Victory in Europe was declared in May 1945, they were reunited in Antwerp. Having survived the London Blitz and military campaigns in Italy and Africa, where Monty suffered shrapnel wounds, they could finally begin their life together with a Bournemouth honeymoon in 1946.

Blanche knew and liked Bournemouth from time spent in England's premier seaside town during a prolonged period of convalescence in the 1930s following a serious bout of diphtheria as a thirteen year old. The town, along with nearby Sandbanks, soon became their favourite part of England.

My childhood years were spent on the Surrey/London border in Morden.

The suburban 1950s providing a safe and secure environment to view the gathering winds of change that would shape the social and cultural landscape throughout the following decade.

Morden incidentally was the scene of the first Rolling Stones' recordings in March 1963, when Brian Jones led the pre-Andrew Oldham group into R.G. Jones Studio to demo a few songs.

From 1950 onwards, I would regularly make the 100 mile journey south to Bournemouth with my mum and dad once or twice a year, for either a week or two holiday, or just a Whitsun Bank Holiday weekend. We always drove as my dad owned a succession of various cars: the most favoured being Standard Vanguards. The travelling time on those pre-motorway roads was around three and half hours.

The theme music for a 1953 BBC radio drama, *The Little Red Monkey*, takes pride of place as my earliest musical memory. This evocative and eerie tune featured a theremin: an early example of an electronic musical instrument and named after its Russian inventor. In 1966 Beach Boy Brian Wilson featured one to great effect in his production of 'Good Vibrations'.

Although, according to family folklore, my earliest reaction to the sound of music occurred as an eighteen months old toddler, waving frantically to the sound of the *Dick Barton* theme: 'The Devil's Gallop!' This could be heard 5 times a week on the Light Programme in the early evening slot, until vacating to make way for *The Archers.*

Next came harmonica maestro Larry Adler's title music for the vintage car movie *Genevieve.* As a child I loved the film, still do actually, and felt added emotional links to it as my mother had known the Adler family before the war, and in the mid 50s, we'd drive down to Brighton each November on the same day as the 'Old Crocks' rally featured in *Genevieve.*

The only radio station that counted in the mid 1950s was Radio Luxembourg: 208 on the Medium Wave, a commercial forerunner of the 60's pirate radio stations. I became aware of it just prior to its switch into full-on pop programming, as an avid schoolboy listener to its daily early evening broadcasts of *Dan Dare – Pilot of the Future!* Based of course on Frank Hampson's wonderful creation for *The Eagle.*

Even though I grew up with a TV in my family home, going to the cinema was, in that era, far more interesting and imagination stretching. Visits to various local Odeons, Gaumonts and ABC's with my parents were frequent, perhaps being an only child they preferred to take me with them. Two outstanding mid-fifties movie memories were provided by the sci-fi classic *Forbidden Planet*, inspired by Shakespeare's *The Tempest*, featuring Robby, the first friendly robot and *Twenty Thousand Leagues Under The Sea*, starring a giant squid!

The movies, Rock 'n' Roll and Bournemouth were to come together for me in 1956. Seeing the Bill Haley *Rock Around The Clock* film in Westover Road made a huge impact. Whilst being slightly anxious, having heard of Teddy Boy 'Riots' at previous screenings up and down the country, and as yet unaware of how relatively safe and corny the Comets' music was, nevertheless they instantly captivated me with their infectious country rock boogie.

Having been around for many years as Bill Haley and The Saddle Tramps, with a name change, a hit record with their version of Joe Turner's 'Shake, Rattle and Roll', and then featuring in the soundtrack of the seminal flick *Blackboard Jungle*, they suddenly found themselves, with both the record and film of *Rock Around The Clock*, to be briefly at the epicentre of the first musical culture shock of the Rock 'n' Roll explosion. Soon swept aside by Elvis Presley's astonishing fusion of white country/black R 'n' B music coupled with a James Dean rebel image, Bill Haley still possessed his immutable 15 minutes of Rock 'n' Roll fame.

By the time I saw him and his Comets for real at the Winter Gardens 8 years later, I was a teenager with considerably more musical savoir faire and he was a cheerful, chubby, kiss-curled chap long past the hysteria generated by that movie. And yet – he was still BILL HALEY! And I was still delighted to see him perform live.

As the 1950s picked up speed and headed towards the sunny uplands of the 1960s, I found myself via an 11+ victory sharing a grammar school with a future Prime Minister. Four years older than me, John Major was still affected by the same ethos, standards and indifference. On becoming Chancellor of the Exchequer he expressed views on Wimbledon's Rutlish Grammar School that I could easily recognise. Formerly a public school, in 1958 it offered a mixture of grammar school qualities and opportunities, yesteryear atmosphere and a distinct lack of empathy that left some pupils, including me, feeling almost invisible.

Fortunately as adolescence beckoned I found a backing track to schooldays that enabled me to continue formal education until the first chance I had to jump ship. Yes – polyvinyl chloride – in the form of 7" records!

Here I must mention the famous Generation Gap cliché. Whilst it was very real for many of my generation, for me, in at least one important instance it didn't exist. Those first records that were to lead to a life of collecting and dealing were Buddy Holly and his Crickets from the U.S. of

A. combined with England's Anthony Newley. Significantly they were to come my way, not by pocket money purchase, but as a gift from my dad, whose own record collection of 78s & 45s, had already introduced me to folk blues innovators Sonny Terry and Brownie McGee, Santo and Johnny's 'Sleepwalk', Earl Bostic's 'Flamingo', Reinhardt and Grappelli, and of course The Comets.

In his late teens, just before WW2, he and his friend Rick von Ericisson spent a summer going from one small French town or village to another, singing and playing guitars for fun and a handful of francs. These amateur wandering minstrel activities pre-dated the Donovanesque troubadours of my time by nearly 30 years! He even managed to see the coolest act on the continent: Django Reinhardt and Stéphane Grappelli's recently formed band The Hot Club of France. Once during the war he sang a song broadcast from Italy on Radio Roma.

But after 1945 the realities and responsibilities of married life required 'proper employment'. He joined the then relatively new and expanding UK end of the American Hoover company, eventually becoming a South London area manager. The firm's Middlesex H.Q. boasted an Art Deco building so splendid that Elvis Costello was to sing its praises on 'Hoover Factory', a track on his *Taking Liberties* LP.

Along with other companies of this size Hoovers had a social side involving dances etc. for their employees and partners. My dad became involved with organising these events and occasionally performing at them. It was not unusual for me to find our small suburban house filled with drums, guitars and sheet music, whilst rehearsals took place.

So, for me, it's not hard to see why the Generation Gap faded away.

By the mid 50s however, Monty took the bold step of leaving this established occupation to open a small shop in Wimbledon, buying and selling records, old gramophones and musical instruments. In an early example of marketing synergies he called it Exchange and Mart, possibly the first in the country to connect with the brand name and image of the magazine.

And yes, this became the source of those original singles and, after both family and business had moved to Bournemouth in January 1961, the way I initially earned a living after schooldays had ended.

Well that's enough about the pre-teen me: now we're in 1960's Bournemouth let's pause for a moment and consider both Bournemouth and that famous decade.

How long is a decade? Obviously 10 years. But sometimes the appellation 'decade' circumscribes an era too closely: it could more usefully be defined for the 1960s as either a longer or shorter period of years.

Looked at one way, musically, the 60s possibly started in the mid 1950s and finished in the early 70s: from an innocent Rock 'n' Roll led youth culture to a post modern 'pop devouring itself' time of ersatz knowingness.

Measured another way the fast moving changes in music, movies, fashion, photography and art, might be said to have kicked off around October 62 with 'Love Me Do', *Dr. No*, Carnaby Street, Bailey and Shrimpton, Hockney and Blake – and run headlong in an almost constant whirl of newness till late 67: the demise of Brian Epstein heralding the eventual Beatles break up, the Oldham Stones giving way to the Glimmer Twins Stones, Antonioni's *Blow Up*, sharp mods meld into fuzzy hippies, the red hot excitement of Peter Blake's *Sgt. Pepper* design cools down to the enigmatic minimalism of Richard Hamilton's *White Album* cover.

Perhaps 61: President Kennedy vows to put a man on the moon – to 69 when America's Apollo astronauts, Armstrong and Aldrin, do just that. A Sixties moment like no other in the four decades that have since passed by; or for that matter the hundreds of decades of human civilisation that preceded it.

Politically, a youth inspiring dawn began with the U.S. Presidential election of J.F.K. in November 1960, to sadly conclude, three assassinations later in 1968 with the Californian ending to his brother Bobby's momentous challenge for the White House, following the death of Martin Luther King earlier that year.

The 60's shock waves that initiated the cherished, and now expected, freedoms of expression for the individual, surfing on the crests of those magical songs and records, are still reverberating around the planet to this day.

Bournemouth was, along with almost everywhere and everyone, touched by that swift moving period of changes. As yet to perform the geographical conjuring trick of travelling from Hampshire to Dorset in 1974, the town replete with 'golden beaches', chines, pleasure gardens, floribunda and trolley buses, was quietly going about its century old business when Beatlemania arrived.

Before reminding ourselves, perhaps a surprise for some people, that Bournemouth played a far from inconsiderable part in the Beatles meteoric progress from Liverpool/Hamburg semi-obscurity to world wide fame and fortune, I need to reminisce about September 1962.

Simple Twist Of Fate

I sometimes wonder what might have been if the relative 'discoveries' of Lord Cardigan and the Earl of Sandwich had been reversed. In a parallel universe we could be eating cardigans and wearing sandwiches!

Or if the building in 1812 of Lewis Tregonwell's family house at the mouth of the River Bourne, had lead eventually to the expanding development of 21st century Tregonwellville, instead of Bournemouth?

Or reflecting on a personally more significant timeline, what the consequential changes would have been if, having spotted a Bird reverberation unit, from his perch on the top deck of a bus transporting him from Canford Bottom to Westbourne in search of a Watkins Copy Cat, Al Stewart hadn't hopped off of it and into my dad's Moordown shop!

The day following his 17th birthday found Alastair Ian Stewart doing just that during one of the few remaining days of his fast fading school summer holidays.

I looked up, as a new pathway through my future world began to open with his smiling enquiry, delivered in what seemed to sound like a slightly American accent: "How much and what is that?" – indicating the guitar effects unit in the window. Having left Poole Grammar and my schooldays behind a few months ago in April, I was 'helping' in the shop whilst trying to work out what comes next. "That," I replied, "is a Bird reverb and it's £15."

Still beaming his distinctive smile, the result of a minor boarding school mishap having removed a small semi-circle from the centre of two top row teeth, he said, "I'd like to try it out." Pausing momentarily to survey the dozen or so guitars currently on display, Al continued, "I think I'll pop home for my guitar first, see you soon." My dad and I exchanged glances: the unspoken thought, "Well that's the last we'll see of you." Wrong!

A couple of hours later, having bussed back to his cottage home near Wimborne, and collected not only his electric guitar but also a small practice amplifier, he returned, General MacArthur style, still smiling.

The next hour of that early autumn day in 1962 established the foundations for a close friendship that the *Bournemouth Echo* would one day describe as having lasted over 40 years and 2 continents. We began a 'conversation' which, like Bob Dylan's *Everlasting Tour*, still continues.

The reverb unit, incidentally manufactured in nearby Poole, was duly plugged in, along with Al's Watkins Westminster amp and his cherry red Hofner Colorama guitar. As the lead guitarist of Wycliffe College's

Snowballs opened up with a couple of Marvinesque riffs, plus a couple of his own, I came to a swift decision: maybe he could show me how to do this. I possessed a black, solid body Futurama guitar, a small Scala amplifier, and so far a singular lack of talent. To be fair I could knock off a few so-so attempts at the Shadows' 'Apache', 'FBI' and 'Man of Mystery', thanks to my dad's patient efforts to pass on some of his own skills.

As Al plucked away we chatted and clicked. He was returning in a week or so to complete one last term at his school in Gloucestershire, before to their mutual satisfaction his incarceration, as Al saw it, ended.

In an attempt to convince him of the reverb unit's (non-existent) qualities I plugged in one of the shop's guitars and played my version of Nero and The Gladiators take on Grieg's 'In the Hall of the Mountain King'. Al was impressed by neither my playing nor the so-so reverberations emanating from the box of valves in front of us. While choosing not to buy it, instead acquiring on another day, a superior Copy Cat echo unit from Don Strikes' Westbourne music shop, he did however quickly accept our offer of a lift back to Canford Bottom, as by now it was closing time and we lived not too far from there in Broadstone.

Having loaded Al's gear into the boot, as my dad drove, Al and I continued to chat; deciding to get together soon, giving me at least the opportunity to learn a few new chords. Before reaching his home my instant friend had informed me that he also wrote songs: maybe I'd like to hear them? He then revealed that, through a tenuous family friend link, he felt confident that Cliff Richard could be his possible conduit to writing a hit! Bizarrely, however dubious I thought this ambitious statement to be, part of me felt that this unlikely character would one day become a hit songwriter, and yes, I did want to hear his songs.

Al's family home was a thatched cottage of considerable charm located at the end of a short secluded drive. Having unloaded amp and guitar, said hello to his mother Joan, and accepted an invitation to visit them shortly, I departed with Al's words following me down their driveway: "Remember to bring your guitar."

On the short journey home I wondered why this new acquaintance seemed significant and why intuitively I believed his certainty that he could write a hit. Over the following years, including many, when it seemed to us both that only we imagined his songs would make it, my thoughts have returned to that September day and the curious fact, that although we had to wait till the next decade, it came true.

Incidentally something Al, rather surprisingly, took musically and perhaps nostalgically from that first meeting was a lasting affection for 'In the Hall of the Mountain King': over 45 years later, as many of his concert going fans around the world would recognise, Al, at the drop of the proverbial hat is likely to interrupt his set list with a quick blast of electric Grieg, delivered with an enigmatic smile.

The last word on our friendship starting on that far off Bournemouth day is perhaps best left to Al Stewart's biographer Neville Judd. Writing in *Al Stewart: The True Life Adventures of a Folk Rock Troubadour*, his in depth study of Al's life and music, published in 2002, he remarks: "Up until this time Al had led what amounted to a very directionless existence. He was unhappy at school, separated from the evolving world of Rock 'n' Roll by what he saw as virtually incarceration at Wycliffe and felt completely unfulfilled. However, this was about to change. It all started with a bus ride one afternoon into Bournemouth.

At this point in his life Al had felt that life had been pretty hard. His time at Wycliffe had been a disaster and he was looking for a way out. He was about to find it. On September 6th, the day after Al's seventeenth birthday, fate intervened on his behalf and he met Jonny Kremer."

"What do you think?" Good question: what were my thoughts? Open in front of me was a lined exercise book, page after page filled with Al's original songs and poetry, created in the main during his 15th and 16th years. They both confused and intrigued me in equal measure. There seemed no way 'Kolei Valley' for example was about to set the pop charts of that pre Beatles/post R 'n' R interlude, on fire. But still that curious instinct prevailed: they were different – they had something. They certainly needed something, and 18 months later in the form of a newly emerging New York talent calling himself Bob Dylan, Al's song writing acquired the catalyst it had been reaching out for.

Replying with polite sincerity I said, "I like that one," indicating a folk-blues with *Hammer Horror* lyrics: 'Stagnation Blues'. Al seemed pleased.

Outside the early autumn twilight had dimmed into dusk, illuminated by the cottage lights shining across the short pathway that led to the small garden hut inhabited by the two of us, plus his guitar, amp, records and books.

A few days had passed and this was the first of several sessions, at either Al's home or mine, that were squeezed into the limited time available before he returned, for one last term, to his bête noire boarding school.

This hut had been made available to my new friend as a kind of 'den': a good move by Joan and Ba (Al's step father) as the tiny bedroom Al occupied in the cottage's roof, complete with traditional low ceiling and lack of 'cat swinging space', was adequate only for a few essentials. Another, and far from inconsequential factor: his loud electric guitar efforts were no longer 'in house'.

It would seem obvious, given as we now know that Al eventually became a celebrated and unique singer-songwriter, to concentrate on these early song writing attempts: but they were and would remain for some time, very much secondary to being a fledgling pop musician.

The sonic landscape we dwelt in during that period as teenage UK males was still possible to sum up in two words: The Shadows. Al, like myself, and all of our contemporaries who possessed an electric guitar, wanted to be Hank B. Marvin.

Three years into a post 'Apache' run of super-hit instrumental singles, The Shadows, led by horn-rimmed Brian Rankin (H.B. Marvin) and his fellow Newcastle ex-pat Bruce Welch, continued to be – vocalist Cliff not withstanding – the coolest act on the scene. Although England was only a few weeks away from the 60's true beginning with the release of a Liverpool combo's first Parlophone record, at that moment it was still this Soho coffee bar originating group that we all wished to be.

Earlier that evening Al's garden hideaway had reverberated to a more than passable pastiche of the Shads: his new Copycat echo unit giving him a chance to emulate the more expensively equipped group's 'Man of Mystery' and 'Frightened City'. They of course did have a slight edge with Stratocaster, Telecaster, Precision bass, Binson echo and Vox AC30 amps.

I'd first seen The Shadows backing Cliff Richard on TV in 1959. Watching the rock highlight of the week, ITV's *Oh Boy* one Saturday evening, my 'Generation Gap' free father pointed to the right of the Ferranti screen saying, "He's the one that makes this," indicating a very young Hank Marvin. The performance that had caught our attention was their version of Johnny Otis's 'Willie and the Hand Jive'. Innovative producer Jack Good, the key man in that period of BritPop, had C.R. centre stage, flanked by Marvin and Welch in a close, screen filling shot. As the vocalist delivered the main lyric the other two had their backs to the audience – then as each pause in the words allowed them to bring the backing chants to the fore, the two guitarists would turn to the camera, with Cliff turning to face away – visually and musically very effective, and obviously memorable.

The following summer they managed, after 3 non-hits (2 as The Drifters), to achieve an exceptional feat at the 4th attempt, to step out of the shadows and into their own brilliant limelight: the 'stepping' being somewhat more than just figurative given their stylish trademark 'Shadows Crossover Step' routine; especially during 'FBI'. Jerry Lordan's tune 'Apache' c/w 'Quartermaster's Stores' hit the top of the charts in July 1960, displacing C.R.'s 'Please Don't Tease'.

Lordan had originally offered 'Apache' to Bert 'Play in a Day' Weedon, who did release his version, but not before the Shads had fortunately taken the decision to make it the 'A' side of their single. A close run thing if the 'Milkman Story' is true. Apparently undecided between the two instrumentals, they played both recordings to Hank's milkman, who perhaps captivated by the opening bongos (played by Cliff), opted for 'Apache'. Good choice: 6 weeks at No.1 in the *New Musical Express*.

My first chance to see this ace group live arrived in early 62 with their performance accompanying Cliff Richard at Bournemouth's Gaumont Theatre, the then recent smash-hit movie and single: *The Young Ones*, ensuring a sold out tour. The audience neatly split between screaming girls (Cliff) and Shads enthusing blokes. Not quite 15 I had somehow managed to acquire 2 tickets, enabling my then girlfriend Ingrid and myself to see them. But only after an enormous amount of logistical planning had overcome the travel/timing obstacles presented by my living in Broadstone and Ingrid in Southbourne. We managed to synchronise bus times, meet up, see the show, then race to catch respective last buses, in time for the following school day.

I saw the group again later that year, this time headlining in their own right at the Winter Gardens.

Ingrid and I had first dated the previous December, seeing *Blue Hawaii* in Westover Road. By 63 she had moved to Scotland. We met only once more, by chance in the summer of that year, in the town centre. She must have wondered what I was raving on about as we briefly exchanged greetings: I'd just seen and met the Beatles that night and everything seemed to be sparkling with electric excitement.

Back in September 62 and Canford Bottom, I'd parked my Futurama guitar alongside Al's superior Hofner, purchased from Don Strike's Westbourne Arcade music emporium: "You should get one of these," he enthused. Noting my desire to improve my guitar playing Al also suggested that I do as he'd done and book a course of tuition with Don. A few months later I did just that; coupled with buying a 3 pick-up variation of the Colorama, another Hofner called a V3 (later known as a Galaxy).

Besides lessons from Don Strike, a professional guitar, banjo and mandolin expert of long standing, my friend was also the beneficiary of the skills and knowledge of a Wimborne guitarist called Bob Fripp. Yes that one: later to be known as Robert of King Crimson fame.

Another exercise book lay nearby Al's slender volume of songs. This I found to be equally interesting. There is possibly no better way of describing the importance of records to us in those days, than by revealing its contents. Not satisfied with the weekly barometer of popular taste provided by the *NME* Top 30, Al would assiduously list the title and performer of each record he played, noting the frequency of plays, and from this info compiled a slowly changing Top 10 of his own. I was very impressed and quickly set about making my own personal record charts.

Alastair, as he was still referred to by his family, duly returned for one last Gloucestershire school term. Staying in touch via a series of letters, many of which would one day be quoted in Neville Judd's fine biography of Al. We met up again in December; just as the infamous 62/63 'coldest winter of the century' was about to begin.

Jon in 1963 with Hofner V3 before listening to Al and putting it back in its case!

Year Of Lightning

There have always been years which seem to shine out in any era: years in which that electrical charge of lightning flashing across the sky illuminates a landscape caught in a moment of fast changing adventure. Sometime those changes of society, art and style arrive with colour and excitement, sometimes not but rather heralding darker wartime days. Sometimes such a year brings a direct and desired conclusion, along with a new, dramatic uncertainty: such as 1945. Six years of World War are over as the Atomic Age begins.

1963 stands out, along with 1967, as one of the 60's 'Lightning Years'. Even in a decade so full of movement and change, these two seem remarkable.

An initial glance back to 1963 reveals a country awakening to the Beatles exhilarating command to Please Please them, shouted from their 2nd single – ending 12 months later with a Beatlemania scream of delight as a nation wants to Hold Their Hand. Along the way the rapid pace of events, both national and worldwide, included the beginning of the end of 13 years of Conservative government, courtesy of Stephen Ward's goodtime girls, Christine Keeler and Mandy Rice Davis; the so-called 'Great Train Robbery' and the assassination of President Kennedy.

All played out, in England at least, to the sights and sounds of Beatlemania. Not to mention the shifting tectonic plates of social/political UK life engendered by the satirical shafts of David Frost's *That Was The Week That Was* and Peter Cook's *Private Eye*, plus his Establishment Club.

Where to begin? Personally, walking the frozen, snow and ice covered Bournemouth streets, one January Saturday morning with Al, checking out the record shops; as new singles tended to be released on Fridays.

The snow had fallen heavily across the country during Boxing Day 1962 and a combination of high winds, sub-zero temperatures and further, sporadic snow falls, resulted in a memorable British winter. There were still exposed pavement corners iced up as late as March before a complete thaw arrived.

That day as I recall we each bought a copy of Jet Harris and Tony Meehan's 'Diamonds'. Just released and soon to be topping the *NME* charts for a six week run. This evidently annoyed their ex Shadows partners Marvin and Welch, as 'Diamonds' composer Jerry Lordan had previously provided them with 2 huge hits: 'Apache' and 'Wonderful Land'. Actually they did release a single of their own version 20 years later.

Alastair Stewart having by now bid a somewhat less than fond farewell to formal education, was enjoying a brief hiatus prior to attempting the impossible feat of travelling two roads at once. No, nothing approaching the quantum physics of *Schrodinger's Cat*; but more prosaically trying to fuse together the necessity of a daytime sales assistant job in Bournemouth's Beales department store with playing electric guitar with the Trappers as night fell.

As the cul-de-sac route of Beales, followed by an equally brief period employed in a Poole office, proved an obvious impediment to being not Alastair, but Al on a starry course to eventual platinum discs, these two roads quickly reduced to one.

As the landmark news events of 63 began to unfold, it's slightly surprising how they were to connect, however tangentially, with Bournemouth. Quite possibly you recall how the Beatles' two visits to the town that year provided key moments for their evolving and amazing story: also Bournemouth's association with the tale of the Great Train Robbery (more of both later). But how did this seaside resort feature, however fleetingly, in the *Profumo Affair*?

A political sex scandal of such intrigue and effect, it has yet to be surpassed in the UK. Even the USA's *Watergate* couldn't produce a stunning leading lady to equal England's Christine Keeler.

Local legend has it that in the spring of that year, the two young women at the centre of a newsprint whirlwind, coupled with pending court appearances, tried to drop out of media attention by staying in a Bournemouth flat for two weeks. They were said to frequent Old Christchurch Road's El Cabala coffee bar but to my chagrin, not at the same time as me!

Miss Keeler did appear, however, in the lyrics of Al's song 'Post World War Two Blues' a track on his 1973 LP, *Past, Present & Future*:

And one day Macmillan was coming downstairs
A voice in the dark caught him unawares
It was Christine Keeler blowing him a kiss
He said "I never believed it could happen like this"

One bonus of Al's brief Beales tenure came in the far from unattractive form of salesgirls. Much to the irritation of the drapery department floor manager, I had taken to dropping in for a chat with Al and the young women working with him on the 2nd floor.

Having fixed a date with two of them, Jeannie and Ginny, you can imagine our surprise on meeting up with them early one evening by the store's staff entrance/exit, to find they were accompanied by a third girl! Fazed only momentarily we set off along Westover Road towards our rendezvous with E. Presley and his then current, and in view of our situation, appropriately titled *Girls!Girls!Girls!* movie. This quintet of two guys, each with an arm around a girl, plus another – described to me by Al as "a spare", soon reached the ABC cinema and its inviting opportunities for dimly lit intimacy.

As 'Return to Sender' serenaded us from the silver screen, and we became more 'familiar' with Jeannie and Ginny, their friend sat with us for a while; when to our amazement she moved across the nearby aisle to a seat alongside a complete stranger and within minutes she and the young man were exchanging kisses etc. too!

Jeannie and Al became, at least for a while that summer, an 'item'; to be referenced by him in his epic song 'Love Chronicles', 6 years later:

The first girl I made love to
It was in a park
The Lower Pleasure Gardens in Bournemouth
In summer soon after dark

Of course there were many various, and potentially more likely places to meet/pick-up/be refused by girls than Beales. Clubs, dance halls and record shops would top the list.

Reading these words today in an era where records shops, as such, are virtually extinct, this might seem unlikely. Likewise in the previous couple of decades when the term 'record shop' basically applied to HMV, Our Price and Virgin Megastore type outlets, primarily stocking CDs, videos, cassettes and eventually DVD's and computer games; in fact almost anything except records, this would also be implausible. But back in the 60s most of the record shops, both the few stand-alone ones and the more abundant retail units within stores were in fact run by young women. Sandie was in charge of Bourne Radio's main outlet in Old Christchurch Road, Anne and Candy ran other branches, Sally King was behind the counter in the town centre's J.J Allen record department. Al and I, not surprisingly, knew them all quite well. By 1964 Sandie in particular proved to be significant and influential.

One of the very best beat bands around town at that time was The Sands

Combo. As I've previously mentioned they had a weekly residency at the Pavilion's *Big Beat Night*, supported each Tuesday evening by Tony Blackburn and his merry men. The Sands Combo evolved into the better known Zoot Money's Big Roll Band, and eventually the psychedelic Dantalian's Chariot. The latter two iterations being recording acts.

Prior to this in 1964 Decca Records released 'The Uncle Willie' c/w 'Zoot's Suite' credited to just Zoot Money; though it featured members of the original Bournemouth group, including for the first time on record: Andy Summers.

The topside of this great, non hit, single was a *Can I Get a Witness* style dance tune, with a B-side featuring a cool jazz/blues guitar solo from Policeman Sting's future ace guitarist.

But he was not the guitarist to be seen in mid 63 if you had wandered along the Pavilion's curving corridors, circumventing the theatre's auditorium, passed by the Hampshire Lounge bar, made your way into the frequently packed out dance hall, pushed through the twisting, shaking, occasionally still jiving couples, and reached a position in front of the stage. There, standing to the right of the stage, would have been 'Rocky' Collis on lead guitar, with alongside him on Fender Precision bass, Roger Bone and Nick Newell on sax; and to their right on piano, vocalist George Bruno Money, performing a jazzy fusion of R 'n' B tinged Rock 'n' Roll, heavily influenced by Ray Charles and Jerry Lee Lewis.

Each performance would initially start without the band's vocalist. Kicking off with a steady riff-free rock beat, they would attract the Pavilion's dancers, focusing attention on the bandstand. Only then would an exuberant Z. Money appear, jumping over the drum kit at the rear of the stage.

I recall one night when he added to this entrance performance a small surprise for his guitarist 'Rocky'. Announcing this to be his, (Rocky's) birthday, to the amusement of the crowd, Bournemouth's Clown Prince thrust a birthday cake/custard pie into the amazed musician's face!

As the media spotlight beamed down on the new wave of Merseybeat excitement it quickly generated an exponential growth in teen and twenty beat groups across the land, Bournemouth being far from an exception, already having a fair number of semi-pro bands on the go. One night that summer provided an unusual opportunity to catch a bunch of them in one go.

It what could be described as *Big Beat Night* on steroids the Pavilion promoted an event entitled the *Band Box Ball* featuring a long list of Bournemouth and Poole based groups including: Zoot Money's Sands

Combo, The Dowland Brothers and The Soundtracks, Tony, Howard and the Dictators, Teddy Valour and The Valiants, Big Ben and The Chimes plus many more.

During The Sands Combo's set they were joined by a 19 year old Andy Summers. I was already aware of his local reputation, but as I stood near the bandstand it was hard not to be impressed by the mature, confident jazzy tones emitting from his large, relative to his stature, Gibson electric/acoustic guitar. The next time I saw the man who would, one day in another decade, perform to Police fans in their tens of thousands, he was playing, essentially for himself, to an audience of two: me and Al.

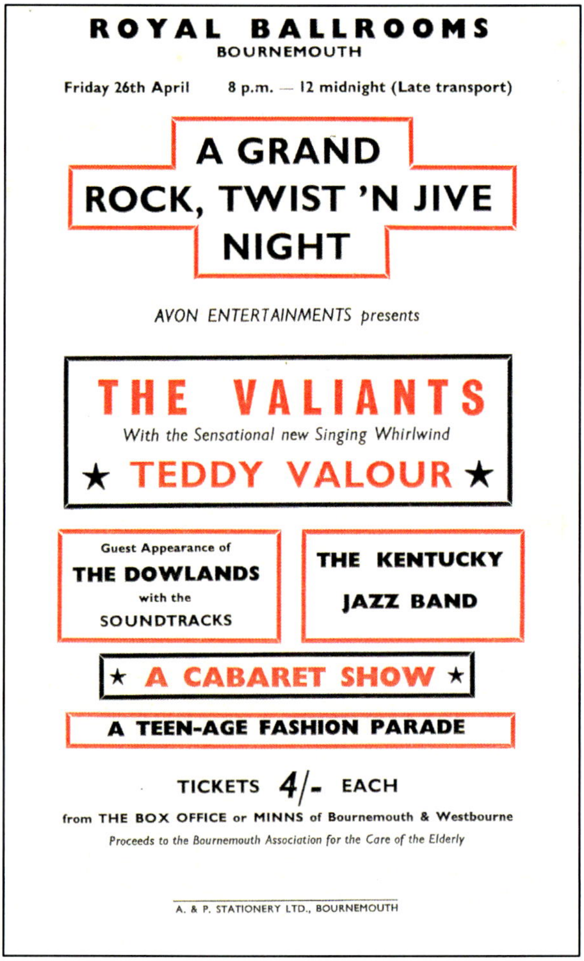

Avon Entertainments Presents.
Tickets available from Minns Music

Minns Music, located in Gervis Place opposite Beales, displayed an extensive range of musical instruments on the ground floor of their town centre shop, including high end guitars made by Fender, Gibson, Gretsch, Guild and Epiphone, alongside pianos and drums. The basement housed a record department replete with the standard 'listening booths' of the day.

Al and I, as you might easily imagine, were often to be found frequenting Minns. Late one afternoon we were chatting to Andy Summers and Dave, Minns Music's manager. As closing time arrived and the shop emptied, the plate glass entry door was locked and the musically versatile Dave embarked on an extensive jam session playing a variety of instruments to accompany the electric guitar improvisations flowing from Andy S. Having parked ourselves in a convenient position near the front of the shop we were obviously more than happy to provide a mini audience.

Jumping briefly into the future to the early 1990s I had another opportunity to be entertained as part of a mini-audience, this time an audience of three, including my wife Abi and Al's fiancée Kris. The performers were Al and Tori Amos, backstage at London's Royal Festival Hall. Al was headlining a sell out concert there that night and Tori was to accompany him on piano.

A pre-concert musical moment presented itself primarily as they needed to rehearse 'Year of the Cat'. Abi and I were meeting this uniquely talented, effervescent, American singer/writer/musician, for the first time, just as she was about to release her debut album, the smash hit *Little Earthquakes*. Prior to this Tori, who'd contributed vocals to Al's *Last Days of the Century* LP and combined with him in writing a couple of songs, had been sharing a flat in London with Kris, while composing the songs for her first solo record.

I remember her amusement as Al and I exchanged the kind of irreverent banter that those who have known us well across the years were all too familiar with.

Meanwhile back at the *Band Box Ball* the proceedings had been opened by The Dictators with vocalists Tony and Howard. They were a highly competent local pop group who managed to overcome the relative limitations imposed by their mainly Watkins equipment: Rapier guitars and Dominator amps. The group's potential was to be recognised the following year when Oriole Records released their single 'So Long Little Girl'.

By coincidence the area's other record making outfit, The Dowland Brothers, were also on Oriole. Later that night Dave and Gordon Dowland, backed by their group The Soundtracks, performed a knock out version of James Ray's 'If You Gotta Make a Fool of Somebody', involving a back to back 'duelling type' routine featuring their lead and bass guitar players.

The Soundtracks lead guitar then was Gretsch Country Gentlemen playing Alan Barry. Alan was some years later to record with Fields, and also played on a 1970 session for Al to record 'Elvaston Place' the flipside of his CBS single 'The News from Spain'.

Before him Roy Phillips from Parkstone had been the group's guitarist. Later switching to keyboards and vocals with Philips Records trio, The Peddlers, and huge Las Vegas based success.

Mike and Pete Giles provided the Soundtracks' rhythm section: Pete bass guitar and Mike drums. By the close of the decade Mike Giles' percussion along with Robert Fripp's guitar and fellow local musician, and friend, Greg Lake on bass had formed the nucleus of the outstanding and original progressive rock band King Crimson, and released *In the Court of the Crimson King*, on Chris Blackwell's Island Records.

A year or so before, in 1968, the Giles brothers and the gifted Fripp had produced an LP of idiosyncratic music for Decca's Deram label: *The Cheerful Insanity of Giles, Giles and Fripp.* The predictably low sales figures accrued by this album provided no indication of King Crimson's eventual mega chart topping.

As these band realignments await us some years hence, staying with 63 we find Bob Fripp performing around town with his group The League of Gentlemen, including another future King Crimson member on bass guitar: Gordon Haskell.

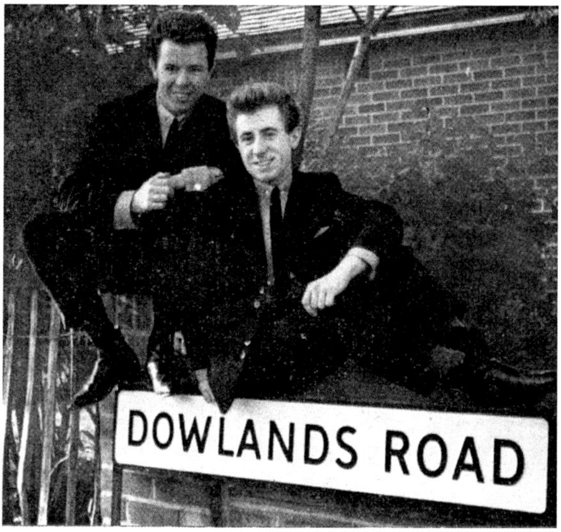

The Dowland Brothers
Bournemouth's answer to the Everly Brothers

The Dowland Brothers, having initiated their musical career at a talent contest hosted by Winton's Moderne cinema, were seen by more than a few people as, not only Bournemouth's, but England's answer to the mighty Everly Brothers. The most significant of these 'more than a few' being the infamous Joe Meek. Of course the battlefield of contestants to be the UK's Everlys was not exactly congested: the Brooks Brothers with a couple of Top 10 hits and at a pinch the Fontana Records, chart topping Allisons who weren't brothers. Still they looked alike, so close enough.

Signed to Meek's RGM Sound, Britain's first independent record company of note, the Brothers Dowland found themselves being produced by the eccentric ex sound engineer, who had created the worldwide smash hit 'Telstar'. As an 'independent' Joe Meek's RGM tended to release his productions through licensing deals with major labels. Or, in the case of Oriole, not so major labels.

The indigenous record companies of the day were headed by the long established giants EMI and Decca, followed by, at some remove, Pye and Phillips. EMI owned a collection of top labels including HMV, Columbia, Parlophone and Capitol. Decca Records: Decca, London American, Coral and Brunswick. Pye, also encompassed Pye International, Pye Jazz and Piccadilly. Phillips' sister label was Fontana. Next to be found on the UK's vinyl food chain were Oriole and Ember, Oriole just ahead of Ember Records. Actually come to think of it some way in front, as Oriole, along with London American and Phillips, was an early conduit to the record buying public in this country for Tamla Motown.

In the years of the Dowland's Oriole records (62-64) the label released Motown's: Contours, Miracles and (Little) Stevie Wonder.

By *Band Box Ball* time, David and Gordon Dowland had 3 singles available: 'Little Sue', 'Big Big Fella' and 'Break Ups'. Not, as you may have noticed, chart hits. Although, almost certainly unknown by the brothers, 'Break Ups' was to be No.1 for some time in that homemade, personal records chart I referred to in a previous chapter, created by, and for, Al.

Staying with the Dowlands for a moment, by early 64 they had their closest run in with Pop fame, thanks to a J. Meek produced cover of the Beatles' 'All My Loving'. Principally a McCartney song and one of many stand out tracks from *With The Beatles* (*Meet The Beatles* in the USA), and incidentally a frequent request on BBC radio's *Two Way Family Favourites* programme.

Not needed by the prolific Lennon and McCartney as a Beatles' single, it seemed destined to remain an LP track. After all this was a period in which mega-selling No.1 'She Loves You' was immediately followed by mega-selling No.1 'I Want To Hold Your Hand'. The Bournemouth duo watched as their version climbed the charts to No.28, with enough momentum to probably go far higher. But wait – EMI had other plans! Not content with their Midas touch Fab Four's records selling in such unprecedented volumes that even the *With The Beatles* LP had entered the Top 20 singles chart, Parlophone released a 4 track EP early in February 64: 'All My Loving'. Yes you've guessed it – the Beatles' EP becomes one of the biggest EP's ever and the Dowland's record doesn't. Ah well, so it goes.

While thinking of Bournemouth and brothers Dowland and Giles, the Everly's performed here in October 63 and I had the pleasure of meeting them.

Hugely popular in England from 1957's 'Bye Bye Love' on through many hits including 'All I have To Do Is Dream' and 'Cathy's Clown', they arrived in town headlining a Don Arden package tour.

The previous year I'd planed to see them at the Winter Gardens, but with tickets purchased well in advance a 'small' snag appeared and unfortunately the America duo didn't. Well 50% of them didn't – and to paraphrase Peter Cook's splendid 'Tarzan' sketch: traditionally for a duo the full complement required is 2! Soon after arriving in England to begin their 1962 tour, Don Everly was overwhelmed by a, at the time unknown to the public, health (drug) problem and returned to the States.

Phil continued with a unique Everly Brother tour and I, in hindsight, regrettably accepted a ticket refund. As a 15 year old, the financial outlay from my limited funds required the close harmonies provided by both their fabulous voices.

As the years have rocked on, however, seeing this highly unusual Phil Everly performance, assisted by the brothers' bass guitarist Joey Page, would have been at the very least an interesting early preview of Phil's later solo career. Writing to me from Wycliffe College, Al enquired, "Did you enjoy the Everly Brother (!) show?" Unaware of my decision to wait and hopefully catch them another day.

That day duly came one Saturday late in October 1963 with one of the era's outstanding Pop Package tours: the Everly Brothers plus Bo Diddley, Little Richard and on their first foray away from the clubs, the Rolling Stones. No chance of me requesting a refund this time!

The tour had begun the previous month and played several towns before reaching this one: initially with a line-up of just Don and Phil, the Stones, Mickie Most, Julie Grant and the Flintstones. The pre-tour box office bookings had been a disaster for Don Arden its 'colourful' promoter. Not exactly a surprise, as the artists and venues had of course been booked earlier in the year, when the full effect of the Beatles led, UK revolution, had yet to shatter, as it very swiftly did, the American domination of all things Pop.

By the autumn of 1963 however, this tour was the first to feel the full force of this unprecedented sea-change. A change which pop and social history now records by the following year had become a tidal wave that British bands surfed on across North America's own music heartland.

Confronting the fact that an Everly's tour, which only a few months earlier would have been a certain sell-out, and now appeared a financial fiasco, Arden had to act quickly and Little Richard was 'parachuted' in. Even this was not enough. Only when Bo Diddley was added to the posters and *NME* ads did the tour swing round and achieve the desired profits.

So for these reasons by the time I'd taken my seat, along with a packed Gaumont first house audience, – perhaps including you? – an extraordinary 100 minutes of Pop/Rock's 'past, present & future', began to unfold.

Encompassing on one Westover Road stage the pinnacle of harmonic pop: the Brothers Everly, plus the R 'n' B rock roots of Bo Diddley; Little Richard, one of that small number of R 'n' R originators, and with a glimpse of the future's shape and sound, the Stones.

Not to mention the second act on this remarkable bill: Mickie Most. Following the show openers the Flintstones' instrumental act, compère Bob Bain introduced a solo, one half of the Most Brothers (no, once again not really brothers), one time 50's, 2i's coffee bar performers.

In fact prior to a successful few years chart topping South Africa's fledging rock scene Mickie M. had been one of the UK's earliest exponents of the then deemed '8 day wonder' gimmick from America, along with Tommy Steele, Lionel Bart and Tony Crombie. Before another 2i's hopeful, Harry Webb, had even decided on being Cliff Richard in preference to another option, Russ Clifford(!), Most had employed a youthful Hank Marvin as his guitarist, along with Jet Harris. At the end of the tour, equipped with the elementary studio knowledge acquired in that far off continent, he stepped away from the microphone and rapidly became, with that extraordinary 60's momentum, one of the greatest pop record producers ever. In 1964 only groups and singers produced by George Martin sold more records in the U.S.A. The Animals' 'House of the Rising Sun' and a string of million sellers for Herman's Hermits took care of that.

Just a quick thought before returning to that enthralling evening. The many problems concert promoting could easily present, highlighted by Arden's tricky situation that autumn, bring to mind an old adage – 'There are 10 ways to loose money in the music biz – all of them via promoting!'

The best way to accumulate big bucks is, and always has been, song publishing. The royalties from great songs go on and on – at least for 50 or 75 years, dependent on which territory of the world you are fortunate enough to be collecting from. As Brian Epstein once said, late in his life, during an American radio interview, when asked "What's the next 'big thing' Brian?" he replied, "A good song – it always is."

By the time the Rolling Stones had come and gone, I was more than satisfied with my 15 shilling (75p) ticket. I'd been aware of them for 6 months or so, since reading Norman Jopling's original *Record Mirror* article, predating their first record 'Come On': a Chuck Berry 'cover', which I acquired from Bourne Radio.

Not exactly well known at the time, but subsequently retold in umpteen books and interviews, Andrew Loog Oldham, chatting with *Record Mirror* editor Peter Jones, just days before the Rollin' Stones' first ever worthwhile publicity went to print, reacting in a 'Shazam' moment of destiny-grabbing insight and energy, took the journalist's tip to head speedily south to Richmond's Crawdaddy Club and sign the group. Thereby releasing a game-changing, Rock 'n' Pop, chain reaction.

But on that crisp, October Saturday night, surrounded by the warmth of a predominantly female, frequently screaming, audience, the heat emanating from the stage was not radiating the Stones' 'Greatest Rock and Roll Band in the World' future, but rather a cut-down version of their recent club repertoire. Restricted by pop package tour time restraints, they raced through their set in 20 minutes, highlighting 'Come On' and their about to be released second single 'I Wanna Be Your Man'.

Oldham's 'chart stuffing' finesse had achieved an initial, somewhat fragile, Top 30 mini-hit with 'Come On' but by now another flash of early Stones' mythology had shone its beneficent light on them.

As their nineteen year old manager/producer paced Soho's streets, having left the Stones rehearsing in Ken Colyer's, Great Newport Street, Studio 51 club, pondering their lack of a suitable 2nd single – Hey Presto! – it appeared. Lennon and McCartney decamping from a nearby taxi, following a Variety Club Awards ceremony at the Savoy, called out a greeting to ALO, instantly renewing their slight acquaintance from earlier that year, when Oldham had P.R.'d 'Please Please Me' for Brian Epstein. The Beatles' song-writing 'power house' then accompanied him back to Studio 51 and offered their potential rivals a half-composed 'song for Ringo': 'I Wanna Be Your Man'. They swiftly knocked off a 'middle eight' on the spot. Now in possession of a follow up single to run with, Oldham, à la Budd Schulberg's *What Makes Sammy Run*, did just that: starting a sprint to the 'Toppermost' of pop's ziggurat.

On this evening, although certain key elements of the iconic Stones' legend were still to be created – Jagger/Richards 'in house' song writing (another ALO move), plus Stones as 'rebels' (with or without a 'cause') – their stage presence was pretty much all there. Bill Wyman already standing stage left, stoically still, slim neck Framus bass held in his trademark style, pointing at the ceiling. On the far side Keith Richards would frequently spin 180 degrees to have his back to the audience for short bursts, probably a semi-shy reaction to the still new and unusual larger stage and audience, compared with the cosy, crowded, slightly claustrophobic, club scene. At the back, of course, partnering Wyman in rhythm, the drumbeats of Charlie Watts. Upfront and Personal: Mick Jagger. But not alone! For substantial periods of their short set, a beaming Brian Jones would rush to the edge of the stage, encouraging the screaming front row girls to reach a few decibels higher. Obviously he'd not got the memo yet: 'You are no longer the band leader!' Jagger, still to embrace his distinctive 'dance' moves, inspired by, or ripped-off, from Charlie Foxx and James Brown, and still maracas free, could do little about it.

The afterglow aura from this early glimpse of Rolling Stones' magic soon evaporated with the arrival of Little Richard. With 6" high pompadour hair and shiny 'zoot suit' jacket, armed only with a piano and a pick-up band, he *Tutti Fruited & Long Tall Sallied* his seaside fans into submission. One of that select, small brotherhood of Rock 'n' Roll originals, along with Presley, Domino, Berry and Jerry Lee, he brought the glory of '50's music power to meet up with the, about to swing, 60s.

During the interval I perused my wisely purchased tour programme (a nifty outlay of a few shillings: currently £85 on eBay) and reflected on my plan to meet the Everly Bros. Catching the first house presented the opportunity to gain backstage access between shows, courtesy of Clive, the Gaumont's assistant manager. We had become acquainted a couple of months earlier, during a frantic few days when Beatlemania hit Bournemouth. Conveniently 'pop packages' of the 50s & 60s invariably played twice a night, doubling the box office take.

Two years earlier, as a 14 year old, I'd met the Beverly Sisters at the Winter Gardens' stage door. Yes, yes, I know: Beverly/Everly/Sisters/Brothers, just a coincidence. I had zero interest in the Bevs as a recording act, but for the previous decade they had been UK TV's leading musical stars and the moment to be a young 'stage door Jonny' was worth taking. Particularly as, for reasons beyond my recall, the twins Babs and Teddie, followed by Joy, elected to kiss me on the cheek, to the slight bemusement of a nearby Billy Wright. Joy Beverly's husband Billy was the many times capped (105 in all) captain of England's football team. They had married in 1958 in Poole, during a Beverly Sisters' summer season at Bournemouth Pavilion. The occasion caused traffic-stopping crowd scenes, nicely illustrating their position as the Posh 'n' Becks of that far off day.

Another stage door moment arrived in June 61, when I came face to face with the amazing Anthony Newley outside London's Queens Theatre in Shaftesbury Avenue. Already with at least two successful careers under his belt and on the brink of another couple of even more significance, he was, as I mentioned before, one of my first record collecting idols. Enthusiastically thanking him for this, that and whatever, as you do, I was delighted to be thanked in return, when he realised my parents and I had driven from Bournemouth and were travelling back the same day. We'd just seen him perform in the recently opened, ground breaking musical *Stop The World I Want To Get Off.* Still in that early 'limbo land', a West End theatre production occupies betwixt failure and success, Newley's musical was, however, receiving rave reviews. Famously for a British musical in those days, it eventually transferred to New York and even greater acclaim on Broadway.

I say Newley's musical, for this highly original tour de force, not only starred this former child star, movie actor, hit record making, TV comedy performer, but the concept was his and the songs co-composed by Newley and Bricusse: including the classic 'What Kind Of Fool Am I'.

During our brief chat he was both genuine and sincere, while still projecting that unique quality of a true star. A few days later a large signed photo arrived at my Broadstone home, sent as he had promised from Decca Records.

Although these stage door occasions had, not surprisingly, given me a buzz, by 1963 I had come to realise that sharing a better moment or two with entertainment artists required being backstage, inside rather than out as this changed the fan/star dynamic considerably.

My thoughts by then had drifted to saying hello to the Evs, when, with the second half underway they were instantly vaporised with the arrival of

Bo Diddley and his thunderous *Bo Diddley Beat.* Well what can one say? 'Hey! Hey! Bo Diddley' I suppose. Just as Little Richard before him, his Roots Rock R 'n' B presence effortlessly dominated the proceedings. Visually stunning with custom built, oblong shaped, Gretsch guitar, maracas playing sideman Jerome Green, and bouffant haired, gold lamé encased 'sister', the 'Duchess'. She splendidly provided the early 60's 'pop sex siren' role (along with Ronnie Spector). Ellas 'Bo Diddley' McDaniel, not content with mythologizing himself with third person lyrics and song titles, also extended this to J. Green with the popular Rock/R 'n' B number 'Bring it on Home, Bring it to Jerome'.

But now it's Everly time! Wearing silver grey, long-tailed three-piece suits, with twin Gibson J200's held aloft to accompany their distinctive harmonising, they commanded the stage. A major part of the brothers' sound was delivered by their vocal harmonies being, mainly, based on parallel thirds, allowing one of them, usually Don, to step forward for a solo line or two when required. 'Bye Bye Love', 'Till I Kissed You', 'All I Have To Do Is Dream', 'Cathy's Clown', with these songs (and others) still humming through me I hung around backstage, missed an initial opportunity to meet them in between shows, and then positioned near their dressing room door – success!

As I chatted to a local booking agent and Jeff Zollo from the *Bournemouth Echo*, with the last notes of the 2nd house final act fading fast, round the corridor corner rushed the two brothers. Still holding their jumbo Gibson's and sweating profusely, those 3 piece 'morning style' suits maybe not such a good idea. You know that saying: 'horses sweat, men perspire and women glow'. Well they were sweating like shire horses! Realising this was not the perfect moment (for them), the five of us exchanged a few words along the lines of: "Fantastic", "Terrific songs", "Thanks". They smiled, murmured a few words appreciating the appreciation and zoomed into the deserved sanctity of their dressing room.

Well OK. fair enough, I'd met them; but what had I expected? Unrealistically to maybe talk about Felice and Boudleaux Bryant, their principal Cadence Records songwriters, pre the switch to Warner Bros; or perhaps their time as US marines (like Presley in the late 50s they had been drafted). Or more prosaically, the long, curly guitar lead, used by Joey, their bass guitarist – in those days guitar leads tended to be straight and relatively short. Realistically I learnt that if you wanted more than a few words, even backstage, your timing as Jimmy Jones sang had to be 'good'.

As I wandered off, musing on this – 'Bonus Time': I'm looking straight at Little Richard! Richard Penniman, from Macon, the 'Georgia Peach', the most exotic of all Rock 'n ' Roll's rare blooms, right here in my home town. Even back then I seldom went the autograph route; somehow it didn't work for me alongside all that 'cool', one tried to project. But what the heck, this was Little Richard; big hair, big smile, still in his stage outfit: "Sign here please." Which of course he did, and yes I still have it.

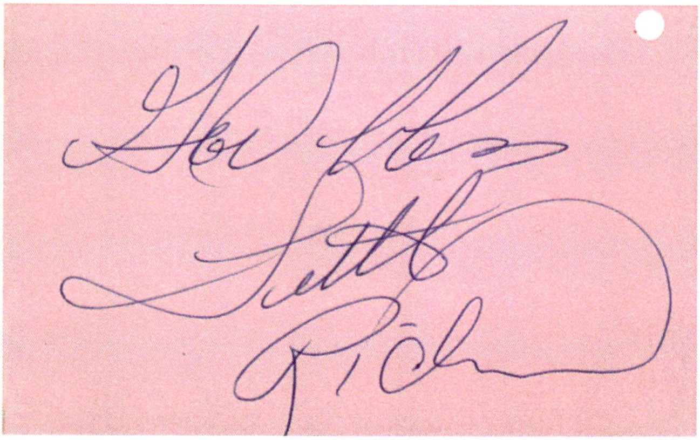

A rock 'n' roll original. Little Richard Bournemouth 1963

The standard package tour schedule frequently required moving directly on to the next town; all the acts travelling on one coach. By now with the audience dispersed, the Don Arden show had boarded their transport and departed. With one exception! As the clock aimed for midnight, a handful of people, including me, were confronted with the slightly surreal scene of a black PVC coated Jerome Green standing in the middle of a deserted Westover Road and wailing – "I missed the bus! I missed the bus!" – before running off into the night.

Back in the 'real world', earlier that year a story had broken that was to run, on and off, for years to come: as everyone was soon to hear, it involved a train, a robbery, and the designation 'Great'.

On August 8th the country awoke to news that a Royal Mail train carrying £2.6 million in used banknotes had been ambushed, not in the Wild West, but Buckinghamshire. Allowing for inflation let's call it £40 million in 21st century money. No wonder the *Great Train Robbery* instantly captured the imagination of Fleet Street.

It quickly disgorged a 15 strong band of 'characters', real life counterparts to the well-known, fictional 'getaway drivers' and including a 'Mr. Big'. A nationwide hunt started for both the gang and that huge amount of stolen cash. But what has any of this drama got to do with sunny Bournemouth? Well simply this: the first and largest amount of money to be recovered was located in Bournemouth; Moordown to be precise. To be even more sat nav accurate, a couple of hundred metres from my Dad's shop! £140,000 – £2 million today.

One of the gang, having rented a 'hide out' flat above a Wimborne Road florist, aroused the suspicion of a garage owner in nearby Castle Lane, by offering to pay 3 months rent in advance from a large bundle of 10 shilling notes. This led, just 6 days after one of the 'Crimes of the Century', to Bournemouth CID carrying out the first arrest of a 'Great Train Robber'.

In the years ahead Rock 'n' Pop managed to gatecrash this 60's 'event' via Phil Collins's *Buster* film, and Julian Temple's *Great Rock and Roll Swindle* Sex Pistols' movie.

By the summer of 63 I had come to realise there were better and easier ways to attract girls then being a 10th rate guitarist. This was made vividly clear to me by Al, following a particularly inept performance at a Branksome youth club. He had turned up to lend support, and more importantly his Copycat echo unit. The group, the Countdowns, included on rhythm guitar another friend who'd come my way courtesy of buying a guitar from my Dad's shop. Richard Berg soon decided, quite sensibly, to put strumming to one side, and eventually became a charted accountant.

We opened with 'Telstar': should have closed with it as well! Week in week out it was possible to catch local group gigs featuring the brilliant talents of Summers and Fripp: there was absolutely no question that I was not prepared to spend the time and effort required to become adequate, let alone good. One initial reason for trying was an almost subliminal urge to be a part of that exciting era of pop music. So for now, having put my Hofner back in its case, I needed other ways to continue my involvement. Basically there were three: local groups, record dealing, and Al.

First groups. The aforementioned youth club, surprisingly not put off by the Countdowns, were keen to book more (and obviously better) local groups. As they had little idea how to go about this I had an opportunity to secure groups for them, and have an ongoing role for myself. My first booking on the club's behalf was – surprise, surprise! – the Trappers. For a fee of £15 they played one Wednesday night in August. The previous evening you could have caught the young Al Stewart and musical chums at Le Disque a Go Go. They went down rather well: particularly popular was their rendition of the then current Surfaris' hit: 'Wipe Out'. So well in fact, that they were immediately re-booked for later that month.

Next: the Sands Combo. As I stood in the peg-boarded semi enclosure of a Minns Music listening booth, trying to decide if the 7" record of that particular moment was worth the outlay of 6 shillings and 3 pence, Zoot Money walked by. He was momentarily distracted by a £1 note I happened to be holding, and whilst making a half-hearted attempt to grab it, replied to my gig suggestion "Yes" indicating 20 quid would be fine. Come the night they were, of course, great. The packed out basement crowd, having been entertained the week before by an artist, Al Stewart, who would one day sell millions of albums, now had Andy Summers, who via the Police would sell tens of millions. Plus, as I recall, a magnet for the 16 year old girls that night, the Sands' drummer Colin Allen. In his time he went on to record with Stone The Crows and play live with Bob Dylan.

Among the teenagers frequenting this 60's youth club were two, Ann and Benny, who even then showed clear signs of civic and social awareness: interesting to note that in the decades to come both Ben Grower and Ann Filer were, each in their time, to become Mayor of Bournemouth.

Record dealing developed out of a primary school comic collecting/dealing enthusiasm. This mini-enterprise centred on hard to obtain American comics. In the 1950s printing restrictions – an overhang from post WW2 rationing – limited UK versions of DC Comics' *Batman* and *Superman*, to black and white editions. The obviously superior US colour originals were therefore highly desirable. At the time a substantial number of American military personal were still stationed in Britain. Due to the marriage of my mother's younger sister Shirley to a USAF sergeant stationed near London, I had access to the imported copies available to these expatriate airmen. This proved extremely popular with my small – both in height and volume – clientele.

All of this came to an end in 1959, with my uncle and aunt's departure for the U.S. of A. One schoolboy customer exclaimed on hearing this news: "But I knew I could always get a good deal from you!" I'd like to believe at least a few of my thousands of future record buying customers would echo this sentiment.

From record collecting to record dealing was a simple step, when, in my mid-teens, I took over running the small area of our Moordown shop devoted to selling LPs, 45s and 78s. There was only one other Bournemouth shop aimed at the local record collecting market; and that primarily for jazz enthusiasts.

Back then the main source of info regarding records, release dates, reviews, artists, and most importantly charts, could be found in the weekly music papers: *New Musical Express, Melody Maker, Record Mirror* and *Disc*. The *NME* being, with a Top 30 chart, by far the most popular. *Record Mirror* and *Disc* were slight variations of the *NME*, with *Melody Maker*, the oldest of these periodicals, essentially for musicians. As the 60s progressed, with the change from beat groups to rock bands, the positions of the *MM* and the *NME* in the print media 'where it's at' competition were reversed.

Following the weekly Top 30 fluctuations was fascinating, but one day in 1961 I came across something somewhat hidden from the general public: a Top 50. Detouring via Poole Music Stores on my way home to Broadstone from Poole Grammar, the existence of *Record Retailer* was revealed during a chat with the young women running the shop.

Situated next to the Regent cinema in the high street, this small shop sold records and sheet music. *Record Retailer*, a 'trade' periodical, was published weekly, only available by subscription and featured a Top 50. Most, if not all, record shops subscribed to the magazine as the reviews and extended chart listings were intended to give an indication of which singles might be hits and sustain sales, therefore making it worthwhile to stock them. My reaction to this was: great! I wrote to the mag explaining I was a private individual (not at that time a record shop), but would like to subscribe – becoming, possibly, the only non-record shop recipient in the country.

Yes you're right, those chart slots from 31-50, could easily be dismissed as trivia: but as time passed the mainstream charts expanded too. Eventually the BBC offering a Top 40. Also worth noting in America the *Billboard* and *Cashbox* charts already provided a Hot 100.

A few years later, in the 'Summer of Love', 1967, I opened my own shop in Westbourne. By then Al was living in London with his girlfriend Mandi, who, as it happened, worked for the *Record Retailer* at their Carnaby Street HQ. Very handy as she would pass on stacks of review copies to me: so if you'd glanced at the window display of my shop the week it opened, looking back at you would have been Frank Zappa, Sky Saxon and Eric Burdon. Needless to say the Mothers of Invention, the Seeds, and the New Animals LPs were all too far out of left field for mainstream Bournemouth record shops to consider handling in 67. Mandi could be seen (still can) on the reverse of Al's 2nd album *Love Chronicles*.

Talking of Al brings me back to that earlier summer of 63, when as an add-on to our friendship I began an ad hoc role as a sounding board for his new songs as they appeared, a PR, when and where possible, and from time to time, advisor on clothes. No, don't laugh, this was really necessary! His interest in sartorial attire was close to zero, mine being the mirror opposite.

An almost overnight proliferation of new looks, fashions and styles had began to dazzle this island, spreading out from the mind of Mary Quant, the hair styling of Vidal Sassoon and the Carnaby Street shops of John Stephen. As clothing emporiums morphed into 'boutiques', Bournemouth, slowly at first, became 'on trend'. The premier local example for a while was to be found next to the El Cabala in Old Christchurch Road. Esquire was small, modern, and unfortunately expensive. Well I say expensive, this like many things in life is, of course, relative. Better value in button-down shirts and hipster trousers was provided from 65 in Gentry, another small OCR shop. The tricky item to acquire locally, certainly in 63, proved to be elastic-sided Cuban-heeled 'Beatle' boots, as purveyed by Anello and Davide.

Although Al and I had little spare cash then, a sad misfortune from the beginning of his days meant he seldom had to pay for clothes. A trust fund, set up by his Scottish banker grandfather, enabled Al to buy any clothes (within reason). The fund was created following the death, in a plane crash, of his RAF officer father, near the end of WW2. This wartime tragedy, occurring 6 months before Al's birth meant he was never to know his father.

Turning to happier thoughts, my influence regarding clothes could be seen in the first Al Stewart publicity photos, commissioned in 1965 by his manager at the time, Tony Stratton-Smith.

In later years this 'style manager' position would be occupied by a succession of Al's girlfriends. 1976 presents a classic example. The white suit he wears on the cover of the Year of the Cat LP became an essential part of his breakthrough image in America: so much so that even as sharp an operator as CBS/Arista CEO Clive Davis bought into this Al Stewart 'look', when he authorised an Arista Records 'signing on advance' of $1,000,000 in 1978. Far from this being Al's idea of suitable attire, it had been chosen for him by his girlfriend Marion, from Bugatti, a boutique in Kensington.

Later on, the same day, they drove down to Bournemouth. My wife Abi and I opened our front door to see a smiling, white suited Al, accompanied by his 'wardrobe mistress', and enquiring of his new outfit, "What do you think of this?" Whatever I replied it wasn't, "Wear it on the cover of your next LP; I'm sure 1.8 million Americans will buy it!"

The first notable composition he sang to me, at the base camp of the Hit Parade Everest he would eventually climb, was a Johnny Cash-style song called 'So I Kept Walking'. During an interlude in the Trappers' Le Disque set Al began his departure from the group scene with this song, arriving a couple of years later as a Soho, singer-songwriter.

Obviously there's a lot more to say about Al and his songs as the 60s unfold: but for now thinking of that club and period, it brings to mind *Home Grown*. Do you remember it? (Sorry, of course you probably hadn't been born yet!) Southern TV's answer to ITV's networked talent competition *Opportunity Knocks*. A kind of 'old school' *X Factor*, without the cross-marketing.

Among the local groups to appear on the show were Le Disque regulars Pam Dawson and the Vulcans also the Johnny Quantrose 5. I remember dancing with Pam one night in Le Disque and the thought crossed my mind, "This is cool, you've been on TV." Oh come on, I was only 16! The JQ5 had another 16 year old, Stan Lee, on drums. In the late sixties we became friends and would often meet up, either in my shop or various jazz gigs round town.

One Bournemouth based winner of *Home Grown* was Tony Fabian, who, accompanied himself on an acoustic guitar and succeeded with a version of Arthur Lyman's song *Yellow Bird*.

Al's first TV appearance would have to wait however 'till 1965 and a BBC TV documentary called *Outcasts and Outsiders*. He sang 'Pretty Golden Hair', a recently written song that included lyrics and a subject somewhat ahead of their time. Filmed at Bunjies in Soho this solo performance, complete with newly acquired Epiphone Texan guitar, provides the earliest footage of post beat groups, singer-songwriter Al Stewart.

Two years later the song resurfaced on his debut album *Bedsitter Images*; this time backed by a full symphony orchestra.

But for now in 63 he was still an electric guitar player in a group. This didn't stop, however, an almost daily dialogue between me and Al as to how he and his songs could advance further along the road to having one recorded. Initially the aim was to write something commercially viable for a contemporary group to record.

A half chance came in 1964 via Al's second Bournemouth band: the G-Men. Featuring vocalist Dave Le Kaz, Terry Squires on lead guitar, Bev Strike (son of Don Strike) on bass guitar and Al on electric organ. They never achieved a record deal, but did cut a demo single in London's Dubreq Studios. The Aside, 'When She Smiled', an attempt by Al to construct a pop song, was sung by Dave. As far as I know only one copy still exists and currently it is in my possession. It was light, slight, and not at all indicative of what was to come: could have been a

Freddie and the Dreamers' B-side!

The first step into the (local) media spotlight as a songwriter came in September 1963 when, in my PR man guise, I arranged an article on the Trappers in the *Bournemouth Echo*. While promoting the group it emphasised the lead guitarist as being a prolific songwriter. Not exactly true! Having quickly added up the songs listed in my friend's school exercise book (see previous chapter), my ludicrous estimate of 40-50 original compositions was then quoted in the paper.

Dave La Kaz and the G-Men Bournemouth Pier 1964
(Al Stewart 2nd from left)

It was obvious to both of us that until he wrote more songs his best hope of making a record remained within a group. Not until 1964 was well underway did Al, while still in Bournemouth, move progressively away from attempting to compose a hit pop tune – though to this day he wishes he had – and towards, thanks to Bob Dylan, becoming a solo performer. A pivotal point in the transformation could be identified with the creation of a second demo; this time recorded in a small studio near Bournemouth town centre in Yelverton Road. But as we're still wandering around 63 let's leave the details for another chapter.

Although the idea of being a serious guitarist had fast faded for me, it still appeared to occupy the thoughts of someone else.

The previous year I had become friends with one of Bournemouth's most extrovert teenagers: Tony Wagner, tall, slim and always fizzing with ideas, seemed to find every day reality just a little mundane. For example the night in 1962 when Bobby Vee headlined a Winter Gardens show. Tony and his family lived in Bath Hill Court, just a short walk from the venue. Not content with possessing a couple of tickets, strolling over to the Winter Gardens and catching the show, he had an idea. First, let's cruise up to the stage door and sign autographs! Yes, I know: who would want our signatures? Well exactly my question. "No one," replied Tony. Obviously we would need to be impostors. His instant suggestion: Peter Jay and The Jaywalkers. "I look a bit like Peter Jay and you could be one of the group."

A Decca recording band, popular as a mid bill act on many package tours, and, unfortunately for them hitless, were not even in town that night. This 'detail' meant nothing to the effervescent 'Peter Jay' now standing alongside me. "Who's the lead guitarist?" After a moments recollection I tentatively murmured, "Buzz Miller."

A short while later, wearing iridescent, short raincoats – collars turned up – and dark glasses, we took a taxi over to the Winter Gardens' stage door; stopping close by a small crowd of girls, hoping for a glimpse of a pop star or two. Instead of which they got us. Assuming we may be in a group, as Tony and I pretended to head for the stage door entrance, one of them enquired, "Who are you?" To which my chum replied, "Peter Jay," and indicating me. "This is Buzz Miller." (If you happen to be reading this Buzz, my belated apologies!) Several girls immediately thrust autograph books in our direction. Never having believed 'till this moment it would work, what could I do? What would you do? We hastily signed: then swiftly retreated to the anonymity of the W. Gardens.

Many months later, seized with the idea of being a pop singer, Tony answered an *Echo* ad, placed by a local bass guitarist, searching for a vocalist + guitar player, to form a group. Ignoring the fact that by then, having realised my limitations guitarwise, this 'guitar player' could not be me, he insisted I go with him to meet this guy.

When we met up the ad-placing musician quickly realised Tony was not the singer he needed, and I couldn't play guitar to the required standard. Not surprising really when you consider the name of his previous group's lead guitarist: Bob Fripp! This was how I came to meet Gordon Haskell.

He was relaxed and surprisingly understanding, everything considered. We became friends for a while and I recall he enjoyed my mother's cooking on occasional visits to our Broadstone home. We drifted out of touch as the sixties rolled on and Gordon left Bournemouth to seek fame and fortune with recording bands such as Les Fleur de Lys, and eventually reuniting for a while with Fripp in King Crimson.

The last time we were in touch in 2001 I invited him to a small gig, organised by me for Al, in Bournemouth's Mr. Smiths club.

This mini, party-like event came in to being as a consequence of Al – not for the first time – reminding me that over the decades of hit records and world wide tours, he seldom had an opportunity to play his home town. Gordon couldn't make it as he was fully focused (unknown to me at the time) on an imminent, long over due, career break through, with his splendid recording of self-composed chart buster 'How Wonderful You Are'.

Tremendous radio play, led by the BBC's Johnnie Walker, launched Gordon's sincere and personal song into a festive No.1 battle with Robbie Williams and Nicole Kidman's version of Sinatra's 'Something Stupid'. He followed this with the equally successful *Harry's Bar* album.

As someone who had owned his first LP, *Sail in My Boat*, since its release in 1969, I was delighted that this talented and genuine guy had reached his musical moment in the sun.

1963: The year the sixties started to fly. Looking outwards from Bournemouth – or indeed almost anywhere in England – the changes in style, music, fashion, politics and humour were displayed in a fast moving panorama. And at the heart of it all of course: Beatlemania.

The Men From Rickenbacker

This might be a good moment to select 'She Loves You' on your iPod or perhaps YouTube any of the myriad clips of the pandemonium surrounding the Beatles the year the 'steady state' pop universe took a quantum leap into a new reality.

The red hot excitement of the mid 50's Rock 'n' Roll explosion had long since cooled to be a low key extension of the entertainment industry. With the exception of Brill Building gems and early Tamla Motown from America, plus the sparkling Shadows' instrumentals in England, there was little to set the pulse racing.

American popular music continued its almost complete domination of the planet's hit records, songs and tonal style. Since the well documented decline of the original R 'n' R buccaneers, the airwaves and musical movies aimed at the young and the young at heart, were now once again safe havens.

Pelvis Presley having endured a Dr. Who like regeneration due to US Army conscription had emerged as a clean-cut *Rocka-Hula-Baby* singer, no longer wanting to take you on a walk to *Heartbreak Hotel's lonely street.* Chuck Berry and Jerry Lee Lewis had disappeared from pop's radar screens thanks to the revelations of their respective sexual follies. And Little Richard had by then begun an on/off battle between his spiritual side and continued rock outrage.

A static, seemingly unchanging, look had also calmly settled on clothes, hair styles and attitudes. Women, both young and not so young, lacquered their hair into bouffant rigidity and constrained their bodies in tight-waisted, petticoat-flared dresses. Images easily available for assimilation by a teen market from movies and TV. For style examples a quick glimpse of Helen Shapiro or Mrs Bobby Darin, Sandra Dee, should suffice.

The young males' rebel look of James Dean and the obvious establishment threatening New Edwardians (Teddy Boys) had given way to neatly cut, side-burn free, combed back hair, coupled with 2-piece, mohair suits, slim ties and suede shoes.

Then a completely unexpected high-voltage jolt struck the apparently 'stopped clock' of youth culture. Like the sudden appearance of a *Big Bang* singularity, John, Paul, George and Ringo materialised. Looking like four of John Wyndham's *Midwich Cuckoos*, quipping like north of England Marx Brothers, and sounding like – well, sounding like THE BEATLES!

We soon realised they hadn't arrived from a galaxy far away, but had a fascinating, revealing back story of glorious butterflies emerging from their Cavern/Hamburg chrysalis.

Of all the tales of modern times the Beatles fable is by far the best known. Retold repeatedly and happily revisited as enthusing generation after generation ensure their place in history. For nearly 50 years now, thousands of books, magazines, films, plays and documentaries, have allowed us all to believe we know the story inside out and back to front. Well, yes and no.

Ask brilliant Beatles' producer George Martin who he believes knows more about the Fab Four than anyone else on the planet, and his reply will be: "Mark Lewisohn." What does Mark have to say on the subject? Let me quote him:

"The Beatles story has been told very often, but in my view rarely very well. A rock and roll group came out of Liverpool and shaped the last half of the 20th century the world over, and their music transcends changing times. The whole extraordinary story needs to be fully recorded and it needs to be done now, while first-hand witnesses are still with us."

Over the past few years I have enjoyed an occasional e-mail correspondence with Mark, and his complimentary comments on my minor role as one of those witnesses have played a part in my decision to write this book. So now I would like to tell you of *The Men from Rickenbacker* and also Bournemouth's far from insignificant association with two important events in the Beatles' history.

August 1963: the Beatles are spending 6 days in Bournemouth. Fifty feet in front of me, standing close by a slightly left of centre, floor standing microphone, Paul McCartney began another song introduction. This penultimate song of the evening was about to deliver a few moments of incandescent, shimmering pop excitement. He'd got as far as, "Now we'd like to do a new song – it's released on Friday," when John Lennon, not for the first time, interrupted via his own mic with an instruction for the group's spellbound, jumping and screaming audience: "Buy a copy!" With a quick nod of agreement McCartney continued: "It's called 'She Loves You'." Slight pause, glance at nearby George Harrison; a silent 1-2-3: *She loves you, yeah, yeah, yeah.*

One of the first ever performances of the world changing 'She Loves You' was underway. Bournemouth didn't need to be told to buy the single, nor the rest of the country: a few days later it entered the *NME* Top 30 Chart at No.1.

With a cascade of yeah, yeah, yeahs, it lit the blue touch paper for planet-wide Beatlemania. Perhaps even now the greatest of pure pop songs ever recorded. Before the year ended it had become Great Britain's biggest selling record ever.

By now the entire Gaumont Theatre seemed to shake and shimmy, as the predominantly female fans erupted once more with a crescendo of shrieking enthusiasm, at the sight of four live Beatles.

It became necessary, for a view of the stage, to stand and abandon the allocated seat provided by a hard to acquire, prized ticket.

Next to me Al Stewart had a singular, clear thought in his mind; the same thought surged through my synapses too. *This is it!* This is the 'perfect storm' of Rock 'n' Pop thrills and emotions; reality-transcending, girl-exciting, troubles of the moment postponing magic. The years of many great records and rock shows, providing a temporary gateway to a parallel universe, distant from real-life realities of school and responsibilities, had led to this prime moment. Recognisable from an accumulation of all that had gone before, but at once uniquely superior, as the voices, words and music of these young Englishmen gave everyone present an endorphin enhancing sense of joy.

Yes, she loves you And you know you should be glad, oooooh!

With moptops only inches apart, sharing a single mic, Paul and George delivered a frenzied, head shaking, Little Richard inspired, cathartic ooooh! Immediately taking up the exhilarating title refrain, again in tandem, with a few feet to their left, the visually balancing stationary John, with his Cuban-heeled Beatle boots, firmly planted in his already established stance.

Earlier that August evening, on their first ever live performance in Bournemouth, the Beatles had performed eight songs including previous No.1 hit 'From Me To You' and a selections of songs from their first LP, *Please, Please Me.*

They'd opened however with George Harrison's interpretation of Chuck Berry's 'Roll Over Beethoven'; a frequent and long standing vocal contribution from the group's lead guitarist, originating in their Cavern days. They would later that year choose to start side 2 of their awesome second album, *With The Beatles*, with this track. They quickly followed 'Beethoven' with 'From Me To You' flipside, 'Thank You Girl'.

Yes, the expected girl-powered screams were there alright – the U.K. press having chronicled almost daily for many months the evolving news story of the hysteria they generated, ensured the requisite reaction. But it was still possible to hear and enjoy the Beatles live; including the humorous lines occasionally thrown out from the stage.

Before the fourth song, 'From Me To You', a small, but nonetheless welcome, musical surprise arrived in the form of 'Chains'. Although featured

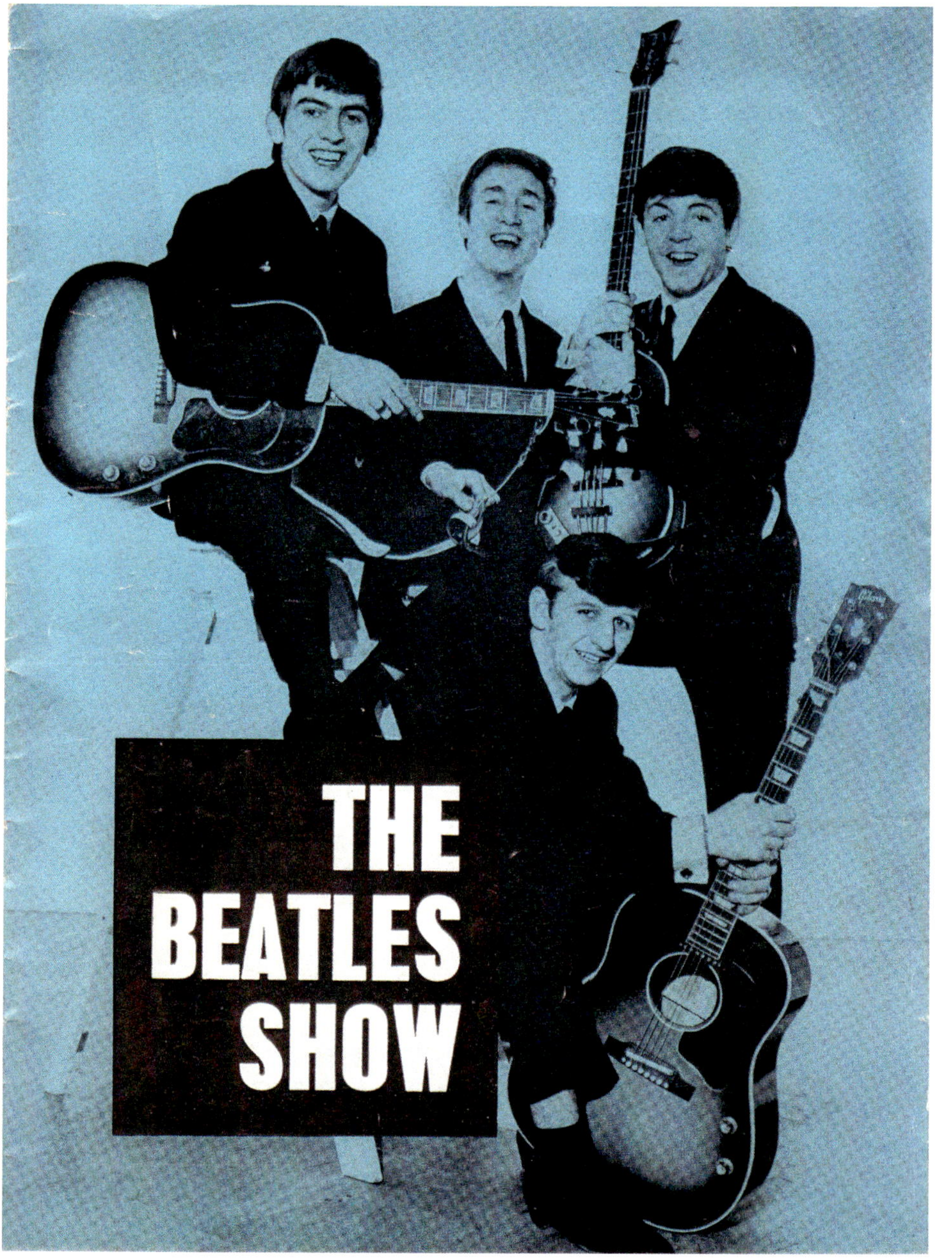

Beatles programme
Bournemouth, August 1963

on the *Please, Please Me* album, their version of the Cookies' American original was not a part of the Beatles regular stage set.

Following a full-on performance of 'From Me To You' the high tempo cooled slightly with McCartney's lead vocal on 'A Taste Of Honey'.

And then one of the evening's stand-out deliveries; a truly great early Lennon & McCartney song (mainly McCartney), 'I Saw Her Standing There', spotlighting the spirit of the Beatles in that era. His heart may indeed have gone 'boom' when he crossed that room to hold her hand, but I'm guessing more than a few of the hearts present that night went 'boom' as well!

Another exception to the group's standard live repertoire came next, with a cover of the Shirelles' 'Baby It's You'. One of two songs from the American girl group they'd recorded in the marathon one day session for their first LP.

Next came 'Boys', originally the B-side of the Shirelles' Goffin & King hit 'Will You Love Me Tomorrow'. This meant it was *Ringo Time*: as this was just prior to Lennon/McCartney deciding to craft a song specifically for their drummer to sing, i.e. 'I Wanna Be Your Man', it was 'Boys' providing Ringo's live show limelight.

Well that makes the eight numbers that preceded the transcendental 'She Loves You'. But what would be this band of joy-bringing troubadours' ultimate statement of their new and unique identity?

'Twist and Shout', although not a Beatle original, coming their way from the American Isley Brothers, still, thanks to John Lennon's semi-shouted exaltation to *'Come on baby now!'* this song, along with 'I Saw Her Standing There' and 'She Loves You', captured the musical essence of Britain's Beatlemania.

It became one of the 5 Beatle records to dominate the US charts in spring 64 when, as American Beatlemania took hold, in a never happened before/ never likely to happen again moment, the group occupied the TOP 5 positions in the *Billboard/Cashbox* Hot Hundred!

A generation or so later, the instant joie de vivre created by the Beatles' 'Twist and Shout' was shared once again when John Hughes, directing Mathew Broderick in *Ferris Bueller's Day Off*, orchestrated hundreds of extras in a street parade to dance, sway and mime to Johnny and His Moondogs' very special vibe.

It's over. The Beatles have finished with their trademark, Brian Epstein inspired, choreographed bow, and left the stage. So that's it – almost.

The still buzzing crowd begin to drift downwards from the exhilarating highs they've just reached and slowly leave the Gaumont auditorium.

Turning to my friend I said, "I don't recognise that small, black guitar

John Lennon's playing – any idea who makes it?" As we stood, confronting a now deserted stage, not wanting the chemistry of the moment to evaporate just yet, I only half expected Al could provide the answer. After all I did know (or thought I knew) a fair amount about the Fenders, Gibsons, Gretschs, Guilds and Hofners etc. that the guitar world had to offer, but I'd never seen a guitar like Lennon's. Although within a year, thanks to the Beatles, its manufacturer would become widely known – in fact as well known as all the other famous guitar makers – at that time probably the only person in Bournemouth who could have identified it was standing next to me. "I think it's a Rickenbacker" Al correctly replied.

I haven't a clue what prompted me to say, "Wouldn't it be great if we could get to talk with him about it?" Perhaps I just didn't want to let go of that elevated 'feeling'. Al gave me a quizzical look. "How?" he enquired. "Just how are we going to do that?" A completely sane response, coupled with a hint of curiosity. As the hubble-bubble sound of young people slowly subsided and the surrounding rows of seats emptied, I realised I had no idea. Why had I just spoken these absurd words? Maybe it was thinking aloud some sort of 'wish impulse'.

Picture the scene: a situation which represented a microcosm of the nationwide scene. From the beginning of 63 post 'Love Me Do' tremors had developed along ever widening fault lines: a Liverpool born volcano had begun to erupt. At first only those (mainly young) people who followed pop music with weekly record purchases and *Thank Your Lucky Stars* and *Juke Box Jury* viewings, plus *NME* scrutinising, knew – to paraphrase the words Bob Dylan would one day write: *'Something is happening and we do know what it is'.*

From the first moment you, me or anyone from 8 to 88, from a tramp to the Queen, saw and/or heard the Beatles it was obvious. This was different. Yes patterns of rock/pop ley-lines could be discerned in their sound; but not either their appearance or reshaping of past influences to create new, fresh and direct music.

Few people outside of Liverpool and Hamburg had known of the group prior to autumn 1962. Those Cavern/Star Club denizens could be likened to Wild West wagon train scouts of the late 19th century: just down the line, across the river, round the bend, the Apaches were going to change your world.

The first sign of that change for me occurred a few days before the October release of 'Love Me Do'. Before hearing the group I saw an ad in a magazine format periodical called *Pop Weekly*. EMI whilst expending a micro amount of money on publicity, completely in line with an initial release by unknowns on their least important label, had, at the behest of Brian Epstein, placed a few music paper ads. Four small, individual photos revealed what appeared to be 'grown-up schoolboys': there was just no visual reference point to any previous popular male hair styles. The occasional art student was glimpsed here and there with a 'Roman' haircut, but these Astrid Kirchherr inspired short fringes were really something else.

The accompanying brief text announced an oddly, but cleverly, named group. John Lennon's desire for a Buddy Holly 'Crickets' inspired name coupled with his instinctive lateral thought wordplay, delivered 100%. Once seen in print the beat group name with a built in job description was quite unforgettable.

Shortly after this I acquired a copy of the single on Parlophone Records' original red label – by January 1963 EMI had re-branded all the company's labels a ubiquitous black. Al, I recall, particularly liked the flipside 'P.S. I Love You'. The audio provided by this 7" of plastic did not really signpost the incredible songs, records, appearances, humour and zeitgeist to come. But it did emphatically sound distinctively different. Different from all the R 'n' R, Pop, Doo-wop, R 'n' B, Blues, Jazz, male and female solo singers, and vocal groups that had come before. This unpolished and immediate music made a direct connection. No invisible barriers of showbiz projection or record company over production – the single obvious reference point to the (recent) past being the unusual use of harmonica, à la Bruce Channel's 'Hey! Baby'.

As 1963 got underway the Beatles, via 'Please Please Me' and 'From Me To You', rode a newsprint energised escalator from pop enthusiast semi-obscurity to national fame and hysteria. No longer were they allowed to be third on the bill to Helen Shapiro or Tommy Roe and Chris Montez, as their early package show tours had dictated. Word of mouth, plus almost daily news reports detailing lengthy ticket queues at any venue announcing a future performance, turned them into bill-toppers.

Britain's Beatlemania did not suddenly 'switch on' with late 1963's Royal Variety Show's, London traffic-stopping, appearance as some historical snapshots suggest but built and built throughout the year, with its brightest flashpoint being the release of 'She Loves You'.

This brings us back to August 19th in Bournemouth and two teenagers in a fast emptying building, surrounded by a huge crowd of Beatle fans gathered in Westover Road and in the alleyways adjacent to the Gaumont. One of whom needed an immediate answer to Al's "How do we do it?" question. It would be impressive to be able to state now, that in the mode of *Blackadder's Baldrick*, I 'had a cunning plan' – but I didn't. Instead he heard me suggest a piece of left-field fiction: tell the theatre manager that Al and I had travelled down from London with Rickenbacker Guitars' related business to conduct with the Beatles, and couldn't get access for our appointment due obviously to the manic teenage hordes currently laying siege to the Gaumont!

Huge crowd of Beatles fans outside the Palace Court Hotel during their August 1963 performances in Bournemouth

If I was looking for an air-punching, gleeful expression of enthusiastic approval, I received in its place a doubtful "OK". Well OK – where do we go from here? As one thought rapidly led to another the next step was obvious: head for the manager's office.

The first house, first night performance of the Fab Four's unusual week long seaside sojourn, was the option with the most appeal at the time we managed to acquire a couple of tickets. If more tickets had been available no doubt we'd have taken a couple of girls, but they (the tickets) weren't. And a Beatles gig was certainly not going to be short of them. And so, in a brief window of opportunity between the night's mandatory two shows, with only ourselves to consider, we found our way to the door of the manager's hoped for sanctuary from the ensuing, ongoing for many days to come, Beatle-generated madness.

"Can I help you?" he enquired, as the door closed behind us. Standing by an office desk, on which stood a slightly incongruous, almost full glass of beer, the middle-aged theatre manager listened to my pitch. "Yes, I'm sure you can," I replied. To his left was another desk, possibly for an assistant. Other than the three of us the room was empty. As this was half time on the first evening of a week-long trip into the unknown hosting this pop phenomenon, probably the interrupted alcoholic refreshment was the right way to go. Perhaps the following few minutes went as they did because dealing with my request allowed a swift return to his pint. Who knows?

With Al standing just behind me, prudently positioned close to the door, for what might easily have been a quickly required (embarrassing) exit, I continued my act with an air of manufactured confidence. I half turned, with a slight wave of my hand indicating Al, and said "This is my colleague, Mr. Stewart, we've come down from London this evening to meet with the Beatles' management on Rickenbacker guitar related business and we can't make our appointment due to this crowd chaos. What do you suggest?"

Looking a couple of years older than my 16 years and wearing a two piece Italian style pale grey suit, pale blue button-down shirt and slim wool-knit dark tie, my appearance and demeanour were not at odds with the contemporary, increasingly populated by young guys, music biz. In other words the fantasy I had just presented was far from implausible.

A second or two elapsed, then without revealing a scintilla of doubt in his voice, he asked, "And your name is?" I answered, "Kremer, Jon Kremer." Then with an efficient movement he reached for what looked like a telephone, but was probably an intercom, and called the stage door. "A Mr." pausing to look at me – "Kremer," I repeated, "and Stewart" – he continued, "A Mr. Kremer and a Mr. Stewart are coming round, let them in."

Moments later, following a few brief words encompassing "Thanks" and mutual agreement regarding this amazing Bournemouth crowd Al and I found ourselves in the midst of said Westover Road crowd.

Some people recognised us from the local group scene and possibly wondered where we were off to, as with the assistance of a couple of the uniformed police officers who where fully engaged with attempting some sort of control, we politely, but insistently, pushed through the other teenagers thronging the alleyway that led to the stage door.

There had hardly been time to draw breath, let alone congratulate ourselves on the seeming success of my '*Jedi Mind Trick*' subterfuge. And now as we approached our immediate destination, two reality check problems flashed warning signals. First, and you may be familiar with this, the Gaumont stage door entrance was located behind gated railings, adjacent to steps that led to Hinton Road. The gate, close to the by now open stage door was unsurprisingly locked and staying locked. Pressed against it, many with autograph books in their hands, a phalanx of enthusiastically noisy girls presented a tricky barrier to further progress.

Shouting from a position in front of the entrance, but behind the iron gate, a voice acknowledged our expected presence and suggested climbing over from the steps. As unlocking the gate and inviting the place to be invaded by fans was obviously not an option, we did just that.

As the stage door closed, with us on the right side of it, the outside clamour subsided to be replaced with quieter, but still hectic sounds and action. Then 'Problem No.2' loomed large. Although backstage, we unfortunately weren't from Rickenbacker, did not possess an 'appointment' and now needed Plan B.

Round a corner or two, not far from our entrance point I spotted one of principal supporting act Billy J. Kramer's backing group, the Dakotas. And yes I did realise his name sounded a lot like mine: though my real name wasn't William Ashton! "Which way to the Beatles' dressing room?" I optimistically enquired. "Oh – follow me."

At the end of a short corridor a fairly unprepossessing door awaited us. Up to this moment Al and I had been exchanging hurried, laughed words, as this slightly bizarre set of circumstances had unfolded. Now what? Like a stretched elastic band snapping back into shape, we decided the best move would be to become ourselves once again. Two young guitar enthusiasts, involved with local groups, KO'd by the Beatles, and curious to know more about Lennon's guitar.

Security? That would be a good question to pose at this point. Well in those days, with the beginning of modern era backstage entourages of minders, P.R.s, tour managers, road crew, promoters, record company execs and sundry other wearers of an 'Access all areas' laminate, still years away, the only obstacle to overcome was the stage-door keeper.

Sure in the unique mayhem surrounding the Beatles that year protection was certainly required to a degree never seen before in England. But this took place mainly in public areas as the Fab Four moved between hotels and venues or studios. This tended to be the responsibility of local constabularies from town to town.

Backstage amongst the various musicians, singers and stage hands coming and going we were ignored. Basically the assumption being if you're there, there must be a reason.

So with only an unguarded door between us and the Beatles I knocked on it. As I was about to try again, it opened. Confronting us was not the half expected Beatle, but Neil Aspinall. The group's old friend and road manager: one day to become the Managing Director of Apple Corps. "Yes?" his straight to the point question.

While he was told of our arcane desire for more knowledge about all things Rickenbacker, I was semi-mesmerised by the sight of Paul McCartney and Ringo Starr just a few feet away. Aspinall must have wondered how we came to be there. Possibly – and of course this is just a guess – he reasoned we must be connected to somebody, in someway, to have gained access; and as they were in Bournemouth for a while, why not go with it.

It being my introduction to me and Al as part of the local group scene and very keen to meet John Lennon and talk guitars. During this brief exchange he'd pulled the door to behind him.

"Wait here," was the non-committal response. So we did.

The next time the door opened a voice I'd last heard inciting everyone to 'Twist and Shout' said, "You want to talk to me?" Before I could reply, John Lennon continued, "I can't ask you in," nodding in the direction of their dressing room, "it's a bit busy in there." Well that seemed quite reasonable to me – in fact at that moment almost anything would!

The three of us than began to chat in the corridor. Al and I trying to be relaxed and cool, without revealing the huge effort this took to achieve. Beatle John stood opposite: cool, calm and collected; almost laconic. Fortunately displaying not one iota of his already well known acerbic wit and sharp temperament. None of the Beatles suffered fools gladly, and it was said that J.L. wouldn't suffer them at all. Instead, as we began to talk of their recently finished performance and our professed enthusiasm regarding his Rickenbacker, he quietly responded, giving the impression that 'guitar talk' didn't appear to interest him too much.

He was wearing glasses, no jacket, and a blue denim shirt, having changed out of his stage suit. The glasses were quite a surprise as, although very short-sighted, he was seldom to be seen in public with them during the first 3 or 4 years of fame.

From 1966 onwards, following a few weeks in Spain filming Dick Lester's *How I Won The War*, he would wear the small, round, wire rimmed, *Granny Takes A Trip* style spectacles that became so associated with him, that many people called them 'Lennon Glasses'. But that day he was wearing black horn-rims, reminiscent of Buddy Holly and Hank B. Marvin. I've always felt that his lack of concern regarding this 'off camera' moment, added an element of shared intimacy.

Well what did we talk about? Our part in the local group scene, playing guitar, Vox amps, Rickenbackers, the Beatles' performance, and a new band that'd just released their first record: the Rolling Stones!

Regarding our entry point to all of this – Rickenbacker curiosity – we learned that it had been bought a few years back in Hamburg, was called a 325, and he liked it a lot: "A great rhythm guitar." Sometime later I realised the models full name was a Capri 325. As I've mentioned the appeal of guitar chat seemed so-so. Apparently of more interest was knowing we'd just seen the show.

"How did it sound – could you hear us alright?" Hard to say if this was a slight, making conversation enquiry or a real request for info at a time when such feedback was still of significance. It really felt like the latter, possibly borne out by their next show. We quickly reassured him: Al going on to describe our position vis à vis the stage.

From where we'd been watching, the amps of George and Paul were directly in front of us; with John's off to the right. This had tended to reduce the volume of the chords emanating from his amp in the overall mix. He seemed genuinely interested to know George's lead guitar was dominating the sound balance, and indicated he'd sort it out.

With a sense of incredulity, Al and I realised the next day our words of 'advice' had been heeded! The *Bournemouth Echo* reviewing both of the opening night's performances, whilst correctly raving over the Beatles' storming success felt moved to comment: "In the second house, John Lennon's guitar was far too loud." As we read these words, sitting in the El Cabala, late the following afternoon we cracked up with laughter – J.L. had acted on Al's critique, inadvertently affecting a Beatles' gig!

Backstage this extraordinary conversation continued: perhaps naturally following our 'mini review', it drifted in the direction of amplifiers. Specifically the Vox amps the group appeared to favour. Nothing unusual there. Back in that pre-Marshall stack era and all the options that were to come, most top bands used Vox. But there was an alternative: Fender Showman amps. They were even more expensive in the UK than Vox; featured top of the range JBL speakers, and had been designed a couple of years before with US 'King of Surf Guitar', Dick Dale, in mind. Vox AC 30s, as their name suggested, produced a maximum of 30 watts: Fender were soon to deliver the first 100 watt amp. As Fenders were often used in studios, Al asked him about their choice of Vox. The response was surprisingly strong and direct. "They're rubbish!"

Al and I exchanged glances. Lennon continued. And although I'm sure this was not the only reason they were equipped with a Jennings Musical Industries' product, this was his explanation: Epstein had a deal with the company, involving the Beatles' images and name featuring in ads for Vox – the obvious quid pro quo being a supply of amplifiers. Lennon's annoyance regarding his AC30 was memorably expressed, perhaps indicating concern with being under-powered alongside George and having the current location's geography in mind: "Sometimes I'd like to kick the bloody thing off the pier!"

This brief diatribe was to live on over future decades, as Al would from time to time delight concert audiences around the world with extracts from our meeting with Beatle John.

The amp talk then lead back to guitars and an out of the blue – once in a lifetime moment as the reason we'd come knocking at his door resurfaced.

But first, as my adrenaline-fuelled confidence reached critical mass, I found myself telling a Beatle that, yes they were fantastic, but there was another group I was sure would become huge. And so, just weeks after the release of the Rolling Stones first ever record I became one of the first to suggest a comparison between the two most important bands in history! And this, face to face, with John Lennon!

Now this could have gone very badly wrong – although I had a good reason (or at least hoped I did) to believe my opinion would be allowed at least, and at best indicate a hint of switched on, in tune, hipness. The reason? Well although the Stones had yet to set the charts on fire and had hardly been glimpsed by more than a few hundred London R 'n' B club devotees, I knew George liked them, had seen a gig in Richmond, and enthused the other three.

John's response? "Yeah we like the Stones." Phew! So that was alright then. I had managed to tell the leader of the most exciting musical act since sliced bread that an almost unknown, yet to tour, pub/club band were going to edge themselves onto the mountain top too.

A bit more chat about the Stones and seeing them play – him, not me at this point – and then my horn-rimmed hero said this totally unexpected thing. "Would you like to see my guitar, the Rickenbacker?" Accompanied by a half apologetic, half matter of fact, "The dressing room's too busy; I'll go and get it."

With this the Beatles' rhythm guitarist disappeared, leaving what appeared to be a Lewis Carroll, 'Cheshire Cat' type, after image.

Slightly stunned by this development, we let the moment freeze-frame us into a couple of Madame Tussauds' statues, until his return.

Lennon returns, Rickenbacker in hand. Then without a hint of concern hands it to me! Well, well, well. From not knowing its maker's name less than an hour ago, I am now holding what was to become one of the most iconic guitars of the 20th century along with McCartney's Hofner violin bass, Jimi Hendrix's Strat, and Les Paul's Les Paul.

Six months later the Beatles would perform to a historic, record breaking American TV audience of 73 million people on the Ed Sullivan Show – the guitar in my nervous grip would then be held by John Lennon.

"Oh, great, thank you. Er, can I try it?"

"Yeh, sure."

It seemed the obvious way to proceed. Slight snag: the owner of this particular musical instrument believed me to be a guitarist with a local group and as referred to in a previous chapter this had been short circuited by my lack of talent. Also, I don't know about you, but when playing guitar I would normally have it strung around my neck or be sitting down. With Trapper Al and Beatle John watching I then had to confront this flashpoint consequence of my 'Must meet the Beatles' bravado.

Adopting a flamingo-like stance, balancing the black Rickenbacker on one knee, I strummed a few chords employing the length of this small guitar's neck and deeply cut-away body followed by a sub Duane Eddy 'shazam' riff.

"Great action. Such a short scale neck."

"Yes," he agreed.

I'd got away with it! Played proficiently enough not to reveal my potentially embarrassing limitations and casually spoken words that guitar players the world over would employ.

With an understandable sense of contained exhilaration and relief, I passed it over to Al. After all here was a genuine musician with the ability to provide substance to our 'We're in groups too' line. As Lennon gazed quietly, my friend played a slightly longer, and fortunately altogether more competent précis of his own skills. Al also commented to J.L. on the guitar's attractions and three quarter size characteristics.

"Got to go – on again soon," John informed us as he recovered his guitar. "Yes, of course. Thanks. Thank you."

He returned to the dressing room and we gradually retraced our dazed steps back into the 'real world'.

As we made our way through the crowds still thronging Bournemouth's streets that warm summer's evening, Al and I would have been amazed to know that as the future unfolded the Beatles' fame would increase exponentially as they sailed on into the history books. That Al would become a platinum-selling, singer-songwriter, with *Year of the Cat* a world-wide smash. And my 'Let's find a way to talk with John Lennon' initiative would move from being a private, personal memory, to being known as '*The*

Men from Rickenbacker' story: to be retold over the next few decades in books, magazines, newspapers, radio broadcasts, tour programmes and live concerts.

The principle reason for this being Al's career in music. Along with, of course, the planet's love affair with the Beatles engendering an ongoing appetite for all and any details regarding their story. Al's success meant interviews: first in music papers, then national press; followed by radio and TV. He would often refer to the time he and his friend Jonny met the Beatles; especially the Lennon/Rickenbacker moment. Eventually, as he always found a positive reaction to this anecdote, he started to include it in his concert performances.

Now this last point effectively caused the '*MFR*' tale to mutate into a far from accurate version. Quite understandably, as the requirements for 'stage entertainment' were some way removed from documentary criteria.

A recent example of this, in our *Wikipedia* world of instant information – sometimes distorted with a 'Chinese Whispers' miasma of inaccuracy – came via *The Times* newspaper. In September 2009, in one of those reoccurring spikes in the continuous graph of 'Beatles News', *The Times*, along with most of the print and broadcast media, reported the release of the entire, digitally re-mastered, Beatles' back catalogue; in mono or stereo, contained in CD Box Sets, costing over a hundred pounds. To mark this occasion – showing yet again the enduring power of the Beatles – this pre-eminent newspaper devoted pages and pages to this 60's group, spread over a week of issues. One double page feature collected interesting stories from people that had met them during Beatlemania. The Al Stewart paragraphs were quoted, not from any of the many interviews, but from his stage act: a colourful re-write in which Neil Aspinall wants to throw us out and John Lennon persuades him to let us stay! Ho hum. Naturally I prefer to recall the various retellings imbued with a little more verisimilitude.

Of the many airings on American FM Radio stations and the BBC, perhaps the most informative broadcast featured on a Radio 1, Nicky Campbell *Into the Night* programme in the early 90s.

For a print version an interesting account appeared in Neville Judd's fine book: *Al Stewart: The True Life Adventures of a Folk Rock Troubadour*. Also an in depth interview with me in *Jackdaw* magazine, came close to capturing the atmosphere of the time.

Al Stewart, quoted in *Troubadour*, gives his take on the challenge awaiting us, just prior, to our backstage adventure:

"The area around the theatre and the Beatles' hotel was just a sea of screaming fans, and that's what confronted us when we came out after the gig. We were on a real high by then and had decided we just had to get to chat to them somehow; but it was really looking to be impossible."

One of my favourite snapshots of the '*MFR*' story occurred in 1991, when it was referenced in a concert programme for the Bootleg Beatles, accompanying a performance by this greatest of all 'Tribute Bands', at the Bournemouth International Centre.

Over the years the *Bournemouth Echo* has run several features outlining the story, including articles by Roan Fair, Jeremy Miles and Nick Churchill.

The most recent retelling of the tale appears in Nick Churchill's excellent volume *Yeah Yeah Yeah: The Beatles & Bournemouth*, published in autumn 2011.

But this was the future. Before concluding that eventful day, Al and I came to a decision: let's do it again! We've met John Lennon – now we want to meet all the Beatles. They were here for a few days and if backstage access can be gained, surely I can talk our way into their hotel? Come on now, it's the obvious next move, don't you think? We agreed to get together the next day to plan 'Meet The Beatles – The Sequel'.

Meet The Beatles

Annus Mirabilis spoke of Philip Larkin's assertion that 'Life was never better than in nineteen sixty-three'. And for more than a few it seemed 'Bliss was it in that dawn to be alive, but to be young was very heaven', as his poetic predecessor Wordsworth claimed over a century before.

In a matter of a few months it seemed as if the world of post-war 50's monochrome had photoshopped itself into sparkling colour. A bit like the opening reel of *Summer Holiday*. It's hard to do justice now to the uplifting fresh feel of 'something in the air'. This was the year the telephoto lens of a world-wide media began to focus on our ancient realm and become overwhelmed and infatuated with the land of Beatles, Bond and Christine Keeler.

While Paul McCartney's banker may not have been 'wearing a mac in the pouring rain' – 'here, there and everywhere' fringe-haired, Cuban-heeled, Beatle clones walked the streets, attired in round-collared, Pierre Cardin inspired jackets.

The afternoon of August 20th found two young 'reporters' from the *Echo*, standing in front of the Palace Court Hotel. Reporters, by the way, the *Echo* was quite unaware it possessed! Keeping them company were a small contingent of hopeful, prototype 'Apple Scruff', girls on 'Beatle watch'.

As Al and I verbally rechecked the simple script lines of our next act, a hotel guest wandered out onto one of the first floor balconies. The excited screams of joy from Bournemouth's teenage fans rose and quickly fell, on realising the figure they viewed from their Pavilion wall perch was not a Beatle.

During our time spent backstage the previous evening chatting with Billy J's Dakotas we heard they, and more importantly the Beatles, were staying nearby in Westover Road's, art deco fronted, Palace Court Hotel. We also gained the unsurprising info that the Beatles seldom surfaced before noon when on tour, unless they really had to. So as they were spending a week in Bournemouth it certainly indicated that we could let the morning pass us by as well.

Across the way the eight storey, bright white, 1930's hotel, replete with frontage-wide balconies for each level, awaited with entrance doors firmly closed. The obviously required 'security' was provided by a solitary, uniformed, member of staff. Mandated to let guests come and go, but to let no one else into the Palace Court that week – especially Beatlemaniacs!

As we approached our first obstacle, I quietly rehearsed to myself: "Hi, we're from the *Echo*, here to interview the Beatles – their manager's expecting us." A few seconds later I heard someone, me actually, say: "Hi, we're from the *Echo*, here to interview the Beatles – their manager's expecting us."

"Yes sir – your colleague is already here. I think you will find him in the lounge on the first floor." As the door was held open and we left the sunlit street behind, I acknowledged the doorman's information, while frantically pondering the word 'colleague'!

As Al and I stood in the foyer we both realised our spectacularly short newspaper 'career' was over. A new, instant, scenario was required. New plan: we are not here for the Beatles; but to meet the Dakotas. Why not?

After all hadn't bass guitarist Ray Jones said, "See you around," just the day before. O.K. here we are: around.

A momentary delay, whilst the receptionist spoke with a middle-aged couple in front of us, and then *abracadabra*! "One moment sir, I'll try Mr. Jones' room." After hearing, no doubt to his surprise, that two visitors were awaiting him in reception, Dakota Ray suggested we come up to his room. Now in possession of his room number and helpful directions for finding it, Al and I, ignoring the lift, energetically (for us), bounded up the stairs to the third floor.

He seemed pleased to see us. The twin-bed room, empty save for the three of us, revealed no sign of the 'trashed hotel room' motif which was to become de-rigueur for the rock world soon enough. We talked briefly of the crazy crowd scenes from the night before, and the girls still waiting in the street below.

Ray, in his early twenties, appeared slightly bemused by it all. Correctly gauging the level the 'Beatle effect' was having on everything; both surpassed and enhanced the status of even a No.1 group such as his. Brian Epstein managed, and George Martin produced, Billy J. Kramer with the Dakotas, had hit the top of the charts with their first single, Lennon and McCartney's song for George on the *Please, Please Me* album: 'Do You Want To Know A Secret'. Note that nice Epstein touch – 'with' the Dakotas; not 'and'.

The Dakotas had gone Top 20 themselves the previous month with a splendid Shadows style guitar instrumental composed by their lead guitarist Mike Maxfield. 'The Cruel Sea', inspired by the title of Nicholas Monsarrat's evocative best-selling tale of war at sea, became a key part of that summer's soundtrack. America's own Shads, the Ventures, cover version re-titled it 'The Cruel Surf'.

Moving small talk to one side I came to the point: "Are the Beatles around?" Glancing at his watch he said, "Yeah. They're probably in the lounge with Tony and Mike. Let's go down."

It transpired the hotel's series of lounges were on the first floor, with one end – the left side of the building if you were looking up from street level – roped off for the Beatles and support acts. Chit-chatting on our way to this inner sanctum, Ray continued to express an almost detached first hand view of the changing, feverish, public reaction the four Liverpudlians were engendering. Prior to becoming a full-time pop musician he worked in a Manchester bank and was fairly well grounded in respect of the Merseymania fantasy land he now found himself in. The Dakotas being from Manchester were the exception to the rule of 1963's B. Epstein managed/G. Martin produced, Liverpool juggernaut. Thirty seven of the years fifty two weeks would see a group managed and produced by these two exceptional men claim the No.1 spot in the UK charts, with the Beatles, Gerry and the Pacemakers, and Billy J. with the Dakotas.

Passing by the, far from insurmountable, thick red rope strung between two gilded supports – which appeared to be keeping the hotel's mainly upper middle class clientele effectively at bay – Ray, Al and I entered a sizable area of rest and recreation.

The recreation being principally supplied by a small bar located alongside the lounge's inner wall. Directly opposite a large expanse of windows, plus balcony door, invited the summer sun to join the party.

Sitting on a long sofa, with their backs to the outside world, were John Lennon and George Harrison. In front of them a coffee table surrounded by large armchairs. One of these hosted the relatively small figure of Ringo Starr. Keeping them company were a couple of unfamiliar faces.

Time for me and Al to beam at each other: this was going quite well! At a right-angle to the Beatles' table the lounge provided more seats and tables. Sitting close by the Fab 3, with McCartney nowhere to be seen at that moment, a brace of Dakotas, Mike Maxfield and Tony Mansfield, beckoned to their fellow musician to join them. As we made our way in their direction we passed, seated by a table near the bar, our *Echo* 'colleague' Jeff Zollo, in the company of Le Disque a Go Go owner, Alan Azern. We exchanged hellos. It was Jeff, the following month, who wrote up my Trappers' PR bit suggesting Al to be a gifted songwriter.

As we sat down John Lennon gave a nod of recognition: probably for Ray; though Al and I preferred to believe it was for us.

Just as the night before, I'd not thought through how the minutes following reaching the Beatles might unfold. Now fortunately, as the 'reporters from the *Echo*' plan had, like mist on a summer's day, evaporated, we appeared to have lucked into a 'genuine' reason to be in this roped off enclosure.

In parlance that would echo around Rock 'n' Pop's backstages & Green Rooms in the future, we were: 'with the band'. The band in question being the Dakotas. As the other band in the room were now so close, for the next hour or two, my attention was split between our table's conversation and overhearing the Beatles'.

We drank coffee, pleased Mike with our enthusiasm for his 'Cruel Sea' hit, and heard a tale of a hotel facility that the Palace Court was not listing on their tariff. Apparently Ringo had already 'scored' with one of the chambermaids: indeed there was some debate as to how many chambermaids!

In later years it became quite well known how much the Beatles enjoyed having 'fun' on tour. John once likened their tours to Fellini's *Satyricon*. It was suggested to me a few years back by Mark Lewisohn, that Lennon had a relatively 'quiet' week in that respect while in Bournemouth, due to the presence of his then wife Cynthia.

By now I'd realised the next table's talk was actually an interview; the other two being journalists. Ray confirmed this. They were from *The Beatles Book*, a new monthly magazine devoted to satisfying the enormous demand for facts 'n' info about the group: a small format periodical, from the same publisher as *Beat Monthly*. Issue No.1 had just hit the newsstands, with No.2 due in September.

John Lennon – who was doing most of the talking – appeared to be filling in background details regarding their time in Hamburg. A bit later on George joined in when they switched to talk of Liverpool clubs. Ringo said relatively little. Occasionally he'd get up and wander about for a while: including stopping for a chat with the Dakotas.

The data gathered by the journalist for *The Beatles Book* was to appear from No.2 onwards. His byline in the magazine was Billy Shepherd. A long, long time after that day, Mark Lewisohn informed me that this was a pseudonym and his real name was Peter Jones. Yes the same Peter Jones from the *Record Mirror*, who a few months earlier suggested Andrew Oldham check out the unsigned Rolling Stones in Richmond's station hotel!

Time passed: still no sign of Paul McCartney. Someone suggested he'd managed to escape the hotel; perhaps as far as the New Forest. Or possibly he was pursuing other recreational pursuits à la Ringo's exploits.

Talking of girls, the afternoon would regularly be sonically invaded by bursts of screaming from the street below. John Lennon greeted one of these expressions of female fandom by shouting, "Shut up!" Of course the girls in Westover Road couldn't hear this, but the other, slightly startled guests of this 4 star hotel could!

Not long after this he walked over to the balcony door, opened it, and briefly stood on the open balcony (these days they are enclosed) inciting the delighted Beatle Watchers to reach a new level of ecstatic volume.

Meanwhile I was hearing of drummer Tony's sister: a teenage singer back in Manchester, who was apparently about to sign a record contract. Her chosen stage name was Elkie Brooks. A first single released the following year didn't chart. But further down the line, after a spell sharing vocal duties with Robert Palmer in Vinegar Joe, she had a huge hit with 'Pearl's a Singer'. Just as with Al, overnight success took a while.

Lennon, by now sitting down again, rejoined the *Beatle Book* interview/ conversation with Harrison. Ringo was standing nearby chatting with Tommy Quickly. Quickly was an Epstein protégé who'd been given a Lennon and McCartney song, 'Tip of My Tongue', plus a slot on the show, to have a crack at the big time. Not to be.

I decided to join them. Needing something to say and noticing Alan Azern had just left, I invited them to a party. A party at Le Disque a Go Go. Actually at that moment a non-existent party! But if the Beatles wanted to come – well that wouldn't be too hard to organise. One of them was a little downbeat and not too interested. The other beamed and said, "Yeah, great. When?" Unfortunately the beaming one wasn't Ringo. He gave me the impression he'd already heard of the idea of a party, but they weren't leaving the hotel unless they really had to. Leaving me to explain to a disappointed Tommy Q. that it didn't look like party-time after all.

At this point I realised something tangible was needed for me to take from this day; a memento of these magic moments. It would have to be autographs.

Following Ringo as he made his way back to rejoin the other two Fabs, I quickly searched my pockets for a pen and something to write on. Thoughtlessly unprepared all I could locate was a pencil and a small piece of thin card. O.K. better than a quill and papyrus – but not much better.

Peter Jones/'Billy Shepherd', had vacated his seat, and momentarily tempting though the idea of plonking myself in it seemed, I parked alongside it instead. Lennon glanced across in my direction, fortunately looking relaxed and affable.

"Would you mind signing this?" Ringo took my proffered pencil and card; then signed Beatle Ringo Starr. Unprompted by me he then passed it across to George. He reached as far as the H of his surname, when – disaster! The lead point of my stupid pencil snapped. "I broke your pencil," George announced apologetically, while turning to his left and politely demanding – not requesting – "John, give me your pen." Which the smiling John did. Continuing to sign, 'Harrison' now appeared in ink. Concluding possibly the longest/slowest autograph in history! By now J.L. having retrieved his pen and added his name, leaning forward over the coffee table returned my unique souvenir. I say unique: it's doubtful if there is another set of Beatle signatures beginning in pencil and ending in ink.

John Lennon, George Harrison and Ringo Starr give me their signatures in Bournemouth August 1963

The *Beatles Book* guy then reclaimed his seat and I rejoined Al, Ray, Mike and Tony.

Almost immediately the three Dakotas announced they were leaving to meet up with Billy J. in the nearby Gaumont, prior to the evening's show. Did we want to join them? Well yes, we did. As the next scene unfolded this simple, obvious choice of action, was to provide a memorable, one-off, fun filled moment. Not the soon to be 'Hello Billy J.' bit, but rather the getting from the hotel to the theatre.

Billy's backing band chose to leave the Palace Court via the main entrance, turn right and a short distance later enter the Gaumont from Westover Road; not the stage door. This would be a common sense, direct route, to employ in a 'standard issue' real world. These *Summer of 63* popmania days (daze?) of course were slightly unreal.

As soon as the five of us reached the open air of the street, a posse of excited, screaming girls detached themselves from the main Pavilion wall cohort and ran across the road, dodging the no doubt bemused drivers.

With surprised smiles forming on the faces of two of us – the other three already accustomed to this reaction – we started to run.

In a mini *Hard Days Night* scenario, we outpaced them, reached the commissionaire-attended Gaumont entrance and rushed into the foyer, as the protective doors closed, curtailing the event.

Nothing was said as we made our way through the empty auditorium and climbed the steps to the stage. Later Al and I confirmed our thoughts had been basically identical: this is the essence of PopWorld and we liked it a lot. I know: what's not to like?

An hour or so before the first house performance the stage was filled with drums, guitars, a piano, mic stands, musicians, plus a couple of stage hands. Al, much to my amusement, momentarily failed to recognise Billy J. sitting on a chair, centre stage, strumming a Fender Strat. The crowded Beatles' dressing room we'd encountered the night before had hosted a 20th birthday party celebration for Dakota Billy. Apparently it concluded later that evening in the Palace Court.

Not exactly rehearsing or sound-checking, but more just jamming a bit someone started up Buddy Holly's *Peggy Sue* rhythm, leading to a short improvised version of Tommy Roe's, Holly homage, 'Sheila'.

We eventually exited via the stage door.

Decades later, quoted in *The Times* in September 2009, Al referred to this 'Meet the Beatles' experience as 'One of the most important in my life'.

Beatles and Bournemouth

The first of two significant Bournemouth-based Beatle History events occurred during their week long stay in the town. It was to reach out from the Palace Court, span the world, and become an iconic 20th century image.

A couple of days after I met them, Robert Freeman photographed the group in the hotel's dinning room: a shoot for the cover of *With The Beatles*, (*Meet The Beatles* in the USA).

Stark, strong and striking, an original art work that instantly re-wrote the existing commercial rules for sleeve design. If EMI hadn't said "No" and allowed Freeman's full concept to proceed, the Beatles would have pre-empted Andrew Oldham's own ground-breaking achievement the following year when he argued Decca into submission and the Stones first LP appeared without any text information on the cover. No title. No group name. Just edge to edge photo.

Far from 'green lighting' this bold creative move, the deciding record company executive had to be persuaded by Parlophone's George Martin to accept the un-smiling, monochrome image at all. Not surprising perhaps as a 'before and after' glance at '50's and early 60's album sleeves reveals an almost total reliance on colour photography and smiling faces.

Impressed by Robert Freeman's previous work with John Coltrane, Cannonball Adderley and other jazz artists, the Beatles and the man who was to photograph 5 of their album covers, were to meet for the first time in Bournemouth. This took place on the Tuesday of that week. Introduced to the group by Brian Epstein, there was an immediate rapport that was to lead on to not only a long standing professional connection but also a social and personal relationship.

So, where did this important and career effecting event take place? Liverpool? London? Hamburg? No: Bournemouth!

Using natural light, travelling at its ever constant 186,282 miles a second, with a heavy, maroon curtain for a backdrop, the photographer positioned the four, black polo-necked musicians, in a close, tele-photo shot. The square album cover format dictating their line-up, with last member to join the group Ringo, positioned kneeling on a stool in front of Paul. The resulting black and white picture – the manufacturing print process having reduced the textural light and shade – revealed four, full-on, Zen-like visages, that seemed to float in a time and space all their own.

On the 22nd of November 1963 a, still obscured, conspiracy changed the direction of the world: America's 35th President, John F. Kennedy was assassinated in Dallas, Texas.

On the 22nd of November 1963 a, still without precedent record release, also changed the direction of the world. With Beatlemania-inspired U.K. advance orders of over 250,000 copies, *With The Beatles* hit the shops.

'*With The Beatles*' Ad Bournemouth Echo

The Beatles' 2nd LP, full to the brim with outstanding original songs and awesome cover versions, repeated its chartbusting success early the following year, when, as *Meet The Beatles*, along with a stack of singles, it encouraged a saddened America, still absorbing the grief of their undemocratic political loss, to find new joy.

The frequently misused adjective 'iconic' could, removed from its religious origins, accurately be applied to this Beatle cover image. It represents the era in a way equalled only by Lewis Morley's, '*Arne Jacobsen*', photographic portrait of Christine Keeler.

It has been clear to see for some time now that four of the Beatles' album sleeves featured photography/designs/concepts that as works of art continue to illuminate and define the decade of their creation. Pastiched, parodied, caricatured and ripped-off, *Sgt. Pepper, Revolver, Abbey Road* and *With The Beatles* are all extraordinary and unique.

Of course all of the group's LPs have featured very special covers; including Freeman's *Rubber Soul* and his innovative, and apposite, *Hard Day's Night* concept.

The friendship that was to continue between the Fabs and their in-house photographer during the next few years received another opportunity to develop, thanks to John Lennon's search for a London home. Knowing of this Robert suggested John and Cynthia should take an apartment in the South Kensington block of flats where he and his wife Sonny currently lived.

If Philip Norman's biography of Lennon is correct this would, indirectly, lead to one of the Beatles' most memorable mid-period songs: 'Norwegian Wood'. The 'playing away' described so hauntingly by J.L. was supposedly with the first Mrs. Freeman!

Talking of wives: in one of those slight synchronicities of life, my artist wife Abi, in the late 1970s, was represented by a London gallery called Graffiti, situated in Great Marlborough Street. At the same time the gallery was exhibiting Robert (Bob) Freeman's work. Specifically a limited edition lithograph of his Palace Court, *With The Beatles* picture. Yes, you guessed correctly: we acquired one!

The print process enabled the tonal balance and texture to be clearly viewed, re-instating the artist's original work previously denied by record sleeve production.

In 1990, the publication of the retrospective volume *A Private View*, a large format book featuring many of Freeman's Beatle photographs, displayed – not surprisingly – his lithographic print on the cover.

Still on the wavelength of art and the Beatles, the late Stuart Sutcliffe comes to mind.

The original '5th Beatle', a friend of John Lennon from their Liverpool Art College days, died tragically in 1962 soon after leaving the group to pursue a full time career as an artist. To please John, Stuart played bass in his friend's band, but never felt like a musician: always painting meant more.

Encouraged by having his early potential recognised by Eduardo Paolozzi, who along with Peter Blake, originated British Pop Art, Sutcliffe decided to paint and not strum. But not before imbuing John Lennon – and through him the Beatles – with an art sensibility that would endow the group with an unprecedented and distinguishing awareness.

Before the Beatles the world of Pop, presumed along with the rest of the entertainment industry as 'low culture', and Art, aligned with Theatre and Classical Music, regarded as 'high culture', possessed no one who breathed the same air. By the time the sixties were over Lennon, McCartney and Harrison had terraformed a new world encompassing a versatile, expanded, one world culture.

The art schools of England were to transform our Rock 'n' Pop from a colony of Showbiz to a musical phenomenon, building an empire of songs on which the sun never set. Viz: the Kinks, the Who, and the Merseybeat band containing the ghost of a genuine artist, that one day would find its choice of a representative logo to be perfectly expressed with René Magritte's *Apple*.

One day in 1990, Abi and I were invited to a private view of Stuart

Sutcliffe's paintings held at Sotheby's. We were impressed with his late period abstract expressionist work: in the direction of de Kooning, and Jackson Pollock. Liverpool alumni attending the exhibition's opening included Roger McGough, George Melly and Beryl Bainbridge.

On the Thursday of 'Beatles in Bournemouth' week the Palace Court Hotel connected Mike Maxfield with an incoming call; incoming all the way from the pillar-box red phone booth across the road.

Having allowed ourselves a fallow, gap day on Wednesday, Al and I had now returned to once more chance our luck. I'd decided to invest a few coins in a little data gathering. Were the Beatles around? Specifically, was Paul McCartney?

Excepting the odd glimpse he was a Beatle that had managed to elude us. Without referring to our extremely nearby location I asked the Dakotas' lead guitarist how was everything and by the way any sign of the lot from Liverpool? And here the dice that had been rolling so nicely for us since Monday fell off the table. "Oh, you've missed them. They've driven over to Southampton to record a TV show." I looked at Al, and indicated the news was negative.

"What show? Which channel and when does it go out?" He replied ITV and 6 o'clock today. Needing to be back in Bournemouth in time for their evening performances the Beatles were pre-recording a promo, miming to 'She Loves You' on Southern TV's *Day By Day*. Accompanying them on their New Forest excursion was new acquaintance Robert Freeman.

Perhaps we should have tried to extend our 'hanging out with the Beatles' on the previous day, but Al and I had been centred on a club gig I'd booked for the Trappers in Branksome Park. A busy week for Al's group; on the night prior to that you could have caught them at Le Disque.

I swiftly headed back to Broadstone to be in front of our 21" black and white TV. Watching England's pop finest lip-synch what must surely have been the first ever TV broadcast of the mighty 'She Loves You', proved to be a slightly weird moment. Watching the Beatles, courtesy of a cathode ray tube, so soon after watching them live and being in their company, felt disconcertingly odd.

That evening, sans Al, I returned to the Gaumont for one last attempt to catch up with the elusive Paul. Navigating my way backstage once more, facilitated by a young assistant theatre manager, who erroneously believed I was somehow part of something or connected in someway with this, that or whatever, I realised the Beatles were onstage in the midst of their 2nd house performance.

For some reason, or rather lack of reason, standing by the stage access door, I gave way to an impulse. Opened it and walked into the half-light of the wings. Ahead to my left the sound of the Mersey Marvels was projecting away towards the audience. I advanced a few feet, carefully avoiding the obstacles presented by the cable strewn floor. At a 45% angle, illuminated by shafts of stage lighting, I could glimpse John Lennon. In the few moments I hovered there I had a) not a clue why or for what purpose I'd put myself in this position, and b) in my confused excitement, no idea what the Beatles were singing. From time to time I've tried to recall the answer to b), but I guess it's not to be: I don't know.

What I do know is a startled stagehand suddenly loomed large in the gloom and demanded to know why I was there. Well obviously as I've just said I hadn't a clue. I gave him an acknowledging wave, a beatific smile, and retreated to the adjacent corridor.

Although no one appeared to be paying any attention to my antics, nevertheless it seemed time to go. Which meant no "Hello Paul, why do you play a Hofner Violin bass – is it because it looks good played left-handed?"

By the time I was able to spend some quality moments with Paul McCartney, I had other questions to ask; and 10 years had passed by and with them the sixties.

South Coast Shadow

"Would you like to buy an electric double bass?" Tall, dark, good looking and short of cash, the bass guitarist of local group the Interns stood in our small Moordown shop accompanied by a fellow musician. Electric double bass – what could he mean? Perhaps some sort of bass guitar. "It's in the van – I'll get it." Which he did.

I'd not seen a musical instrument like it; not even in photos. A plank-like solid body, the height of a ¾ size cello, metal and wood, with a protruding spike at one end and a short version of an acoustic double bass fingerboard at the other. Complete with electric pick-ups, as per a guitar; but unlike a bass guitar, no frets.

He sat down on an upturned piano accordion case and plucked a few un-amplified notes from it. It looked extraordinary, but who might want to buy it? Not an acoustic double bass playing jazz guy. Not back then. A bass guitarist in a band almost certainly wouldn't know how to play it. He looked slightly down when I said, "Thanks, but no thanks".

I later found out that Don Strike's son Bev provided a similar response in their Westbourne shop.

That would have been that: an unremarkable moment, easily forgettable. Except then, while talking of bands and bass guitarists, the Intern implied, current financial circumstances not withstanding, something, as Bob Dylan could have said, may be 'blowing in the wind'.

The Tornados, still a major name following their worldwide 'Telstar' smash hit the previous year, were easily the No.2 instrumental group in Britain: second only to the Shadows. They were also until recently short of one bass guitarist. Peroxide blond Heinz Burt having been induced by an admiring Joe Meek to leave the group and become a 'one hit wonder'. Actually the well strange producer probably didn't put it quite like that.

According to the unsuccessful electric bass salesman he'd turned down the chance to join the Tornados as Heinz replacement. I'm sure you, like me, at that point had to ask why. After all the Tornados, were the Tornados – not the Interns!

So I asked why. He answered enigmatically. He believed there was a chance of something better round the corner. I pondered this whilst wishing him well as he and his upright electric bass left the shop.

Then John Rostill joined The Shadows!

'Licorice' Locking, had wanted to leave his position in England's chart topping Shads for a while and when he did the need to replace him was urgent. They were in the midst of a season at the London Palladium with Cliff Richard, and soon to leave for the Canary Islands to shoot scenes for CR's follow up movie to *Summer Holiday*, *Wonderful Life*.

Locking, previously a part of Marty Wilde's Wildcats, had joined at the behest of drummer Brian Bennett; himself a former Wildcat, to occupy the centre stage spot vacated by founder member Jet Harris: an unusual position for a group's bass guitarist. A quick glance at the line-up of most 60's groups indicating stage left to be more likely. For example: the Beatles, Stones, Who, Kinks etc. Jet, the man who gave the name Shadows to the UK Drifters, when the US vocal group asserted their prior ownership of the name, possessed a dominant personality, perfectly suited to his central role. So for the next 5 years that was where John Rostill stood, with Hank B. Marvin to his left and rhythm guitarist Bruce Welch to his right.

But first he needed to pass the audition.

A year or two before, while playing bass with another group, before his Bournemouth days, Rostill had been favourably observed by Hank and Bruce. The Shadows were topping the bill and had taken a moment to catch their support act from the wings.

Unknown to him he now featured on a short list of possible replacements.

Top of the list being John Paul Jones. He said no. As a young Decca Records' session musician he played on former Shadows Jet Harris and Tony Meehan's 'Diamonds' No.1 hit, and therefore was known to the Shadows. He chose to stay a session player for a while – most notably for Andrew Loog Oldham's Immediate Records – before joining up late in the sixties with another musician from the 'Diamonds' recording; and with Jimmy Page formed Led Zeppelin.

At this point a member of Cliff & the Shads management was dispatched to Bournemouth to locate John Rostill.

After the Interns had performed to a Le Disque Saturday night crowd the bass-hunter from London invited John to drive through the night and take an early morning opportunity the next day. He did and rendezvoused with Hank, Bruce and his destiny. After just one number he was in.

The guy who'd not long before told me he felt sure something better than hooking up with the notorious Joe Meek was 'round the corner', was now a Shadow.

"It's a funny old world," some people say from time to time. Indeed 'Funny Old World' was the title of John Rostill's one and only solo single, but shocking, literally, and sad, would be more appropriate words for the end of his world.

The Shadows split up in 68, having found little space remaining for their special, but slightly dated showbiz image at the high noon of counter culture alternatives. They reformed in 1973 and, a couple of recent 'Farewell Tours' aside, are still with us. But John was sadly not to be a part of this.

In the group's hiatus years Hank and Bruce continued to appear occasionally with Cliff Richard, and also for a while recorded and toured as Marvin, Welch and Farrar, an acoustic harmony group. During this time John Rostill's excellent bass skills had taken him to Las Vegas and extended residences performing with Tom Jones.

By '73 he was back in England and on the brink of a successful song writing career, co-composing with Bruce Welch. One of his songs later that year became Olivia Newton John's breakthrough million-seller in America.

It was Bruce Welch, returning to John Rostill's home recording studio, the following day after a session of demoing songs, who found his fellow ex Shadow, apparently the victim of a tragic electrical accident.

Published in 1988, *Funny Old World* is also the title of a John Rostill biography by Rob Bradford, including my name in the acknowledgements.

Ironically the Shadow originally deemed a 'too fast to live – James Dean style crash' waiting to happen, Jet Harris, was working as a barman in Bournemouth around the time of his successor's demise. Surviving many, and varied problems, in and out of the music biz, the Shads' first bass player was to live on to reach his seventies and an MBE. Funny old world indeed.

Beatles and Bournemouth Reprise

As the shocks, sensations and snowstorms of 1963 prepared to rollover into 64 and leave the Kennedy Assassination, the Keeler/Ward Scandal, Great Train Robbery and Worst Winter Weather of the century to memory and the history books, there would be one more Bournemouth Beatles event of significance.

In early February 1964 the Beatles flew to America for the first time, on the wings of Pan Am and 'I Want To Hold Your Hand'. They landed to be greeted by hysterical scenes at New York's recently renamed John F. Kennedy International Airport, followed by similarly enthusiastic crowds outside the Plaza Hotel.

On the transatlantic flight they had expressed an understandable amount of uncertainty to their fellow passenger Phil Spector. Why would America go ape for them, when during all the many previous years British recording acts had amounted to almost zero? Why would America the originating star-filled home and foundation of the Beatles' music accept a British Beatlemania transplant as the new, true way forward? They soon had the zeitgeist shattering answer.

In less time than it would take Israel to defeat overwhelming odds in 1967's 'Six Day War', the song writing, singing, guitar playing, drumming UK heroes conquered the US of A.

They commanded the airwaves. Dominated the record charts. Broke TV viewing figures. Also monopolised print media and TV/Radio news broadcasts. Nothing on this scale, within this short a time frame, had happened before. So far the world still waits to experience an equivalent pop music phenomenon.

OK, what's all of this have to do with Bournemouth? Quite simply: the Winter Gardens. The Winter Gardens plus NBC, ABC and CBS.

Before the Fabs whirlwind could make what at the time seemed an almost instantaneous takeover of American hearts and minds, even equipped with the gargantuan No.1 asset provided by 'I Want To Hold Your Hand', first US consciousness had to become aware. Aware of what exactly? Well this English group's existence for a kick-off.

Due to the short-sightedness of EMI's US outlet, Capitol Records, only a relatively small number of Beatles' records had reached the turntables of young Americans. Not until their 5th single did Capitol wake up and go into overdrive. By then something had caught this insular label's attention: the

Beatles in Bournemouth, returning to the town for a one night stand in November.

Staying outside the town centre at the 5 star Branksome Towers Hotel, the Fabs second time in Bournemouth that year was almost as 'Day Trippers'. But significant moments of that Saturday 16th, Winter Gardens, appearance were to be captured by America's 'Big3' TV networks, NBC, CBS and ABC, and transmitted coast to coast the following week. Check YouTube for a sample of the first sight 'n' sound America received of England's Beatlemania.

The screaming fan hysteria, inside and outside Exeter Road's concert hall, was filmed, primarily for transmission as a UK news event, rather than an entertainment item. Viewers on the other side of the Atlantic would have to wait a little longer for the Ed Sullivan Show performances to fully understand that, yes, this was a news phenomenon, but one rooted not in fluke and gimmick, but a newly-minted, fresh take on the look and sound of contemporary pop/rock.

The very first major impact on the cerebral cortex of the occupants of our former colony was made by the Beatles in Bournemouth. So this important stage in the group's meteoric progression, coupled with Robert Freeman's Palace Court Hotel, *With The Beatles* photography, writes Bournemouth into the Beatles' geographic history.

One more Beatles and Bournemouth connection exists regarding George Harrison. During the August 63 Palace Court days I hung around, George felt unwell with a rough throat for a day or two, causing him to spend time in his room recuperating. Understandably not wanting to be bothered too much, but with some unexpectedly free hours to fill, he wrote his first Beatles' song: 'Don't Bother Me'. Featuring on *With The Beatles* this Bournemouth song provided the first step on a song writing road to 'Something', 'Here Comes The Sun' and 'While My Guitar Gently Weeps'.

Downliners Sect, Action and G-Men

A week after the Winter Gardens event the Beatles' second LP hit the shops. If you bought your copy from Bourne Radio, as I did, there was no chance that this record could be confused with any other previous LP's release.

Approaching this Old Christchurch Road corner shop's entrance door, opposite Horseshoe Common, a temporary loudspeaker relaying 'It Won't Be Long', 'All My Loving' and the rest of *With The Beatles*, from the basement to the street, caught your attention. Down the stairs, having passed by the ground floor's display of radiograms and TVs, lined up behind the counter, already in carrier bags and good to go, were dozens of copies, confidently waiting to be snapped up. Someone had obviously caught the moment and taken record retailing to another level.

This brings us to Sandie. Hip, dark-haired and with a hint of Françoise Hardy, obviously Sandie was a young woman with quite a lot going for her. And if you were a young male in a band, the added attraction: she ran a record shop!

As I mentioned a while back these emporiums tended to be shops within shops (or department stores), and managed by young women. Don't ask me why, I didn't know or care – it just seemed a perfectly natural, good idea.

Sandie's basement domain boasted the standard racks, peg-boarded walls, and listening booths of the day. Walls alight with rows of 12" square colour: LP sleeves displaying images of singers and groups, interspersed with a few cool B & W covers featuring modern jazz musicians. Of course as 1967's Beatle led LP bonanza was waiting in the future, the 7" single was still the vinyl king. But for the purposes of our Bourne Radio visit let's take a closer look at those covers.

Unlike W.H. Smiths, or Beales, or indeed most stores' record departments in the early-mid sixties, whose walls would be festooned with mid-range popular offerings for the middle-aged Sinatra fan, musical soundtracks from hit stage shows and films, lightweight pop, plus a sprinkling of contemporary MerseyPop, this shop was very different.

The transformation of the thirty three and a third rpm LP, from primarily a platform for classical music, soundtracks, jazz and so called 'easy listening' music – quite hard to listen to if you ask me – to a rock 'n' pop trumping all format, took place across the sixties.

As with so many changes that mattered the Beatles led the way. Starting with the enormous and rapid sales for their 2nd album and peaking with the historic *Sgt. Pepper*, by the time of *Abbey Road*, 12" long-players outsold 7" singles costing only a fifth of their price.

Nineteen sixty nine's *Abbey Road*, by the way, was the first UK LP to be released in stereo only. Another sign that the consumer boom in reasonably priced hi-fi units, coupled with pop/rock's progression from Phil Spector's 2 minute 30 second 'teen drama symphonies' to 45 minute plus demanding song-cycles and 'concepts', had completed 60's music's capture of the LP.

So in late 63/early 64, the available album pick 'n' mix presented by most record shops would vary only slightly from shop to shop. Not Bourne Radio. Yes, the Beatles and other contemporary pop, but also, thanks to Sandie's musical awareness, taste and knowledge, import modern jazz from *Blue Note* and *Riverside*, folk-blues + urban blues, and a virtually unknown singer/writer from Greenwich Village: Bob Dylan.

Knowing Dylan had written 'Blowin' in the Wind', Peter, Paul and Mary's US hit, was one thing – being stared at by a 'Huckleberry Finn' style choirboy was something else. Displayed alongside his first album was the recently released *Freewheelin'*, complete with the visually intriguing Mr. D, ambling along a snowy New York street, anchored by his muse, Suze Rotolo.

Nowhere else for miles around stocked these records. Indeed, for some of them a London trip to Dobell's or Collet's would be required.

Al and I were transfixed by these vinyl offerings. For Al this soon changed gear to infatuation: with both Bobby Dylan and Sandie.

The next step was to listen to these records and here another Bourne Radio plus came into play. Instead of standing in a semi-enclosed booth to hear the sounds delivered from a behind the counter operated turntable, you headed for a small cubicle ensconced in a corner of the shop. Here awaiting your arrival, record and sleeve in hand, resided a seat, wall speakers, and a shelf-mounted record deck.

And so it was here, insulated from the nearby real world of fellow shoppers, I first entered BobDylanWorld.

As he spoke of 'walking in the green pastures of Harvard University' and sang of requesting his 'baby, to let him follow her down', before informing me of a pre-Animals 'House in New Orleans', apparently called the 'Rising Sun', it seemed as if this was a simple 'one to one' communication, just for me. I imagine that this would have been an almost universal experience for anyone hearing that young/old blues voice and those words back in the days before 'Times were a changin'.

Unable to splash out on buying these LPs there and then – allowing for inflation, think of an impecunious student today trying to impulse buy a couple of X-box games – I played a few more tracks before relinquishing my portal to this newly found world.

I caught a disturbing weather forecast, warning of 'Hard rains' and the first of Dylan's songs that Al and I liked to refer to as his 'of' songs: 'Masters of War'. Later there would be 'Chimes of Freedom', 'Gates of Eden' and others. In time I did acquire his first two albums, and realised a couple of things.

First, although unaware of his name, I'd seen and heard Bob Dylan perform back in 1963's snowy January. Flown in from New York by the BBC, he featured in the role of coffee bar singer, during the broadcast of a play called *Madhouse on Castle Street*. And yes, the scruffy looking young American on his first trip outside the US, did stand out, as he delivered four songs (including an early airing of 'Blowin' in the Wind'), punctuating the play at intervals, in the manner of a Greek Chorus.

The second, and obvious, realisation was that other people were discovering/had discovered Bob Dylan. Even if many back then weren't sure how to pronounce his name: Dylan, like Dylan Thomas, and sounding like TV's 'Marshal Matt Dillon', or di – lan?

Among those who possessed the eponymous *Bob Dylan* LP were the Animals. Their inaugural single being 'Baby Let Me Take You Home', a reworking of Rick von Schmidt's 'Baby, Let Me Follow You Down', sung by Dylan on side two, track two. Track three being 'House of the Rising Sun'; the Animals second record.

As it appeared to me that they were working their way through Dylan's 1st LP, seemingly track by track it was a little disappointing they didn't go for a hat-trick with track four: 'Freight Train Blues'!

Source material aside, Newcastle's, Eric Burdon led, R 'n B stars, along with producer Mickie Most, created a stunning recording of 'Rising Sun'. From Hilton Valentine's opening guitar notes, to Alan Price's final keyboard chord, this tale of a New Orleans' bordello is a true classic.

So, Al Stewart, Bob Dylan and Sandie. It would take no great leap of imagination to realise that here was the catalyst for Al's career in music to change direction from a sprint along rockpops' fast lane to a long distance journey down folk-rock street. And, leaving aside a penchant for 1950's Lonnie Donegan, this indeed would be where that fork in the road occurred. Or as Bournemouth's musical bard would say in later years: "I stopped wanting to be Al Beatle and instead become Al Dylan."

The recognition took hold quickly that powerful songs delivering intelligent themes of conviction, ideas and sometimes romance, could be written from a revealing first person perspective, as a counterpoint to pop/rocks musically exciting, but at the time relatively lightweight lyrics.

But for Al acquiring the ability to craft such songs from inside the bubble of a beat group's song structure demands proved to be elusive. Let's face it, you couldn't reasonably be expected to attempt the composition of a new pop 'classic' (or even a camouflaged rewrite of 'I'm a Hog for you Baby'!) before lunch and then compose a pastiche of 'Don't Think Twice, It's All Right' before sunset.

It slowly developed over the next year or two, but his 'Eureka' moment would have to wait till Bournemouth beat band days were over and in 1965 he overheard the guy in the room next to him putting a song together. The then unknown singer-songwriter, sharing London accommodation with my friend, was called Paul Simon.

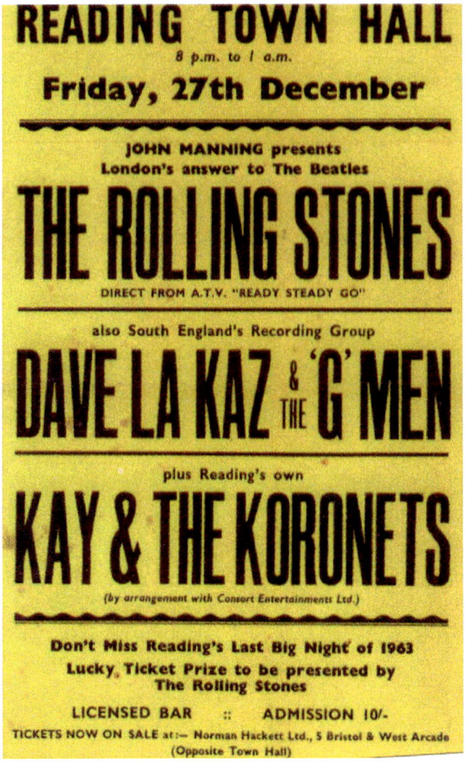

But that lies ahead. Back in Bournemouth and early 64 the discovery of Dylan and a new route forward, coincided with Al having left the Trappers and become a member of one of the town's premier groups: the G-Men.

Among the G-Men's several attractions for Al were a superior vocalist, the splendidly named Dave la Kaz, the fact that bass guitarist Bev Strike's father owned Don Strike, Westbourne's musical instrument shop, and the group being represented by a professional booking agent.

One snag: the G-Men line-up already contained Terry Squires, a more than competent lead guitarist. Nevertheless as the band members knew and liked Al, he decided to join them as a second guitarist.

At this point access to various instruments and PA systems courtesy of Bev's family shop led to the group acquiring a Vox Continental organ. Launched onto the market only a year or so earlier, this highly desirable compact, and relatively portable, keyboard was valve free and transistor based, possessing a slender bright sound.

An obvious asset for any group: slight problem for this one being an apparent absence of anyone able to play it! A problem soon solved when they realised their new recruit could play the piano (a bit). This meant a quick visit to Bourne Radio for Al to check out Sandie's inventory of Jimmy Smith LPs. The innovative jazz organist had recently signed to Verve Records and released a terrific version of the theme from Laurence Harvey's *Walk on the Wild Side* movie and for a while was almost as big an influence on Al as Bob Dylan. I recall one gig in early 64 opening with Vox organ playing Al joining in the vocals on 'Can't Buy Me Love'. Bit like the Dave Clark Five's Mike Smith.

So, far from Al junking his electric guitar for a round-hole steel strung acoustic there and then, he was to continue trying to find his way with a beat group for a while longer.

The G-Men were represented by Avon Entertainments, an agency located on the second floor of an Old Christchurch Road building situated between the El Cabala and Bourne Radio. This asset meant a steady stream of local, and not so local, gigs. They'd regularly play in Swanage – or Duckage, as Al tended to call it – and occasionally as far away as London. Once in Reading the group filled the support slot for an up and coming Rolling Stones.

Optimistically, but incorrectly, promoted as a 'recording group', Bournemouth's G-Men provided minimal competition that night for the Stones, even though the headliners were still being billed as 'London's answer to the Beatles'. Only one member of Jagger and Co. showed any inclination to acknowledge Al that night. Brian Jones appeared an amiable exception, happy to have a chat and talk guitars.

One of the London trips resulted in booking recording time in Dubreq Studios. The group cut two tracks: 'When She Smiled' and 'With You', with la Kaz on vocals. The A-side of the resulting acetate being Al's first 'recorded' song and, as I've previously described, this provided a representative example of his then pop composing skills.

I'd often find myself walking up the steps to Avon Entertainments alongside Al to check out the gigs situation. He, more than his fellow musicians, was totally focused on all and any aspects of his beat music career. During one visit Sam Newgarth who ran the agency ventured the observation that Al could 'make it in the biz' and I should manage him! Well Sam, that's not quite how the future turned out, but you no doubt would have enjoyed scenes in Los Angeles FM radio stations in 1977, when I was introduced as "the man who discovered Al Stewart", as *Year of the Cat* continued to cruise the top of the US charts.

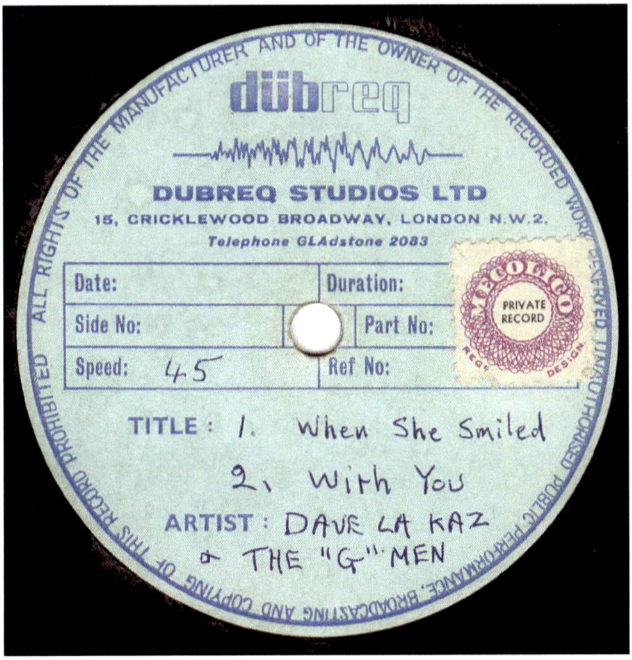

Acetate demo 45 of Al Stewart's first recorded song 'When She Smiled'

Most days of most weeks during 64 would find Al meeting up with me, around 2 p.m., in my dad's shop. By then the later a.m. hours had ceased to exist for Al. Parked at the back of the shop we'd chat, laugh, strum guitars, play cards, read newspapers and plan the evening, disturbed only by the occasional customer.

Klabiash was one card game in particular he and I forever associate with those carefree afternoons. We played with my dad, who had taught us this old European game's rules and arcane terminology. Like rummy (which we also played) it could be enjoyed without gambling.

My dad would also join in the guitar sessions and I still have a few tapes to remember them by.

Sometimes we'd partake of a late breakfast (Al) / lunch (me), in the nearby, optimistically named, Silver Lounge café. It was here a fixation with pinball took hold, climaxing many years later with Al buying his own machine from an LA emporium and installing it in his first American home.

Like many friendships ours was based on common interests, including guitars, girls, records, groups and laughing. Along with the shared frequency our pop trivia thoughts seemed to utilise, a mutually beneficial sense of humour was in place. One example of the two coinciding occurred around then as we walked past a local Wimborne Road pet shop.

American R 'n' B artist Rufus Thomas had one of the first US hits on Stax Records with 'Walkin' the Dog', followed, believe it or not, by more 'dog' songs, such as 'Can your Monkey do the Dog?' In the UK Georgie Fame had released his first single for Columbia Records: 'Do the Dog'. As Al and I strolled along Moordown's main street a recent pop-joke observation came to mind – 'Dog Music' would be the next 'big thing' (no, we weren't serious). Al being Al had even written a song with this in mind: 'Barking up the Wrong Tree'. The pet shop window sign that had caught our attention indicated the availability of personalised metal name tags. It simply read: 'Dog discs cut here'. When our laughter subsided I had to dissuade my musical friend from entering the premises and saying "I've written a 'dog song' I'd like to record – how much?" Of course, in time it fell to another domestic animal to provide him with a Top 10 theme.

Evenings tended to revolve around clubs, movies and ballrooms. In possession of a handy small rectangle of card, dispensed to one representative member per local group, we could frequently gain free access to Le Disque. As the cash we often had available amounted to 'not very much', this along with a couple of cinema connections, proved useful.

As Al put it, when quoted in his biography *Troubadour*: "Le Disque a Go Go – I certainly spent a lot of time there with Jonny Kremer".

Rather then risk boring you with a longish list of names that played the club round 63-65, I'd like to recall a few more moments that the highlighter pen of memory is bringing to my attention.

Tubby Hayes was that rare talent: a British jazz musician who was truly world class, and in January 64 you could find him in the company of the Lennie Wright Trio in Holdenhurst Road's cellar club.

A multi instrumentalist saxophone, vibraphone and flute – it was his tenor sax playing I was there to hear. That same year his reputation would gain repeat appearances at keynote New York jazz clubs, such as the Half Note Club, and later Shelly Manne's LA club. Then in his late twenties, it was a great opportunity to catch this hard-bop stylist before the effects of drink and drugs ended his days a decade later.

An early warning signal was on view that night as between each number the musician reached into his jacket pocket and withdrew a quart bottle of whiskey, taking a sustaining swig before continuing to enthral the packed, alcohol-free, unlicensed club.

In 1965, following the previous year's Mods v. Rockers seaside battles, the cool new groups came from the mod world. Early in 65 The Who released 'I Can't Explain': a terrific Kinks influenced record, produced by Shel Talmy (the Kinks producer). Talmy arranged for the high back-up vocals to be sung by Ken Lewis and John Carter, annoying Roger Daltry in the process. Previously known as the dual vocalists with Carter-Lewis and the Southerners, by then they'd become the Ivy League, but not before releasing a flop single on Oriole Records, featuring on lead guitar an unknown Jimmy Page.

Soon after the Small Faces debuted with 'Whatcha Gonna Do About It'. The scene then seemed set for mod band No.3: The Action. But, as we know, not every act that looks a certain winner then goes on to claim the prize. And so it was to be for the London based, pop-soul band.

Following The Who's early 65 Le Disque a Go Go gig, The Action played the club towards the end of the year, around the time of their first single, 'Land of a Thousand Dances'. Watching singer Reg King performing with his 'right hand held to his ear' affectation, mod suited and booted, they seemed to me to be well equipped to fulfil the, then current, music biz buzz they'd generated. As mod came and went, and The Who and Small Faces left it behind, they also unfortunately left behind the hitless Action. Several singles over the next couple of years failed to bother the charts. Even a name change to Mighty Baby and a tilt at psychedelia didn't do the trick.

A similar fate, perhaps surprisingly, awaited Bournemouth's Zoot Money. Easily the best band in town, by 1965 his Sands Combo had decamped from the south coast and by the time they'd reached Soho, and Wardour Street's Flamingo Club had transmuted into Zoot Money's Big Roll Band, complete with ace local guitarist Andy Summers.

Armed with the support of a Flamingo residency provided by the club owning brothers John and Rik Gunnell, plus a recording contract with EMI's Columbia Records, the scene seemed set fair. The Flamingo had already launched Georgie Fame and his Blue Flames to chart topping heights, to be followed by the equally successful Chris Farlowe and the Thunderbirds. Surely Zoot Money described by Alexis Korner as 'Bournemouth's answer to the world!' would be next. But just as the Action being third behind The Who and Small Faces didn't happen, the Big Roll Band couldn't reach the fame level of Blue Flames and Thunderbirds. Again, like the Action, not even leaving in their case jazzy R 'n' B behind in 1967 for another name change to the psychedelic Dantalian's Chariot could produce more than a low Top 30 chart placing.

This becoming a star must be harder then it looks!

Zoot Money's Sands Combo rebrands as the Big Roll Band including Andy Summers

The same could be said of another mid 60's group who had 'smash hit' written all over them. The Downliners Sect. An effectively named London R 'n' B band they looked likely to emulate their predecessors the Stones, Yardbirds and Pretty Things. Umpteen singles and LPs later the answer was no.

I'd first noticed them a while before they'd landed a proper record deal when a small *NME* ad offered an EP, enterprisingly for those days, pressed and released by a one shot indie label, Contrast Records, showcasing their London club act, entitled 'Nite in Great Newport Street', recorded in Studio

51. The night the Downliners played Le Disque I felt fifty-fifty about the sight and sound projected by the group. Yes, a great R 'n' B sound; but not distinctive or original. The leader singer, Ray Sone, while totally adequate, did not display a persona to compete with the Yardbirds' Keith Relf or the Pretty Things' Phil May, let alone Michael Philip Jagger. Interestingly he'd got the vocalist job in preference to either a young Rod Stewart or Steve Marriott.

He did however show an unusual characteristic regarding temperature. The busy club being quite hot, meant one of the last things you might expect to see would be singer Ray performing centre stage and wearing, not a jacket, but a three-quarter length, belted, blue leather topcoat! Standing fairly stationary, from time to time, he'd reach into an inner coat pocket and retrieve a harmonica. But however tropical the surrounding climate seemed for everyone else the coat stayed on.

As their set progressed it appeared each song alternated between a 'Bo Diddley' rhythm and a 'Can I get A Witness' riff. During a midway break in the evening's session I chatted with lead guitarist Don Craine – the one that favoured wearing Sherlock Holmes style deer-stalker hats in publicity photos. He remained amiable even as I remarked on the Sect's lack of sonic variety.

Returning to the stage with the rest of the group, he then repeatedly made a visual comment to me on my well intended 'constructive criticism'. Smiling in my direction as I continued to view the band from a nearby position on his side of the stage, Downliner Don made pantomime glances at his guitar's fingerboard as though posing the question, "This O.K. – What do you think?"

A good solid band, with a great name, capable of delivering a rousing version of Bo D's 'Cops and Robbers', but not the stuff Hit Parade dreams are made of, is basically what I thought. Anyway it's time to leave this basement and take a look at mid-sixties Bournemouth above ground.

Mods, Miss World and More Moments

'Lonely Doll' on HMV Records (Capitol in the USA) – Do you remember this 1965 worldwide hit? I certainly don't! Possibly because the bit about *worldwide hit* isn't true. And yet the recording artist was *world famous*, albeit for only 15 minutes of Warholian fame the previous year.

I had the pleasure of finding myself face to face briefly with the chanteuse in question a couple of times round town. Pleasure being perhaps an obvious word to use when meeting Ann Sidney, Miss World 1964.

I'm sure Poole's Miss World Ann Sidney was never a lonely doll

Local nineteen year old beauty Ann, having captured her crown and received acres of newsprint in return, was invariably referred to as 'Ann Sidney – from Poole, Dorset'.

You've probably noticed that although this book's geographical title highlights Bournemouth, the inclusion of Poole references fit naturally, as the relatively nouveau former and its next door neighbour seaport, on the map since the 12th century, share time and space like a binary star system.

The inoffensively coy and quaint parades of bathing belles in so called beauty pageants, or insultingly misogynistic degenerations of womanhood, depending on point of view, have long been consigned to the backwaters of last century's 'pop culture'. But back then this televisual spectacular was in its heyday. Created in the UK as an additional aspect to 1951's *Festival of Britain*, by 64 *Miss World* generated huge viewing figures putting it on par with annual events like the *Eurovision Song Contest* and the F.A. Cup Final.

Long after most winners had faded from view in the British Isles, partly due to being only the second contestant from this country to triumph, Ann Sidney remained on the B/C celebrity list. The record aside, she maintained an, on off, long running TV & Movies career. Look carefully in Mick Jagger's late 60's flick *Performance*, James Bond's *You Only Live Twice* or an episode of TV classic *The Avengers* and Poole's world-beating beauty queen can still be seen.

Brunette Miss Sidney, however, was not the dark-haired female subject of a new, heartfelt, Al composition. One day in June as he sang 'Dark Haired Girl' I realised his unrequited desire for Bourne Radio Sandie was far from abating,

The ballad, never recorded and now lost in time, whilst failing in its immediate aims Sandie-wise, did point towards 1969's considerably more accomplished *Love Chronicles* songs. Soon after this he split for London town, not to stay, but to escape from Bournemouth and his feelings for a while. Three weeks to be exact.

Al snaps his fingers as the beat goes on

My pal Al stayed in touch via a couple of letters, updating me on his first try at being a solo performer in the capital. Not a success. At one impromptu gig at a pub called the Black Lion the crowd declined to applaud and chose to laugh instead! Perhaps he shouldn't have sung a recently written, slightly under the influence of new mentor Dylan, song: *A Child of the Bomb.* A too serious, immature, sketching of a post nuclear apocalypse world. Not a bad try. It was after all the cold war era, the fifties 'Ban the Bomb' movement still in full flight, and following the Cuban Missile Crisis two years before, a time when possible atomic conflict remained a background fear.

Undeterred by the Black Lion knock-back, he then approached Jeff Kruger's Ember Records, offering them the chance to have a 'bomb singer' on their label. They declined and he returned to the seaside.

Back in Bournemouth Al tried one more time to use a song as a flag to attract Sandie's attention. This time instead of attempting an original song he went straight to the Dylan songbook. Knowing of the object of his affections considerable enthusiasm for Bobby Zimmerman, he alighted upon 'The Times They Are a-Changin'".

One day in August 64 he recorded the very first Al Stewart record. Not a tape, nor a demo as part of a group; but a two sided 7" record under his own banner.

At the time the town possessed a small recording studio just off Richmond Hill, in Yelverton Road. Rustling up both the required sum to pay for an hour or so studio time – including a couple of demo copies, and three other local musicians, he produced a ¾ time take on the title track of Dylan's recent 3rd album.

Of greater interest to me was the flipside. Another crack at writing a pop song, Al's 'The Sky Will Fall Down'. He gave me one of his acetates complete with the label legend reading: The Stewart Group and crediting those playing on the disc. Three guys from Bournemouth, all three worth a mention here for one reason or another. Al of course sang and played rhythm guitar. On lead guitar G-Man Terry Squires, who went on to join the New Overlanders. Bass player Pete Ballam from the Trappers, in the late sixties released an LP as part of psychedelic group Bram Stoker. Lee Kerslake drummed his way from Al's initial, unreleased single, to a stack of albums and international tours with Uriah Heep.

I don't recall what effect, if any, this effort had on the leader of the Al Stewart Group's intended, but at least it created a fascinating curio.

No he didn't make it with Sandie, well not then. Many years later, with a couple of albums to his name, he met up with me for a dinner date in our favourite Bournemouth restaurant, the Continental, in Holdenhurst Road. Accompanying him was, yes you've guessed it: Sandie. I think we were all pleased to realise that long after the moment of its beginning, the circle had finally been completed.

Although 'The Sky Will Fall Down' presents itself as the earliest recording of singer-songwriter Al Stewart, and as a record it was, there exist even earlier original song performances on tape.

Recorded in my family home 6 months or so before 'Sky', on a 4-track reel-to-reel, Telefunken, on ¼ inch, 7" spools of tape at 3¾ ips. I'd often record Al and myself plonking around on guitars during his frequent visits to our Dolphin Court flat. By the beginning of 64, while still an electric beat group guitarist, he'd taken to rocking up to my door with his semi-acoustic 2nd guitar and a newly written song. My ears providing him with an initial response to balance with his own.

Flash forward to another decade and we'd be standing in Abbey Road's Studio 2, listening to playbacks of recordings en route to the *Year of the Cat* album. First checking producer Alan Parsons' view, Al would turn to me as if 64 was the day before yesterday, and enquire, "How did it sound to you?" *Plus ça change, plus c'est la même chose.*

The downbeat 'Child of the Bomb' was magnetically caught in that Branksome Park abode, as was the comparatively up tempo 'Swansong of the Millionth Man'. Sitting in front of a single mic with a single cutaway, cello-bodied Voss guitar around his neck, Al would proceed to give it his all. While I tried to monitor the erratically flickering, almost useless, basic recording volume meter.

We'd tried, unsuccessfully, to record voice and guitar separately utilising the tape machine's primitive track to track facility, but it proved to be frustratingly impossible to mix. One previous attempt to lay the melody line of an Al instrumental original, 'Kerguelen', accurately on top of the chords, resulted in this hauntingly melodic, jazzy tune, acquiring an unwanted disconnected ethereal sound.

The Voss guitar, an instrument not unlike a Hofner President, had one pickup, made by a firm called Roger. Al nicknamed it *Roger Voss*. A bit prosaic compared to B.B King's *Lucille*, but there you go. He kept it until 1965 when the chance of a gig at Bunjies coffee bar, a tiny Soho folk music cellar, necessitated a change to a flat-topped, round-hole, Epiphone Texan.

Naïve though the 'Child of the Bomb' lyrics were, their owner sang them with sincere conviction; an attribute he brought not only to the words of songs, but to most other words too. Conversations though were always lit up and lightened by an ever present, slightly off centre, humorous look at life.

'Swansong' presented a kind of response to the questioning anti-war theme of Dylan's 'Blowin' in the Wind': Al suggesting however long it would "*take till they know*" that he'd wait to be told that one day "*man had thrown away the battle-drum*". Well pop-pickers, I told you he was sincere – and a serious tone often imbues sincerity.

While the reality of hostilities remained fortunately for us safely contained in the words of songs, if you believed England's newsprint media in the spring/summer time of 1964, we should head for the nearest Saxon hilltop fortress, as the Vikings were coming! OK, not the Vikings, but the twin tribes of British youth: the Mods and their nemesis, the Rockers.

Though not exactly a storm in a teacup, or a parka on a Lambretta, the Mods v. Rocker's Bank Holiday, seaside battles that year have taken on a mythical slant magnifying their on the ground, blow by blow, significance.

They certainly happened, and were later stylistically embossed by Pete Townshend's Quadrophenia double album, and movie of the same name. But more interesting to recall would be the taste in music of Mods 2.0 during that fairly short interlude prior to devolving into the far more violent skinheads.

Also rather then dwell on the often heavily outnumbered, Rock 'n' Roll loving, Teds on motorbikes, a glance across the Atlantic to their older and more threatening US counterparts, the Hells Angels, would be more interesting.

Originating on America's west coast as a semi-lawless band of roving post WW2, Harley-Davidson loving delinquents, thanks to Marlon Brando's *Wild One* movie, they made the UK Rockers seem a touch anaemic and not really a part of the fast changing 60s.

In 64/65 the Ben Sherman shirted, mirror-bedecked Vespa ridding Mods, had their record players and dance clubs alive with the sound of, not only home grown Who and Small Faces, but an energising potpourri of soul, Tamla, Ska and Bluebeat. They even had, in the form of *Ready Steady Go*, a TV show to call their own.

Clotheswise their predecessors, the first Mods, known originally as Moderns for their liking of cool Miles Davis and Coltrane, had the edge on Mod 2.0. They were 20th century Beau Brummells who'd never risk their sartorial ensembles on a dodgy scooter.

A pop music connected example of the first flowering of Mod can be seen in a 1962 *Town* magazine article featuring a London 15 year old called Marc

Feld. By 65 having signed to Decca Records and changed his surname to Bolan, the precociously hip Marc warbled 'The Wizard' as his initial, unsuccessful, attempt to achieve a hit. The hits eventually came via an ersatz hippy image created for his pre- T.Rex persona, Tyrannosaurus Rex.

The use of 'mod' as an adjective denoting something fresh, cool, where it's happening and contemporary, predates the mid-sixties when it entered the everyday lexicon of this country's population. I have reason to note this personally when, from time to time, I re-read a yellowing, slightly crumpled, clipping from the *Bournemouth Times*, published in 1961, its alliterative cross-heading proclaims: '*Monty's Mart Is For Mods*', and describes my dad's newly opened and quite new to this area, venture into Moordown retailing.

Yes, a thousand Mods descended on Brighton during Whitsun Bank Holiday weekend, May 64, chased Rockers, acted up for the TV news camera men, and a few hundred stayed on to explain their choice of recreational pursuits to the local magistrates' court the next day.

That same weekend a smaller number reached Bournemouth and indulged in a little mayhem around the pier and undercliff seafront, before the town's well prepared custodians of the law, in appropriate numbers, managed, using a precursor to 'kettling', to contain and disperse their outlaw day trippers in the Lower Pleasure Gardens.

The supreme legacy of Mod resides not in a few south coast ructions or even images of crisp clothing, but in music: principally Pete Townshend's Who. Not just for *Quadrophenia*, which incidentally he regards as a pinnacle in his career, but in the very essence of this Top 4 sixties group. The other 3? Surely along with the Beatles and Stones: Ray Davies' Kinks. The Who fuelled not just by amphetamines, like many of their early days' Shepherd Bush followers, shone brightly with art school driven insights into Metzger's *Auto-Destruction* ideas, and Bridget Riley/Victor Vasarely Op-Art imagery.

Let's leave this chapter with a Who/Bournemouth connection. In keeping with all the great English 60's groups the Who, far from being a one man band, were full of stars. In Keith Moon they possessed, not just an explosive drummer – literally on some occasions! – but a man who created Rock's reputation for extreme, wild and weird, off the wall antics. Later to be taken to Gold Medal winning status by Led Zeppelin.

In 1966 he fell for, and soon married, an attractive Patti Boyd look-alike; a teenage hairdresser turned model, called Kim. Together through tempestuous times for the rest of the sixties, until by the early seventies she called time on their extraordinary marriage. They met in Bournemouth.

Elves and Animals

"Bournemouth 515313." A voice so well known to me no introduction was required, and indeed none given, ignored my telephone identification and queried, "Are you still coming to the Tiles' opening?" Even though the day had been up and running for some hours by then I still needed a few seconds to compute Al's question. Tiles? Opening? Yes! Yes of course, weeks before I'd semi-agreed to do this. The *Melody Maker* had been flagging it up as an event not to miss and here was my London based alter-ego making sure I didn't.

This March day in 1966 the largest beat group club *Swingin' London* had ever known was about to throw open its doors and invite you to, not only be rocked by the Animals, but also do a little shopping. The previous largest live music club in the metropolis, the Marquee, was easily eclipsed by Oxford Street's underground extravaganza. Tiles Club not only possessed a stage suitable for presenting Eric Burdon's chart-topping, R 'n' B, crew, but also a subterranean parade of shops! Hard to believe, but true. Bored with the band? – well obviously not on this opening night – but stay with this and imagine you are: check out the record shop or maybe one of the clothes boutiques, both male and female, or perhaps try on some shoes.

"You mean it's tonight?" "Yes," Al replied, "I want you to meet Stratton-Smith, he'll be there, we might be able to sell him the Trackmarks idea." I looked at my wrist, a Seiko watch confirmed it was now PM, and although I now owned a car, driving into central London at short notice did not appeal. I'd have to check the train times. "I'll have to check the train times – call you back."

With the trains checked, the return call made, and a small overnight case packed, I found myself enjoying the relative splendour of the Bournemouth Belle for the next two hours as its Class 47 diesel engine thundered through the New Forest.

Connecting with Al at Waterloo, we headed for his Soho bed-sitter in Lisle Street. As the clock had by now ticked on to nine-thirty and the Animals were due on stage at ten, we dropped off my stuff and sped round a few corners to Tiles.

The long queues of young punters, as shown by Pathé News on cinema screens the following week, had been absorbed by the cavernous enterprise as Al and I descended the stairs into waves of musical sound and chatter. As record after record played, with the headliners nowhere to be seen, we pushed our way though the throng to the shops: also not surprisingly packed out.

Then, intermittently obscured by the bopping bodies, Al caught a glimpse of his manager, Tony Stratton-Smith Esq. Standing a little to one side of the action, with a barely noticeable aura of aloof distinction from the slightly younger generation surrounding him. Al while making the introductions inadvertently confused him by mentioning I'd just arrived from Bournemouth: he thought for a moment I was a member of the group his artist had been so enthusiastic about. With this clarified we chatted about the idea of co-managing the Trackmarks. At this point I guess a little exposition is called for.

Besides pursuing his musical career as a performer Al had been quite taken by the idea of finding a group that he and I could manage/produce, knowing how nicely it fitted with my Andrew Oldham fantasy. I guess that night we were attempting to cast Tony S-S as Eric Easton – the experienced biz professional to be a foundation for our flights of fancy.

"Any idea what's happened to the Animals?" Apparently, he informed us, they were still knocking back pints in nearby Wardour Street's *The Ship*, a then fave-rave pub for groups and music journalists. The Trackmarks? Stratton-Smith didn't say yes – didn't say no. Did say the name was poor; suggested if any of this happened changing it to the Tracks. Well yes, a far better name: crisp and a bit Mod.

The next move would be to return to Bournemouth and run it all past the group. Now in case you are wondering if this enterprise then flew – and as you've never heard of the Tracks, I assume you know it didn't – it didn't. Why? Well in our naïvety Al and I believed all we had to do was tell the band this great opportunity, being managed by Stratton-Smith, Stewart and Kremer, was not to be missed and bingo!

Enter reality in the shape of the drummer's dad: he who, having shelled out for at least some of the band's musical equipment was keeping tabs on his 'investment' by acting as their manager, seemed far from bowled over. Not interested in this 'London' management unless he received a suitable, sliding scale, percentage for himself. Well, as this was beginning to sound like no fun at all and more like serious work with little chance of a pot of gold at the end of it, we faded from the Trackmarks/Tracks future. It turned out they did not have one, at least in terms of breaking out from the local scene and making records. Mr Kerslake's son Lee – Al's 'Sky Will Fall Down' drummer – eventually became, as I've previously mentioned, a part of million-selling heavies, Uriah Heap.

Before returning to Tiles, I feel a, hopefully suitable, digression coming on. We are all daily *time-travellers* in our thoughts and writing about this mid-60's Bournemouth-based band beginning with T reminds me of another; this group from Poole and in the late 70's, at least for a while, a 'hot' item.

Tours. PowerPop, post-punk, Mod flavoured, self-promoting, indie band par excellence. In that period following McClaren and his Sex Pistol's pop/rock scene reboot, a gateway temporarily opened, a bit like the Merseybeat 60's. This allowed a short timeframe for New Wave pop.

Unlike the sixties this time around there would be no waiting about for an A and R man to descend from the heights of a major label and make you a recording deal that not even Marlon Brando could have refused. A deal by the way that 9 times out of 10 resulted in either no successful record sales or if you charted, a royalty rate calculated in fractions of a penny, and a two singles contract, swiftly cancelled when the follow up tanked.

Tours had developed, as many of their contemporaries had, from the pub-rock scene, which had both pre-dated Punk and in many ways survived its demise. Poole musician and song writer Ronnie Mayor had, being in his early twenties, a few years' local experience to give him confidence, and with his group Tours a vehicle to take a new original song somewhere, somehow. The somewhere turned out to be everywhere and nowhere. The how remains a classic pop/rock biz mini-tale of the time, much as 'Language School' is still a pop classic.

If you're familiar with this record, and it's your cup of tea, then I'm confident we are both on the same page here. If not, you might like to click on the ubiquitous, fab, InterWeb, and see how you think it stands up, 30 odd years down the line.

Shortly after inviting Richard Mazda, another adventurous local songwriter/guitarist to join Tours, the group succeeded, at their second attempt, to produce a shining recording of Ronnie's song. They then proceeded in the spirit of the day to press, distribute and promote, 'Language School' themselves.

To those familiar with Bournemouth's many foreign language schools and the continental ambience the students – especially the female ones – brought to the town, the title and lyrics of the record were spot on.

With an initial pressing of a thousand copies sold out in less then a week, plus the influential support of the BBC's John Peel, in the summer of 1979 Poole's power pop purveyors went from zeroes to contenders in about the time it takes a record company exec. to exclaim: "Who are they? Where are they? And why haven't we signed them?"

Around this time I mentioned them to Al. He was visiting England from his home in Bel Air and had called round to our home in Queens Park to play me and Abi a few unmixed tapes from his forthcoming album. On hearing 'Language School' he turned to me with delight and said, "Call Luke – this is just what he's looking for." Coupled with a typical Al sixties flashback, "You and Luke should manage them."

Well let's pause for a second or two. OK. Luke? Luke O'Reilly, Al's manager during the late 70's Double Platinum years. Luke, who a couple of years before had said one evening at a party in Los Angeles that he, Al and I, were the 'Three Musketeers'!

At that time, when the seventies were about to give way to another decade, one of those erstwhile companions of d'Artagnan, Al, had followed *Year of the Cat* with another American Top Ten million seller: *Time Passages*, and was fully engaged with the production of his next LP, *24 Carrots* and co-producing an album for his band, A Shot In The Dark, and therefore no longer looking for a group to manage to pop stardom. Another musketeer, O'Reilly, had recently become captivated by the idea of duplicating the vast sales 'My Sharona' had generated for the Knack, an ex LA bar band: hence Al's remark on hearing Tours. And then there was me.

Happily married, with a recently born son, Daniel, a popular Bournemouth record shop, and any thoughts of managing a group left behind back in the sixties. Now here was Al still buzzing with a concept close to the one I've been outlining from 66. Substitute Luke for Al and Tours for Trackmarks and you can see why the one has reminded me of the other.

I really wasn't too serious about any of this, but it sounded fun, so let's see what happens.

A few transatlantic calls later Luke, a guy around the same age as Al and myself, has flown over, reached Bournemouth, and been introduced to the group by me. Tours then had a late night meeting with us at the Carlton Hotel, following a town centre gig that had impressed O'Reilly.

In retrospect I probably wasn't the only one not taking things seriously. For a start the group did not, at the time, know me personally, or my long standing music biz connections; only, rather confusingly for them I suspect, Bus Stop Records my Westbourne shop.

They'd heard of Al Stewart alright and realised the LA based manager I suggested to them was the real thing – small problem, they already had a local manager/friend who, in the way of indie bands of the day was almost as integral to the group's fledgling success as the musicians. Also they were very close to signing a record deal with Virgin Records.

As we sat around a long, lounge table, in this 5 star, East Cliff, hotel, Luke, imagining them as the Knack, offered to sign Tours to Kinetic

Productions, his US company. I would manage the UK and he America. The first move would be arranging a USA West Coast tour as a support act to a more established band. This, standard at the time, intro to the States, would allow necessary opportunities to meet 'n' greet DJ's at FM radio stations. Also, and importantly for this deal to proceed, Kinetic would record the group with release through a major label.

Central to this being the re-issue of their fab, publicity generating, John Peel favoured, 'Language School'. Peel, who I'd met several times in the 60's, played the record day after day that summer, frequently announcing it to be his 2nd favourite record, only topped by his 'all time fave': 'Teenage Kicks' by the Undertones.

How did Tours view Tours? Quite differently to the power pop group their would-be managers glimpsed. They were firmly tripping along a Pistols/Clash route. "What would you say if we wanted to put out an LP with a blank, black sleeve?" – An example of one anti-music business question. Followed by: "We'd refuse to do *Top of the Pops*." Told you it didn't seem that serious to me.

Luke O'R zoomed back to sunny California, Richard Mazda stayed in touch with me for a while, including showing up with new demos to hear after Tours fell apart. Fell apart – how, why, when?

Not long after the Carlton get together they signed to Virgin, refused to re-release their pop classic song, issuing instead another R. Mayor song, 'Tourist Information'. Good, but not as good. And not a hit. Even superfan Peel neglected it. Virgin weren't pleased with a least 50% of Poole's finest and a fractious Mazda and Mayor were certainly not pleased with the single's sound, nor its Virgin Records supplied producer.

Ronnie left the group and formed a new group, Da Biz. Richard released one more single on Virgin with his new band Cosmetics. So that was that. Another unfortunate music biz tale of what might have been.

What might have been? Who knows?

Two years earlier Abi and I watched from the side of the stage as, a then unknown, American group performed their first show outside of the US, in a Bournemouth town centre venue. A warm-up gig for Blondie, just prior to touring England with fellow New Yorker's, Television. Although their first and second LPs were great it was the third *Parallel Lines*, packed with enough hits for a *Greatest Hits* album, which secured Debbie Harry's band deserved superstar status. Much credit was correctly directed to the record's producer Mike Chapman, who also produced the Knack.

Before it became certain that any involvement with Tours was not to be, Luke and I talked of who we believed Kinetic's Tours producer should be:

Mike Chapman. Yes, I would have been as curious as you, and presumably Ronnie and Richard, to have heard the results and, maybe, the hits.

'We gotta get out of this place'. Surely not, you've just arrived! As Eric Burdon gave the Animals' Top 10 hit from the previous year, his deep-toned, gravel-voiced, full attention, Al and I edged our way through their Tiles' audience to be near the stage.

One of the many attractions the 1960's had to offer an enthusiast for contemporary UK PopRock – and at that time we're probably talking about most of the western world's teenage population – would certainly be, if you got the timing and location right, the chance to catch this sort of action up close: the polar opposite of stadium rock gigs and festivals of the future. The latter being a little like watching the former through a pair of binoculars the wrong way round.

Bass playing Chas Chandler, who after the group split later in the decade would become the manager/discoverer of Jimi Hendrix, stood directly in front of us. Seated just behind him Dave Rowberry, who'd replaced original keyboard Animal Alan Price, following an early example of the music biz mantra/cliché: 'Musical differences'.

After the Animals had finished delivering the goods with a mix of hit singles and R 'n' B LP songs, Al and I made our way through Soho's post midnight streets to the hovel he then called home.

Remember that line about the 'broken window pane' in the title track of Al's first LP *Bedsitter Images*?

One floor up, small, dingy, and surrounded by dwellings populated by 'ladies of the night', it was, nonetheless a first breath of freedom. A place of his own free from the obvious constraints of a family home, let alone the impersonal community life of a mid 20th century English boarding school.

He pointed out some mail that had arrived addressed to the previous occupant. Slightly to our surprise it was for Clinton Ford, then a well-known BBC radio singer on programmes like *Easy Beat*. Somehow it was easy to imagine any voice reaching you via the airwaves as being in the possession of someone who could afford somewhere better.

Before slumping to sleep off the exertions of a long day I picked up a book my friend was in the midst of reading.

I wonder how many people are left on this planet who haven't heard of *Lord of the Rings*. A billion or two probably. Leaving a few billion more that have. By the turn of the century it would regularly top 'best book of all time' polls. In one of those highly subjective and ultimately meaningless exercises it was even nominated 'Book of the Millennium'! As indeed a similar opinion survey decreed John Lennon's 'Imagine' to be the 'song of the Millennium'.

In the new century the trio of Rings movies effortlessly broke box office records, but this happy state of affairs for publishers Allen and Unwin, and the Tolkien estate, would have seemed unlikely back in the spring of 1966. Following its first printing in 1953, the lengthy 3 volume saga – which incredibly its author would later regret not making even longer – sold slowly.

For several years J.R.R. Tolkien's epic tale sold in the region of 3 copies a week, principally to libraries. Just the reaction that a 'Sword and Sorcery' story might expect to receive in an era of post war austerity in the year England was captivated by the real life/real time 'fairy tale fantasy' of Elizabeth 2's coronation. Also the very genre it was to reside atop of didn't exist: *Lord of the Rings* created 'Sword and Sorcery'. Its only precursors lay in the words of Mallory and Spencer. So at that moment I'd never heard of it.

The hardback book I was flicking through was volume 2, *The Two Towers*, and bookmarked around midway. "Oh, you've got to read that." In that tired moment I had no response to Al's enthusiasm; just glancing at a couple of paragraphs: it seemed almost biblical. Unlike Al, who by then had acclimatised to all-nighter life, needing to bring the day to a close, I murmured something non-committal before returning Frodo and Gandalf to the table top.

The next day, before a late morning breakfast at nearby Patisserie Valerie and catching a train back to the seaside, I picked up volume 1 and began at the beginning. As you possibly know the author initially employed his knowledge of linguistics to fashion a story written in the style and tone of his earlier book *The Hobbit*, and written in a series of letters to his son. The first hundred or so pages are not really indicative of the darker depths the adventure goes on to explore. Still I was hooked.

Back in Bournemouth I located the trilogy in a small Old Christchurch Road bookshop. Possibly the only copy on sale locally that day, as the launch of the Rings cult was a year or two away and requiring first a single volume paperback edition and significantly 1968's American university students discovery of Tolkien's tale, making it a huge bestseller.

In 1972 I took advantage of a chance to upgrade my *Lord of the Rings* to a single volume, limited edition, containing the three books plus maps, printed on ultra thin Indian rice paper. Great to hold in its black card slipcase embossed with a green and gold Tolkien designed Numereon symbol, but almost impossible to read without shredding the pages!

As the Bournemouth-based book you are currently holding is just that:

based on events, people and memories of this town all those years ago I'd better mention the synergy with the world famous Oxford professor.

For many years prior to his retirement from university life Professor Tolkien and his wife had loved to visit Bournemouth and frequently stayed at the Miramar Hotel on the East Cliff. So perhaps it was not surprising on leaving Oxford they would choose to live in this area. When the time came, in 1973, for him to leave both Middle-Earth and this world for the Grey Havens and beyond, this fantastically successful author was living in Lakeside Drive, Branksome Park.

Again, talking of this book, the reason for mentioning elves in this chapter's title, has by now become apparent. Specifically one elf: Tolkien's Legolas.

When at last the chance to make a record came to Al in summer 66 he wrote and recorded, 'The Elf', inspired by the aforementioned character that had leapt from the page to his musical thoughts and then the grooves of 7 inches of Decca vinyl.

Although Stratton-Smith was not to find success with, or for, Al Stewart – finding huge amounts of it in the later sixties with Genesis and his own record label, Charisma Records – he did fix up Al's Decca deal and besides generating a highly collectable rarity (check eBay), started his recording career.

Let's catch up with this song and others in another chapter. If it's summer 66 and you're in Great Britain you are probably noticing something very unusual is happening. Unusual and to date unique. England's footballers are about to win the World Cup!

The Summer Before The Summer Of Love

Quantum theory would currently have us believe matter in the form of sub-atomic particles can appear seemingly out of a nowhere nothingness: as long as it instantly disappears again. I guess in the macro world we inhabit entropy's timeline reassuringly suggests a past, present and future, with memorable events preceding, and indicating an eventual outcome yet to be.

Thanks to human beings possessing an ability to recall the past somewhat superior to a goldfish's alleged 2 second memory span, history books, however subjective, can be written.

The historians of the nineteen sixties have consistently pinpointed 1967 as a supernova moment in a spectacular decade. Completely correct: but 1967 did not appear from nothing and nowhere.

For the rock/pop world and its attendant fellow traveller, the evolving sociological/political counter culture, the 'swing year' was 1966. Yes 67 was *The Year*, a high-water mark reached as though seen through a shimmering prism of illuminating colours; but it would be rewarding to revisit the changes and subsequent shifts of direction 66 brought to the mid-sixties scene. Actually to get a good run up to the action of that influential year a step back to 65 would be handy.

Year three of Beatles' Britain would ostensibly find Bournemouth's music scene continuing on its merry beat band way. Top Ten names would regularly appear at the Gaumont or Winter Gardens. Club venues and ballrooms were still popularly presenting national names on their way up/down/or sideways; and of course local groups.

On one level the tunes, lyrics, styles and ambience stayed a steady course, with a few slight modifications to the sea charts provided by 63's and 64's trendsetting navigators.

Trendsetting, now there's a quintessentially early mid-sixties word. One Bournemouth group even took it for their name. Managed by Roy Simon, a local businessman, signed to Parlophone Records, it featured at various times the brothers Mike and Pete Giles, plus club owner Alan Azern on piano; due you remember Trendsetters Limited?

1965 began with Georgie Fame's January No.1 'Yeh Yeh', to be followed by Denny Laine's Moodyblues, 'Go Now'; both wonderful representatives of the year's key records. As 65 progressed they were followed by significant chart toppers and 3 LPs that clearly showed the times were indeed a changin'.

After a lengthy fallow period following the demise and diminution of Rock 'n Roll's original 50's stars, s-e-x returned to top the agenda. Sure it had always been present as an element of pop music, from New York's Sinatra Bobby-Soxers of the late 1940s, through the first 'Pop' singer: Johnny Ray – onto Cliff and then the Fab 4's *Screamagers*. But not since Presley's splendid gyrations were deemed unsuitable for viewers of America's Ed Sullivan Show had sex overtly been the top card in PopRock's deck.

Mick Jagger and the Stones changed that decisively: lyrically, sonically, and in live shows, with summer 65 No.1: 'Satisfaction'. A few months earlier in March their previous, self-composed, No.1 'The Last Time', follow up to late 64's 'Little Red Rooster', had began to emphasise just what the band's vocalist had in mind. No one needed to be a mind-reader now. This new style, semi-androgynous, '*Satisfaction*' popsex, was full-on. The Rolling Stones appearance at Bournemouth Gaumont during August 64 had given me a chance to experience the projection of their casual, instinctive, but insistent, sexual message. A message clearly received by the not unattractive, late teens girl seated alongside me.

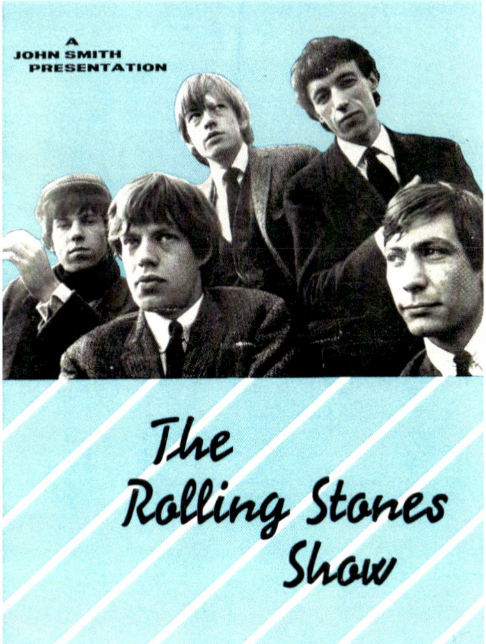

Rolling Stones programme
Bournemouth 1964

The Stones set including a recently released cover of the Valentino's, 'Its All Over Now' and Chuck Berry's 'Around and Around', was a sound and visual event best absorbed as more than a sum of its parts.

Individually attired, having initiated the rock group look of freedom from the previously standard uniform look of showbiz suits, their performance, from start to finish, was a total immersion, fusing together act and audience in a high volume and highly charged atmosphere of sex.

As Mick Jagger attempted a mini high jump, crossed with a scissors kick, the female next to me – a complete stranger – whilst loudly articulating her desire for M. Jagger, in what appeared an almost trance-like state, reached out and squeezed my thigh! We exchanged glances; nothing was said. Following the Rolling Stones departure and the apparent completion of her catharsis, she gave me her phone number before disappearing in the crowd. Yes, yes those were the days!

Actually it would have been personally beneficial if that particular day had been delayed a month or so. By September, having turned 17, and passed a driving test, I bought my first car. And as any male from my generation would recall, the portable privacy on wheels this allowed, was a terrific asset.

Still enamoured with the American automotive glamour their cars provided, I acquired the nearest affordable UK equivalent: a 7 year old, Ford Zodiac Mk.2, replete with white-wall tyres, an automatic Borg-Warner gearbox, and a two-tone finish in turquoise and ivory. I kept it for several years and the costs of running and maintaining this asset ensured I was perennially short of cash.

The sex the Stones brought to 65 was added to by March No.1 'Its Not Unusual'. With a name acquired from Albert Finney's hit movie, Tom Jones, giving a nod in the direction of the previous decade's Presley moves, offered a slightly older female age group, the imaginary thrills Sean Connery's *James Bond*, suggested.

Two of the previously referenced 1965 'keynote change' LPs arrived inside two refreshingly original sleeves. Released just a few months apart, and destined to improve, influence and reshape the art of popular music: they were both the work of Bob Dylan.

Bringing It All Back Home and *Highway 61 Revisited*, from the cool confidence evinced by Dylan's cover photography to the extraordinary songs and thoughts these two 12 inches of vinyl revealed, these LPs were unprecedented.

Released in the year he famously 'went electric' (neatly ignoring Bruce Langhorn's electric guitar on Bob Dylan's first single, 1962's 'Mixed Up Confusion'), these recordings were to be pivotal, not only for this pre-eminent singer-songwriter's musical career, but the entire world of modern records and songs. The quartet of songs featured on *Bringing It All Back Home*, side two, recorded in January, in just one or two takes, were densely packed with lyrical imagery and performed with such crystal clarity that to this day they sound new and original. The seven minute tour de force polemic of 'It's Alright Ma' remains, for me, the pinnacle of this truly great 20th century artist.

Also side one's extraordinary 'Subterranean Homesick Blues': possibly the first Rap record, a few decades ahead of the rest. A Dylan song and performance which generated, via D.A. Pennebaker's *Don't Look Back*, a unique precursor to the rockpop promo video age.

That year's second Dylan album included the tremendous 'Like A Rolling Stone' and moved the recently formed 'Planet Folk-Rock' into a new orbit.

Assisted by Paul Butterfield Blues Band guitarist Mike Bloomfield and organ debutante Al Kooper, sound and energy was generated with an embedded, embittered torrent of words, sufficient to create an unforgettable foundation for all of rock music yet to come.

The 'thin, wild, mercury' sound Bob Dylan heard in his head, and, like Pandora's Flying Dutchman seemed destined to endlessly search for, was contained within the grooves of his *Highway 61 Revisited* LP.

Both LPs retained Dylan's fascinating stream of consciousness sleeve notes begun on the reverse of *Another Side Of Bob Dylan* the previous year.

Al Stewart, by now living in the East End of London and having initiated his career as a solo acoustic guitar performer no longer seeking to play an electric guitar in a group, found himself in conversation with another singer-songwriter. The fellow artist at the time was sharing accommodation with Al at the home of Judith Pieppe and did not share my friend's enthusiasm for all things Dylan. Especially not his rambling sleeve notes.

Sitting opposite me a few days later, with his Epiphone close at hand, Al recalled Paul Simon's views. Simon knew Dylan from around Greenwich Village, and they were far from similar personalities. Basically at that time he appeared to find the ex Hibbing hobo an ungenerous person whose words he regarded as 'rehashed Ferlinghetti'.

Although now dwelling in a series of low rent metropolitan abodes en route to his *Bedsitter Images* Soho bed-sitter, Al still spent quite a lot of time in Bournemouth during 1965, and even more during a 'flat spell' in 66. This meant the pattern of our friendship continued much as before. But now, instead of regaling me with tales of bumping into Ritchie Blackmore and the Outlaws in Charring Cross Road, it would be quotes from the temporarily transplanted American from the room next door. Or showing me the new guitar tuning he'd acquired from Bert Jansch; who in turn had learnt from Davy Graham.

The aim during his initial, 'break into the music/record biz' London campaign had been to join a pop group or R 'n' B band as a guitarist, probably playing rhythm. An audition for an embryonic Procol Harum, the Paramounts, saw him turned down by Gary Brooker. One group that could have claimed Al Stewart, and therefore turned him away from an eventual *yellow brick road* pathway to his own Year of the Cat-Land of Oz, were called the Bo Street Runners. Recent winners of *Ready Steady Win*, a *Ready, Steady, Go* spin-off, the Runner's prize from Associated Rediffusion's TV talent contest for groups was a record release on Decca. He didn't join and their record didn't sell. Instead, singing an impromptu 'The Times They are a Changin' soon after in a Soho coffee bar cellar, he was offered, and accepted, a weekly residency in Bunjies. Notwithstanding the fact that to fulfil his commitment required learning all the songs on Dylan's 2nd and 3rd albums in the space of a couple of days.

Now the potential beat band journey to being *Al Beatle* was effectively over; and if he was not destined to be *Al Dylan* he did of course become *Al Stewart.*

The days spent in Paul Simon's company were to prove as valuable to the development of Al's song-writing skills as the long distance instruction received from Dylan's recordings. Moments after first meeting Simon and enquiring "What do you do?" the then unknown, London based, future superstar, having replied, "I guess I write songs," pulled up a chair, unpacked his guitar from its case and sang to his audience of one 'Flowers Never Bend With The Rainfall'.

Later that year during a Bournemouth visit to my home, Al pulled up a chair, unpacked his guitar from its case, and sang to me a brand new Paul Simon song, apparently completed a few days earlier in the room adjoining Al's in the flat they were still occupying. This was rather groovy as it allowed me to become one of the first people to hear 'Homeward Bound'!

Now I'm sure you've heard the story of the song's composer sitting on a station platform, tired of gigging round northern England, longing to return south to girlfriend Kathy, and while waiting for a train, knocking off 'Homeward Bound'. Well true – up to a point. The point being the famous song may indeed have its genesis on Widnes railway station, but Simon completed it back in London.

Whereas, for example, Henry Mancini popped a photo of Audrey Hepburn on top of his piano and during 15 or so minutes of reflection wrote 'Moon River'; or Johnny Kidd and his Pirates spent a similar time concocting Britain's *Greatest Ever* Rock 'n' Roll record, 'Shakin' All Over', (joint with Sammy Samwell's 'Move It'), this was not how Paul Simon worked. Then, as now, a musical perfectionist who carefully considered every word, as distinct from his New York acquaintance Dylan, who can be seen in Pennebaker's *Don't Look Back* documentary busily typing lyrics seemingly at the speed of thought.

Prior to receiving a phone call from CBS that was to relocate him back in the USA, Paul Simon claims he enjoyed some of the best days of his life while singing, writing, performing and producing in England. The phone call informed Simon he was No.1 in Boston and inside the Billboard/Cashbox Top 100: time to come home. 'The Sounds of Silence', previously recorded twice acoustically, once solo, once with Art Garfunkel, now, courtesy of a CBS engineer, had a lightweight folk-rock backing, gifting the record its chart momentum. Back in New York, with 'Sounds' a Hot 100, nationwide, No.1, Simon & Garfunkel embarked on their second career as a duo: this one somewhat eclipsing their young teenage hit(s) as Tom and Jerry.

In 65, *The Paul Simon Songbook LP*, including 'The Sound of Silence' (Sound singular, not Sounds), was released in England having been recorded quickly with minimal costs. Following this, on a truly tiny budget Paul Simon produced his friend, another American artist now on the London contemporary folk-blues scene, Jackson C. Frank, for UK Columbia Records. The eponymous album, featuring 'Blues Run the Game', was to be the tragic Jackson's only LP, selling just a few hundred copies. The emotive and evocative 'Blues Run the Game' however was to be recognised over time as a special song, as representative of that mid-sixties scene as Davy Graham's 'Angi'. Recorded, but not then released, by the wonderfully talented, but also sadly neglected, Nick Drake, among others.

Those others included, perhaps not surprisingly, Simon & Garfunkel, and as recently as 2010, Laura Marling.

The Bournemouth connection? Well slight: but amusing.

Not unexpectedly the Jackson C. Frank LP received little initial publicity. This seemed to me to be a missed opportunity to proclaim the musical input of the second guitarist on the recording session: Al Stewart. As this was to be my chum from Canford Bottom's first appearance on a released record, complete with his name on the sleeve, I couldn't let the moment pass.

Al would always acknowledge the enthusiastic support he received from my parents and this particular bit of PR was initiated by my mother: "We should call Stan Sowden, he writes the *Echo* 'Entertainment Page'."

In possession of the information regarding splendid (actually minimal) guitar playing by a local area musician, on this record they'd never heard of, the *Echo* column duly reported this, attached to a hilariously misleading cross-heading. It proclaimed Al to be *The Man Behind The Strings*. Kinda indicating he was an equivalent to the then Bournemouth resident Mantovani; or perhaps EMI arranger, Geoff Love!

The newsprint also included my name and contact details for any interested local 'talent' to get in touch, with a view to being supposed beneficiaries of our desire to be pop impresarios. Total number or responses: zero.

Another cause of laughs around then involved Art Garfunkel. He'd joined up again with boyhood friend and partner Paul in London and was at the *Jackson C. Frank* LP sessions. Unbeknown to me, and certainly not intended by me, Al had winged an idea of mine past Artie. It came from one of those small hours of the morning type conversations you have, when words of chat that sound inspired are not likely to seem so bright in the light of a new day. Talking to Al I remarked on the increasing number of *House of the Rising Sun* recordings by then in existence and casually mentioned it would be nice to have a compilation LP consisting only of versions of *Rising Sun*. Well I'd have bought it! Shortly afterwards I received a letter from Al mentioning that, by the way, Art Garfunkel didn't think much of my suggestion – well thanks a lot, it wasn't exactly either a suggestion or serious! Although this still amuses me, you know even now I would quite like a *House of the Rising Sun* LP.

Several big names of the early seventies were holdovers hit-recordwise from the sixties, when major success proved elusive, e.g. Elton John, Rod Stewart and Marc Bolan. One of the biggest and certainly most inventive could be seen as early as 1965 if you happened to be frequenting Bournemouth Pavilion that summer.

I'd first caught a glimpse of David Bowie, then Davie Jones, on BBC TV's *Tonight* programme, one evening in 64: not singing then, but publicising the problems brought to him by his ultra-long hair. By June 65 as singer with Davie Jones and the Lower Third he could be seen and heard each weekend performing at the Pavilion.

This coincided with a decision. To avoid clashing with the Monkees' Davy Jones, he engaged in the first of his many transformations: Davie to David and Jones to Bowie. Then the Lower Third became The Buzz, (great mod sounding name), and in 1966 group membership segued into solo performer, and of course mega-stardom. Still, this town offered a chance to be near the beginning of it all.

The second of Pop's three mid-sixties golden years, 1966, had a flying start, given the perfect 'baton' handover, from 65. The Beatles had entered their phenomenal second phase, almost imperceptibly at the time releasing the special artistry they possessed from the bounds of MopTopMania.

First signs that, like their friend and peer, Bob Dylan, the group had amazingly upped their game had come with *Help!* The song, LP and movie, all contained significant information that while ostensibly delivering more highly desired Fabness, new levels within the structure of Pop sound and image were also being attempted and achieved.

John Lennon's dilemma had begun to surface: having conquered the world as Beatle John, behind a terrific façade of confident public relations, he still felt long standing inner-world conflicts. 'Help', the song, combined both the sonic highs of exhilarating Beatle music with a revealing lyric, confessionally crying for assistance and adding to the insights provided by 'I'm a Loser'.

Help! the film, while not continuing the ground-breaking *Cinema Verite* of its quasi-documentary predecessor *Hard Day's Night*, colourfully extended the Beatles celluloid personas, director Richard Lester's innovative techniques providing a template for US television's *The Monkees*.

But, in retrospect, an ultimately more important aspect of the movie is displayed during a restaurant scene that allowed George Harrison to become aware of a new musical instrument: the sitar. The starting point for a one-time Merseyside assistant electrician's journey to the banks of the Ganges; and eventually trying to alleviate the suffering of millions with his *Concert for Bangladesh*.

The LP *Help!* along with a version of the single offered two more superb, direction-changing songs. McCartney's 'Yesterday', destined to vie with Hoagy Carmichael's 'Stardust' and George Gershwin's 'Summertime' as the most recorded song ever, and the proto-type heavy metal music sounds accompanying Lennon's intensively sad words for 'Ticket to Ride'.

But just before the calendar flipped to another page they released *Rubber Soul*, conclusively establishing Lennon, McCartney, Harrison and Starr were still ascending, and with them the cultural excitement of the sixties.

Utilising a combination of electronic production tools, such as heavy compression – soon to be de rigour on psychedelic-era records and contemporary folk-rock influences, the Beatles fashioned an outstanding album, which, while still a collection of disparate songs, nonetheless indicated a new role for the LP. Each track was worthy of comment, and leaving aside the captivating 'Michelle', three seemed to leap from the turntable and once heard never to leave the public consciousness: 'In My Life', 'Norwegian Wood' and 'Nowhere man', all John Lennon songs.

All set to go, 1966 would not disappoint. With the two formats of 7" 45 rpm singles and 33 and a third LPs as their platforms, the Pop records of that year, as distinct from Rock or any other popular music genre, would reach their apogee, and offer a lingua franca to the world. The desire for Western pop music and blue jeans would create a foundation for the young people on the other side of the then *Iron Curtain* to construct an emotional blueprint for a life outside of walls; either ideological or dividing Berlin.

No I haven't forgotten you are reading a Bournemouth based book, but as we all sat around waiting for the World Cup Final to fill our black and white TV screens, Marshall McLuhan's *Global Village* meant Pop music's universal democracy allowed everywhere to be plugged into what's going on. This town, while still buzzing with local action, had, with the departure of Zoot Money, Andy Summers, Al Stewart and Tony Blackburn, begun to make its mark on the national stage.

The summer of 1966 was not all love, sunlight and the joy of great records being released virtually every week. The media of any period bring, all too frequently, news to shock and sadden; but without intending to diminish by omission any other news story of the time, two stood grimly out.

Later that year the Aberfan disaster overwhelmed the nation's emotions with the loss of so many young lives in a, totally avoidable, catastrophically horrendous accident. A few months earlier the country was shocked with a completely different newsflash: three London policemen had been shot dead. This senseless event in our relatively gun-free British Isles caused widespread outrage and sympathy for the victim's families.

A reaction to this in Bournemouth took the form of a charity concert to raise money for those families. The Winter Gardens' summer season headliners were the hugely popular Morecambe and Wise and they, joined by their supporting acts, combining with all the performers from the town's other summer shows at the Pavilion and Pier Theatre, announced a one off, Midnight Matinee, to be held at the Winter Gardens, with all proceeds going to a newly set up charitable fund. My parents and I joined the, obviously sold out, audience to enjoy this unique amalgamation of three variety shows.

Just prior to this night, while queuing for tickets, I had an unexpected town centre sighting of one of Hollywood's superest of superstars.

It wasn't necessary to walk up the curving incline to the concert hall to buy show tickets thanks to a small booking office outpost down in Exeter Road. Half aware of the chit-chat passing between two women just behind me, I became fully aware when one of them exclaimed: "That's what I call a real man." Turning to my left, four people – two couples – were walking past a few feet away. One couple were unknown to me; the other quite the opposite. Looking as if he'd just stepped out of Hitchcock's *North By Northwest* movie, Cary Grant, accompanied by his then wife, actress Dyan Cannon, looked terrific. No idea why he was strolling through Bournemouth.

Jon with Alex Cummings
Bournemouth boutique opening 1967

I do however have an idea why, that August, I called Alex Cummings, a *Bournemouth Times* journalist. I'd see him round town, here and there; there's a photo including us, taken at the opening party for a menswear boutique on Poole Hill – that's the sixties for you: even a party to open a clothes shop! Eventually he was to become the editor of Bournemouth's weekly newspaper, prior to its demise. That day he responded enthusiastically to my suggesting he write a feature on a Bournemouth personality; one who had just released his first record. And so the first Al Stewart, solo artist, newsprint publicity, including a photograph, came to be.

Backtracking a few days, Al, on receiving his, just pressed, copies of 'The Elf' from Decca, zoomed down to the south coast to excitedly share them with me. The Tolkien inspired song had been produced by Mike Leander and featured Jimmy Page on electric guitar.

The flipside to Al's original song was 'Turn Into Earth', a dirge-like Yardbirds' tune from their second album. The composers' credit read: Samwell-Smith, Simon. The Simon being Rosemary Simon – Yardbird bassist Paul Samwell-Smith's then girlfriend, and not, as some people were to suppose Paul Simon. Incidentally she was a P.A. to *Ready Steady Go* producer Elkan Allan.

Al, Alex and I duly rendezvoused at the *Bournemouth Times* building in Branksome. At the time the newspaper's offices were in Poole Road, opposite a ten-pin bowling alley. Bournemouth's main facility for this, fairly new to England, American pastime could be found in Glenfern Road; substantially larger and open 24 hours a day.

Before Alex interviewed Al in the bowling alley's coffee shop and learnt of fairytale elves etc. I set up a visually linked photo session with a photographer in the grounds of the *Bournemouth Times*. Scouting around the nearby trees for some props to enhance the pic I happened upon a couple of large pine cones and one of those twig-like 'witches broomsticks'. The resulting image of Al holding these complemented the accompanying text perfectly.

In our mutual delight that, at last, Al had made a record, we both naïvely believed this was it: next stop Top 10. Realistically we should have paused, considered the facts and perhaps recalled Zoot Money's Decca debut from 64. The facts being: few radio plays, one TV appearance on a BBC TV *Children's Hour* programme, a couple of small reviews, virtually no ads or publicity and the small (literally) matter of an initial pressing of only 500 copies!

Before accepting that this single would be, at best, just the beginning of a journey to a life of hit records for Al, an attempt was made to gain a potentially more suitable TV audience.

Three summers before Southern Television's *Day By Day* had featured the Beatles and 'She Loves You' in the programme's occasional music slot. So wouldn't it be nifty if they could be persuaded to present Al and his Elf to the South's viewers? As route A to achieving this was a non-starter for a no-hit unknown, we tried route B.

Al Stewart's first single 'The Elf' 1966

Pat Sloman, the programme's leading female presenter was attractive, thirtyish and although the daily TV show broadcast to this region from Southampton, conveniently she resided in Branksome Park. Also, slightly surprisingly, her phone number was not ex directory.

On hearing I represented a singer with a newly released single about an elf; Ms. Sloman's encouraging response was to invite me round to hear it. At the appointed time she opened the door of her flat to admit me, plus record, plus Al. Vivacious Pat loved the record, said she would play it to the producer, and seemed happy to let us overhear a phone call received from, apparently, her boyfriend. Amusingly informing him she was busy entertaining two young men!

She kept the record. We left. Al appeared on *Day By Day*. 5 years later!

1966's great TV moment, football's World Cup Final, on the penultimate day of July, added that extra special something, to gift this era in England a golden national memory. As Captain Bobby Moore and his team mates captured the *Jules Rimet Trophy* with a 4-2 score line it seemed as if they had conjured Roy of the Rovers from the comic book page to the Wembley turf. Be nice if it happened again – maybe next time.

Those sunny summer days of 66 needed a soundtrack to the visual excitement of England hosting the World Cup tournament and the Kinks provided it perfectly with Ray Davies' No.1 hit 'Sunny Afternoon'. A quick glance at the charts from June to August would easily justify 1966's claim to being a peak period for pop music and the 7" single: e.g. 'Daydream', 'Summer in the City' – Lovin' Spoonful, 'Monday, Monday' – Mamas and Papas, 'Wild Thing' – Troggs, 'Paint It Black' – Rolling Stones, 'Paperback Writer', 'Eleanor Rigby', 'Yellow Submarine' – Beatles, 'River Deep Mountain High' – Ike and Tina Turner, 'Bus Stop' – Hollies, 'God Only Knows' – Beach Boys. Oh, yes, and the greatest PopRock LP of all time.

OK I know, all these *Greatest of All Time* statements are always highly subjective and are more a starting point for discourse rather than a defining conclusion, but for 45 years one album has, by featuring on top of umpteen 'Greatest Album Ever' lists, proved to be a genuine contender.

Revolver. The Beatles answer to the question: have they peaked with *Rubber Soul*? Well no they haven't! By the time of its August release thanks to innovative promotional use of radio, the sparkling new achievements of the fast maturing ex-Fabs were apparent to one and all.

For many years now extensive radio play is an expected precursor during the weeks preceding a potential hit's release, be it CD or download, but not in the sixties. Not until several of the *Revolver* tracks featured on top radio programmes starting in July. I remember hearing the first broadcast of McCartney's (with a little help from his friend J.L.) 'Eleanor Rigby' on Simon Dee's BBC programme and realising in that instant that this was yet another of those exciting sixties musical leaps onto a new mountain top.

Being able to possess the LP a few weeks later repeated playing revealed every song to be a winner. For example Paul McCartney's Jane Asher song

'Here, There and Everywhere': ask him to name which of his compositions he rates as top favourite and the answer tends to be this one. Or perhaps 'Yellow Submarine', released as a single c/w 'Eleanor Rigby': amongst those providing background voices are Brian Jones, Marianne Faithfull, Donovan and Beatle stalwart Neil Aspinall. 'For No One', complete with crystal clear Alan Civil horn solo. And pointing the way forward to new, uncharted territory for the popular song, last track, 'Tomorrow Never Knows'.

To top it off this fabulous album came contained within an equally outstanding and original sleeve. Combining contemporary line drawings of the Beatles with a collage of photos from recent years, Klaus Voormann, old friend from Hamburg days, and about to join Manfred Mann on bass guitar, created an LP image for the group to rival Peter Blake's famous *Sgt. Pepper* the following year.

Last word on *Revolver* and the summer before the summer of love: *Q Magazine* names this record No.1 LP of all time in the year 2000. In 2002 *Rolling Stone* reaches the same conclusion.

Ritzy Music & Discotheques

The bandstand still stands to your left as an early evening walk through the Lower Pleasure Gardens has brought you to the Pier and a decision: turn left – the IMAX building; nominated by Channel 4 TV programme *Demolition* as the worst building in England, or go right towards the B.I.C. Well obviously not left. Bournemouth International Centre at least will from time to time provide the musical entertainment you require.

Now let's imagine, just for fun, a downloaded, still to be invented(!) Apple App has enabled the smart phone currently pointing towards the West Cliff approach to dissolve the contemporary buildings and landscape, replacing them with the sight and sound of the 1960s.

The sixties reality this digital tech magic would reveal would soon become apparent as a further, slightly uphill stroll, brought a major Bournemouth music venue into view.

The Ritz: for 4 years from 1966 until a 1970 name-change to the Hive, provided a constant stream of top, or about to be top, bands. Bands that due to Bournemouth's then lack of a university would in all probability have swerved the town as its absence would have left national booking agencies nowhere to place them. The university/college circuit that developed increasing importance during the late 60s for the explosion of hard rock R 'n' B bands, psychedelic outfits and everything in between, featured many of the groups booked to play the Ritz.

Face to face with the English Channel a bow-windowed, fifties style, ex-hotel ballroom, replete with flashing Ritz sign warning not of hazards to passing ships, but rock music was contained within. Fancy spending a quid to keep company with Jethro Tull or Ten Years After? Perhaps the Spencer Davis Group, Taste or the Groundhogs. Maybe Desmond Decker or Peter Green's Fleetwood Mac. All these and many more performed during 68/69 at this West Cliff venue.

No doubt the September 68 appearance of one band caught the attention of local musician Greg Lake. Immediate Records' P.P. Arnold's backing band The Nice, so named by Andrew Oldham with a nod towards another of his labels acts, Steve Marriot's Small Faces single 'Here Comes The Nice', were led by explosive keyboard player Keith Emerson. Throw in, so to speak, Atomic Rooster's drummer Carl Palmer, a couple of years later, and hey presto! Emerson, Lake and Palmer.

Following a critically well received debut album the previous year, at the time of their Ritz booking the Nice were close to peaking chart-wise with their hit interpretation of Leonard Bernstein's *West Side Story* music: 'America'.

Guitarist Greg with two records on his C.V. from 67 and 68 as a member of first the Shame, then the Shy Limbs, was en route to accepting an offer from an old school friend, to join his new band as a bass guitar playing vocalist.

In 1969 Wimborne's Robert Fripp formed Progressive Rock originators King Crimson; they played a gig in Hyde Park, released *In the Court of the Crimson King*, and almost at once found themselves atop the album charts as the sixties segued into the seventies. Although a London band, at Crimson's core were 60's Bournemouth musicians the Giles brothers, Greg Lake, Gordon Haskell and of course, ex League Of Gentlemen, guitar maestro Fripp.

"Extraordinary how potent cheap music is," remarked Noel Coward long ago. Extraordinary indeed has been the ongoing effect on the lives of so many of us delivered by this 'cheap music'. The intended implication of Coward's adjective was not to insult the popular songs of the day, but rather admire the lasting and strong emotions revealed by supposedly transient music: not opera, not classical symphonies, but the often casually created tunes and words, incorrectly supposed to have a short shelf life.

Beat music of the sixties as it continued to permeate the hearts and minds of the young world could not exist in a vacuum: it needed an audience. Those rhythms and lyrics, whether performed live or stored in a handy portable storage device for later retrieval – a black vinyl disc, needed sentient beings to hear, view, be moved, and remember the musically stirred emotions the performers generated.

Let's for a moment look away from the main stage of Bournemouth's Ritz, even if the then current No.1 hit-makers Fleetwood Mac are performing 'Albatross'. Amongst the smoky, swaying, punters it's a fair bet we might spot three Ritz regulars: Eric, Alan and Dave. No, you haven't forgotten them; they were never the missing members of Dave Dee, Beaky, Mick and Tich: just superfans whose life-long love of far from 'cheap' music presents a microcosm of the ongoing depths and delights the sounds of the sixties provided.

David Partridge was probably not known by the other two pop punters, but as 'Dave Carson' he performed as an occasional DJ when the re-invented venue became the Hive and he became Bournemouth's Murray the K. For many years before this he'd been well known on the local music scene, not as a musician, but rather a personable character with a penchant for Blues 78s, Stones and Beatles, and most of all Roger McGuinn's Byrds. Sartorially stylish in Cecil Gee suits, Dave could be found one moment being requested to leave Bourne Radio's basement record department having initiated a heated debate with an *Echo* reporter on nuclear weapons, and on another organising an impromptu game of 'Test Match' cricket on Bournemouth beach suggesting to a couple of passing policeman they might like to join in as the 'Australians'!

When the Bootleg Beatles played the B.I.C. in 1991 it was because Mr. Partridge promoted the gig – just for fun: he wasn't a concert promoter; he just wanted to see the next best thing to the real Fabs. Such is the powerful hold 60's music continued to exert on this fan.

Eric Billett and Alan Burridge, firm friends from schoolboy days, by then in their late teens, were enthusiastic live music patrons and also record collecting regulars at a small Westbourne emporium providing 'Pre-owned vinyl for the cognoscenti': in fact within a week or so of my Poole Road shop's opening Eric had become one of its very first customers. Perhaps no better example could be offered to illustrate the long term effects of rock-a boogie than revealing the name, over 40 years later, of this record shop's final customer the day it closed forever: yes, of course, Eric!

What of Alan as the years rolled by? Did the excitement of seeing the Move, Fleetwood Mac and other Ritz faves, fade with time? Certainly not: in 2009 he published *Bournemouth Rocks*, a compilation of local gigs he'd enjoyed, many with Eric, and also reminiscences of weekly visits to, what would become, Bus Stop Records.

At the beginning of a new decade as the 60s' slow fade into the 70s began, I attended the opening night of a newly built large entertainment complex in Glenfern Road, containing Le Cardinal, Maison Royale, the Outlook, and the Badger Bars. In the following years these music venues/restaurants/bars would be re-branded as Chelsea Village, Stateside Centre, and eventually the Cage.

Although providing the town centre with substantially increased opportunities for social interaction and dancing, to either live bands or records, they failed to continue the 'cool', *where it's at*, atmosphere delivered by sixties discotheques. Instead they began a trend towards middle-of-the-road style music venues, which for all their glitz and glamour could not be confused with the 'where it's happening' vibe encompassed by the smaller 60's equivalents.

Eventually a new generation arrived in the 90s, removed far enough in time from the sixties to generate their own, distinctive, dance clubs, with the advent of *Rave Culture*.

Although the origins of records providing music to dance to in public, as an alternative to 'live' musicians, began as far back in the UK as the late 1940s, it needed the 60's records and go-go vibe, coupled with club-size venues, to make the hipster-trousered and mini-skirted clientele feel 'on trend'.

In time the word 'Disco' would acquire pejorative connotations both as a 70's music genre and as an often amateur, or semi-pro, mobile 'DJ' for party time hire. But in the 60s as the seeds of Regine's original early 50's Parisian, Whiskey a Go Go club and England's first discotheque, London's Saddle Room, opened in 1961 by Hélène Cordet, blossomed into imitators across the land, these new style clubs represented a significant element of *Swingin' Sixties* charisma.

By 1964 Bournemouth could offer Le Kilt; just off the Square and close by the town hall. Adjoining the Anglo-Swiss restaurant with its cosmopolitan clientele of continental students, the tartan-themed Le Kilt was popularly managed by Adrianno Rossi, and owned by Louis Brown. Over the next couple of years Adrianno moved to managing Papa's at the Lansdowne; a newly opened discotheque occupying the premises of the now no longer Le Disque a Go Go, eventually taking it over and renaming the club: Adriannos. By the psychedelic summer of 67 Louis Brown had opened a second town centre club on Poole Hill called Samantha's.

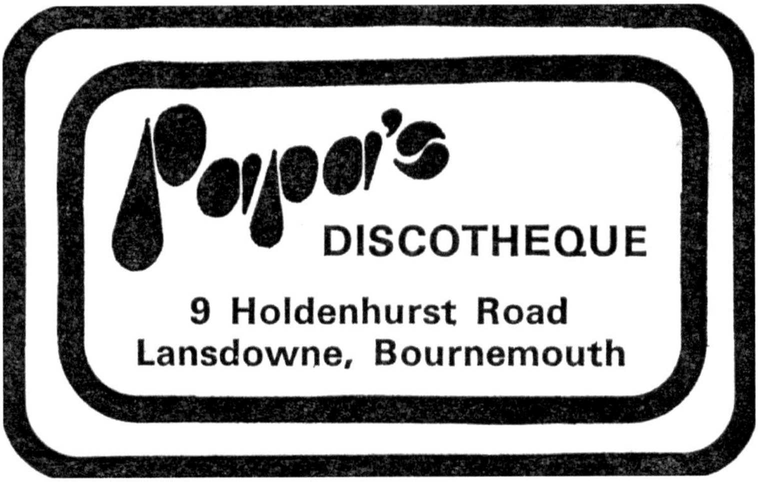

He already owned the Scotch of St. James in London; the epicentre of high-end pop-club night-life. Situated in Mason's Yard, behind Fortnum and Masons, and close by John Dunbar's Indica Gallery, the Scotch was the mid-sixties favourite hang out for the Beatles, Stones, Who, Animals, and anyone deemed cool enough to gain entrance to its mock Scottish-baronial interior. This strictly limited admission club had followed on from the Ad Lib as the pop culture elite's nite-spot of choice: the kind of place that *Time Magazine* had in mind in that famous '*Swinging London*' issue.

'Psychedelic Phil' was in charge of Samantha's and, although we didn't know each other, by a quirky coincidence he knew my dad from London in the fifties. Phil had been a stunt man in those days and as a 12 year old I'd seen him crashing from a Wild West saloon balcony on the Dominion stage during a *Wyatt Earp Show*, starring Hugh O'Brian as the TV marshal come to life.

One evening Phil entertained my parents in his club of flashing lights and, weird though this was amidst the far younger generation of clubbers, it also seemed quite relaxed and natural.

For a few years there was only a slight overlap of patrons seeking live sixties music from Le Disque, the Pavilion, the Arcade Ballrooms or Poole's Cellar Club, with the Soul and Ska loving hipsters grooving to the sounds of Stax and Motown in the discotheques. This changed a little by the late 60s as a club like Samanthas mixed DJ nights with live bands. The Nite People would play one night and Andy Peebles spin soul sounds on another.

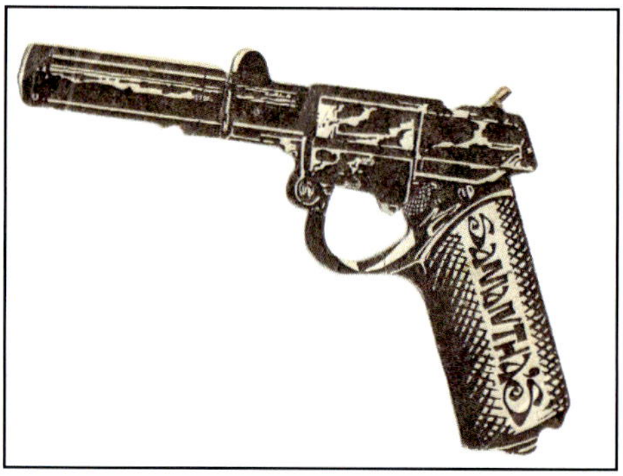

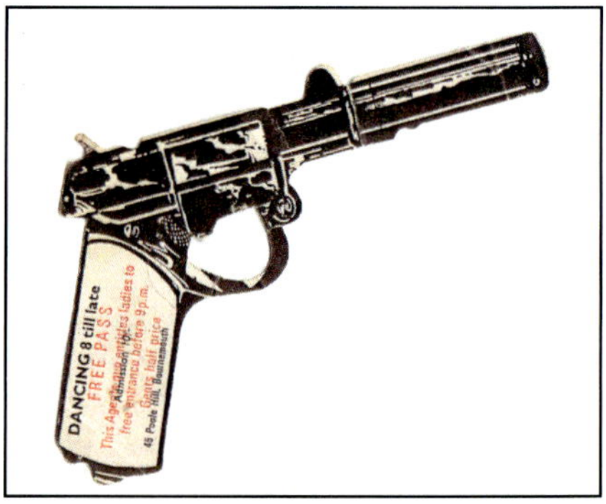

Two sides of free pass for Samantha's psychedelic club 1967

'Larry Page the Teenage Rage' may not have hit the top as a UK RockPop contender in the late fifties, but in a similar career move to his contemporary Mickie Most, as a record producer in the mid-sixties the sun did indeed shine for a while. When Reg Presley, the leader of Andover's finest, the Troggs, captured on a semi-notorious bootleg recording, *The Trogg Tapes*, revealed the group's inability to make hits anymore was due to the absence of Larry Page and his 'pixie dust', he highlighted the special touch producer Page had brought to singles such as 'Wild Thing'.

Utilising some of his cash from the splendid 'Wild Thing', and several other Troggs hits, Larry P. and Dick James, launched their own record label, Page One Records. Local faves, the Nite People, signed to Page One and released a distinctive and eclectic album in 1969: *PM*. Fronted by vocalist/guitarist Jimmy Warwick, with Chris 'Fergie' Ferguson on drums. I shared many a late night last Bournemouth bus to Poole with Fergie back in the early 63 Manfreds at Le Disque days.

In common with the Troggs, the Nite People had previously released several singles on Fontana Records. Unlike the Troggs their 'Page pixie dust' free records weren't hits. *PM* however, while still failing to shift more then a tiny quantity of units, was an exceptionally varied LP of, mainly, cover versions, from skiffle to early ProgRock, via Tamla Motown: Lonnie Donegan's 'Rock Island Line', the Four Tops' 'Reach Out I'll Be There' and Frank Zappa's 'Peaches En Regalia', plus 'Delilah' and Jimmy Giuffre's jazz classic, 'The Train and the River', all on the same album!

Samantha's club favourites the Nite People

Samantha's Andy Peebles possessed both passion for, and knowledge of, 60's soul music. In the late 60s/early 70s I'd see him here and there round town, often in clubs or my shop, buying, selling, and talking about records.

One Bournemouth party we'd both been invited to celebrated the 21st birthday of Sue Cotton, a granddaughter of BBC radio bandleader Billy. I wonder if he remembers meeting Billy Cotton's son, Bill Cotton, that evening. An interesting thought, as Bill Cotton was then Controller of BBC Light Entertainment and the quietly determined Andy would one future day present a well known programme within his fiefdom: *Top of the Pops.*

Just as Tony Blackburn before him had left Bournemouth for life as a pirate in 64 on Radio Caroline, then on to the then brand new BBC Radio 1 in 67, and eventually a presenting slot on *Top of the Pops*, Andy Peebles would leave the south coast and also reach BBC radio and TV, in his case via broadcasting on Manchester's Radio Piccadilly. A nice fusion of Samantha's' DJ and star band came together in 69 when the Nite People presented him with a signed copy of their newly released *PM* LP, dedicated to the Emperor Andy; an affectionate allusion to top radio disc jockey Emperor Rosko.

'*The Huge World of Emily Small*', ring any bells? Probably not. This 1967 LP debut by the Picadilly Line on CBS sold about as well as the Nite People. And yes, unlike Radio Piccadilly they spelt the group's name with just one c. A PsychPop collector item created by a pair of singer-songwriters: Rod Edwards and Roger Hand. A year or so and a label change to RCA later the duo had re-branded as Edwards Hand. Produced by no less an eminence than George Martin indulging in a little light relief from the Abbey Road tensions wrought by the Beatles' *White Album* sessions. He produced a second LP for them the following year: still no record charts were stormed.

Backtracking to late 66 and a conversation between two ever hopeful music entrepreneurs, sitting in a Ford Zodiac parked near the Lansdowne one rainy evening. Earlier that day Al had played me a couple of demos by Rod and Rog, two recently acquired chums from Soho's Les Cousins contemporary folk club, and fellow house-mates for a while as his domestic London wanderings continued.

One of their demoed songs was called 'Twigs' and they certainly sounded as if they were in with a chance. Al thought so: "I want to make a record with them," he informed me. "We could hire a studio and you and I could produce it." Still that sixties-long refrain. He'd even thought of a biz name; an amalgamation of our surnames: *Streemer Enterprises.*

As we chatted in my car our mutual enthusiasm was tempered by one seemingly ever present ambition-thwarting problem: no money. Well not exactly no money; more no spare £100 cash, the minimum sum calculated for this idea to proceed. More like 2K today. I had yet to open my shop and Al was still playing small clubs; also the vehicle we were sitting in was continuing to remove pound notes from my wallet with the facility of a Dickensian pickpocket.

No conclusion was reached that night, but we never found the funds and some time later Al, backed by his new manager, Roy Guest, finally had a crack at producing a Rod and Rog demo. He'd written a song for them, more than somewhat in the style of Dylan's *Tambourine Man*, called 'Primrose Lady'. Even with the quality advice of top session guitarist Big Jim Sullivan this novice fugitive from Bournemouth beat groups couldn't produce the goods in the few studio hours available to him. Glad it was Roy G's cash and not mine. By late 1967 Al and the Picadilly Line were both managed by Folk Directions and signed to CBS Records.

I sometimes think back and wonder if this was an opportunity missed. Then quickly accept a reassuring thought: if George Martin couldn't produce a hit for them, no one could!

The exclusivity not surprisingly desired by mid-sixties clubland in-crowds could on occasion create a tangential and long lasting effect.

I had arrived relatively early one night in October 66 at the Scotch of St. James, utilising a tenuous Bournemouth connection with owner Louis Brown, admission had presented no problems. A couple of hours later, having knocked back one or two over priced whisky miniatures from the comfort of a high backed leather sofa, I and my mellow mood had descended to the small dance floor area below.

To the left what appeared to be a gilded coach: actually an elaborate base for the club's DJ and turntables. Across the dance floor in the far left corner a tiny stage. A stage that had recently introduced Chas Chandler's new unknown protégé, Jimi Hendrix, to London's pop elite.

As the sound system relayed the Four Tops' current No. 1 'Reach Out I'll Be there' – not for the first time that night – I relaxed on more of the Scotch's abundant supply of button-backed leather and casually surveyed the small group of tables to my left. On a raised, very slightly enclosed, corner area a few tables were fully occupied by that evening's clutch of Pop V.I.P.S. An in-crowd within an in-crowd, like a *Swinging London* version of a Russian doll.

That late autumn night's pop music celebs were representative of virtually any night at the Scotch of St. James. A Stone, two Who, and an Animal. By 2.00 a.m. Bill Wyman, Keith Moon, John Entwhistle, and Alan Price, were all merrily chatting and drinking, never going near the minute dancing area.

I however did, and found myself during one bout of exercise on the crowded dance floor, shoulder to shoulder, with a jolly Bruce Welch and attractive blonde.

All of this had distracted me from my main reason to be in the Scotch that night: a midnight meeting with Al Stewart plus Picadilly Line Rod and Rog. With the appointed time continuing to recede, and knowing of Al's usual punctuality, I remained, without the benefit of a 21st century mobile phone, unaware of the reason for his no-show. The clock ticked on and my attention was taken by a P.A. announcement from the gilded coach ensconced DJ: he had a pre-release copy of the new Beach Boys' single, this would be the first chance to hear it. Great. Then the club was filled with the sound of 'Good Vibrations'. Instantly amazing – Beach Boy Brian's tip top response to the Beatles' goal post moving *Revolver.* Goal posts that the following year the Fabs would move, forever, out of sight with *Sgt. Pepper.*

Round 5.00 a.m. I left, passing by the Indica Gallery where John Lennon a few days later was to meet Yoko Ono for the first time. Still no sign of Al, who, by the way, knew Yoko and her then husband Tony Cox.

Later that morning I had the answer. The three of them had shown up as arranged and the equivalent of present day door security had said: "No. You can't come in." An annoying, small matter, soon forgotten. So you might think. Thirty five years later quoted in *The True Life Adventures of a Folk Rock Troubadour*, while describing the happy times his *Year of the Cat* American success had enable him to enjoy in Sunset Strip's welcoming rock clubs, Al still remembered, "All those nights at the Scotch of St. James where I waited outside and even Jonny Kremer could get in and I couldn't!"

1967

Nineteen sixty seven: a famous year in a special decade. 'The Summer of Love'. 'Strawberry Fields Forever'. *Sgt. Pepper's Lonely Hearts Club Band.* The Redlands' Rolling Stones become Rock 'n' Roll outlaws. *Monterey Pop Festival.* Farewell to Brian Epstein. Hello to Pink Floyd and Jimi Hendrix. *Blow Up.* Patrick McGoohan's *Prisoner* begins. Al Stewart plays a solo concert at the Royal Festival Hall and releases his first LP. And I open my first shop selling records and guitars.

Early in 1967 Al holds just released Incredible String Band LP *'5000 Spirits'* while I wear momentarily fashionable satin shirt

It's quite OK if you didn't notice that last item; but I'm sure the others caught everyone's attention, either at the time or through the retrospection of history's magnifying lens.

Just as 1963 had sparkled with myriad zeitgeist forming moments, the events of 1967 by the year's end had created a super new enhanced Pop Culture that appeared a light year or two removed from its beginning.

The world had the Beatles and the Beatles had the world. It seemed as if almost everyone everywhere felt connected through their music and personas to a tuned-in decade speedily rewriting the rules and rhymes of previous years. The population of Bournemouth being far from an exception; not a surprise considering the town's connections with the Mersey Marvels earlier touring time. Nick Churchill's book *Yeah Yeah Yeah: The Beatles & Bournemouth* pays informed testament to that.

Those touring years had now ended, with the group's penultimate live performance on a San Franciscan night the previous August. The final public hurrah yet to come on the rooftop of their Saville Row Apple H.Q. late in January 1969.

By 67's inception, with a spectacularly unique story already written, they had embarked on a new 'tour'. This one through their psychedelically illuminated minds never slipped anchor from the safe harbour of Abbey Road studios.

The last world tour's unwarranted and undeserved trials and tribulations delivered to their door by the despotic politics of the Philippines, coupled with the fanatical ignorance of a handful of record burning dwellers deep in the heartland of America's old Confederate states meant the peace and safety of this London base was urgently required.

Fortunately for all concerned – both band and worldwide audience – they conjured up another, if anything, even more impressive chapter. The first indication that the wizards that would be glimpsed during the opening reel of the *Magical Mystery Tour* movie had a fresh and strangely original path to travel had become apparent with the last track of *Revolver*. 'Tomorrow Never Knows' was unprecedented and flashed an early warning sign: something very different is on the horizon.

That 'something' was to be a 7" double A-side single which simultaneously delivered a work of pop music transcending Art, a strong contender for Greatest 45 rpm Record Ever, whilst signposting the single's eventual demise at the insistence of the all-conquering LP: John Lennon's 'Strawberry Fields Forever', back to back with Paul McCartney's 'Penny Lane'.

Never intended for release as a single by the Beatles, but as an initial instalment for their next LP; an epic slowly taking shape and destined for eventual summertime release. Amazing to consider the marvellous *Sgt. Pepper* expanded to include these songs: but this was not to be.

Given the keys by a grateful EMI to use the company's landmark NW8 studios 24/7 if they so wished, and with memories of the one day session to complete their debut *Please Please Me* album possibly in mind, they did so wish. By February 67 an avaricious and impatient record company was ravenously hungry for 'product'. Art for art's sake etc. but as Bob Dylan suggested, "Money doesn't talk it swears." Parlophone's parent company persuaded Brian Epstein to persuade the 'boys' to acquiesce and so this more than fab work of art exists as a single entity fixed in amber forever between two astounding LPs.

'Strawberry Fields Forever', from its 1966 beginnings in Spain as Lennon strummed an acoustic guitar between takes for his movie *How I Won The War*, via an unprecedented 55 hours of innovative studio time, finally emerged as a deeply personal tone-poem, with deliberately stumbling lyrics referencing childhood emotions and adult identity uncertainties. I have always believed this to be Beatle John's aural masterpiece.

To possess this piece of art on a cheaply bought piece of plastic, originally contained within a picture sleeve, was already a high point of 60's record buying opportunities; but to flip it over, fire up your Dansette, and hear Paul McCartney's evocation of the Beatles' Liverpool yesteryear, well, what can one say – thank you, thank you very much!

'Penny Lane's' warm words of fond remembrance for a geographical location populated with a cast of real life characters directed by author Paul continued a theme initiated by partner John's 1965 *Rubber Soul* song 'In My Life'. Both songs reveal a sincere and poignant reflection on a long gone time.

A by-product of this double A-side would prove to be a significant influence on soon to be unveiled English Psychedelia records, as distinct from the *Alice in Wonderland* tropes of America's hallucinogenic inspirations.

That same February in 67 found George and Patti Harrison travelling home one evening from a day-long social gathering at the Sussex dwelling of their friend Keith Richard. A well-timed decision to hit the road denied them the chance of being somewhat more than spectators at the notorious *News of the World* generated Redland's Raid.

From Fleet Street's Marianne Faithfull *Mars Bar Fantasies*, to eternal *Rock Rebels Status* for the Rolling Stones, via William Rees Mogg's 'Who Breaks a Butterfly on a Wheel', *Times* editorial, this quintessential 60's saga reached its climax in a summertime trial.

As the counter culture's young knights, Jagger and Richards triumphed in their joust with the establishment they left behind a sadly damaged Guinevere. Fortunately, in time, she recovered her mojo and became a celebrated performer in her own right. I met Marianne once in the mid-seventies backstage at an Al gig: we briefly talked of intellectual pop people

– as Al and I thought of her; she reacted with incredulity and instead nominated Al. Mars Bars weren't mentioned.

Now the *News of the World* is extinct: not hard to imagine a little Hip Hip Hooray from a couple of Stones and Ms Faithfull.

As this pivotal year began Bournemouth's music and fashion scene continued to enjoy pop package tours stopping by to try out the, sometimes hard to accommodate, Winter Garden's acoustics: while local groups paraded their own wares alongside tribute band style renditions of Top 20 hits in clubs and ballrooms. Their audience still decked out in button-down shirts and ever popular mini-skirts; as yet to turn the page to paisley tab collars and flowing floral prints.

For this town's stand out event of 67 most of the 12 months must float by: ten and half to be precise. But before revisiting November 15th we need to travel through the mid-year metamorphosis known as the *Summer of Love*. This precursor to that late autumn date is an essential element to creating the new wave of styles and sounds that allowed an exceptional night of state of the art PsychRock to astound Bournemouth.

If rock biz were not a generic term but rather a brand *RockBiz*, à la *Coca Cola* or *Google*, its logo might easily have as its attendant catchy corporate tag line: *Sex and Drugs and Rock and Roll.*

Ever since Rock began to roll in the mid fifties sex had been a key element of its mission statement, but not drugs. Sure on the jazz side of the fence dope of all sorts had been a handmaiden to innumerable musicians and more then a few audience members, but even as the early mid-sixties Greenwich Village prototype-hippie folk rockers and West Coast surfer bands and their followers upgraded their vocabulary to joints from reefers and West London's Mods amphetamined their way round Shepherds Bush loaded with Purple Hearts, there was still little recognisable impact on the sounds and style of PopRock. This needed hallucinogens: specifically it needed LSD.

Although originally synthesised in the 1930s, and associated with enthusiasts such as Aldous Huxley and US psychiatrist Timothy Leary, this drug, still legal till 66, remained out of view of the general public till events on both sides of the Atlantic during the summer of 67 caused the media to declaim the dawn of a new social divide between the 'straight' and the 'non-straight'. Not that simple really.

As Al and I talked over the supposed intriguing possibilities back in 66 after reading an article in *Time* magazine around the time Cary Grant was revealed to be an advocate, we came to the ego-preserving decision to give it a miss. A decision that sadly many people, including Peter Green and Syd Barrett, did not reach. In a full page *International Times* article close to the *Summer of Love*, Al suggested he preferred to get 'High on ideas'. Allowing for a hint of pretension, mainly due to being quoted out of context, this was surely a saner, safer, route to travel, than Leary proposed in his mind-mapping *Politics of Ecstasy*.

By the way, yes it is slightly weird to recall that the cleanest of clean cut male movie stars Cary Grant, round the time I glimpsed him taking a walk through Bournemouth, a few chapters ago, was also a secret tripper.

But the pros, not many really, and the cons, a heck of a lot, of LSD aside, its incontrovertible effect on the winds of change that blew through 1967's pop culture would prove to be, if not deep and long lasting, spectacular and scene changing. Changes that in themselves would indeed be long lasting.

Shakespeare's "*Summer's lease hath all too short a date*", so too sixty seven's brief psych flowering. Nonetheless the cross-pollination resulting from those San Franciscan herbaceous headbands would seed musical and technological changes impacting on, at first the culture of the Western World and eventually effect communities on a pan global scale.

Ultimately the most significant sociological re-shaping, drugs aside, came from tangential tech developments; an evolution which ironically would digitally damage the record industry's long term standard business plan so severely that at this moment its shape and very existence seems uncertain.

In architecture *form* may indeed *follow function*, but to trace the pathway to the future from 67 it might be worthwhile considering form following content.

The shift from 45s to LPs that accelerated from the Beatles *Sgt. Pepper* starting gun, initiated changes to music and production, the storing and retrieval of music, the collecting of music, plus art and commerce.

First and foremost the music. In a splendid house in Belgravia, the home of era-enhancing Brian Epstein, as the sunny month of June approached, and with it the release of the Beatles new LP, John, Paul, George and Ringo held court. A photo op album launch party. Unlike the MBE adorned pantomime-military costumes of their alto egos *Sgt. Pepper's Lonely Hearts Club Band*, the now somewhat more than fab Fabs are attired in Chelsea cool from the likes of Michael Rainey's *Hung on You*, with three of them – not Paul – still sporting Zapata moustaches.

The Peter Blake/Jan Haworth designed sleeve, courtesy of uber-scene maker Robert Fraser, is on display revealing for the first time a glimpse of its unique and original imagery, a photo montage front cover to a, gatefold sleeve, completed by another first, all the lyrics on the back. A perfect complement to a loosely themed collection of shiny, bright, compelling, and though frequently introspective, basically hopeful songs.

Like Neil Armstrong's *Giant Leap for Mankind* lunar declaration two summers later, this LP made a Pop Culture jump the equivalent of Bob Beamon's 1968 Mexico Olympics long jump record shattering achievement: a World Record that would outlast not only the sixties, but the seventies and eighties too. For the Beatles and *Pepper* over 40 years into their history books' journey we had better start thinking Mozart style centuries.

How could this be produced in the relatively primitive, not to say archaic, studios of the mid-sixties – even Abbey Road? Well it couldn't. Hand in glove with the Beatles' creative ingenuity, George Martin with his engineer assistants, improvised and initiated technical facilities to match and allow the new sonic demands of Lennon, McCartney, Harrison and Starr.

And so, like a double-helix, modern music and studio technology began its ongoing march into the future, like the expansion of time and space, seemingly inseparable. As the years came and went the form of both recording studios and the medium for storing music would continue to evolve.

At first analogue, then digital, changes would present multi-track studios, capable of assembling a track second by second from a mountain of takes; plus alternatives to vinyl records for domestic playback and collecting.

Following in the magnetic ferrite oxide footsteps of pre-recorded open spool tapes came music-cassettes and the even more unfortunate 8-track cartridges, developed by a US consortium led by Bill Lear, of Lear Jet fame.

The 8-track designed initially for in-car play would, believe it or believe it not, pause in the middle of a recording, switch tracks, then continue, as if nobody cared: well they did care, so this format correctly went the way of the spinning wheel.

Better, but still not a serious hi-fi contender even with the necessary Dolby hiss reduction added, the narrow, slow speed, poor quality tape, pre-recorded cassette did, as a blank format present the record industry with its first major revenue threat. Convinced they were missing out on substantial sales due to home taping from records and radio in desperation many companies resorted to printing a skull and crossbones/cassette image on each LP's inner sleeve.

If the record companies of planet Earth had possessed a crystal ball a glance at the non-paying Download world of the 21st century would have a) told them not to give two hoots about cassette cash lost, and b) to be amazed at how collectively their lack of timely action would come close to costing them the whole ball game, while unnecessarily handing over a sizable percentage of their revenue stream to someone called Steve Jobs.

Long before a generation arrived who, not unreasonably, decided that music, like water, was free – except of course like water it's not free, just someone else is paying for it, the record industry was still ahead of the curve.

For example C.B.S. Records, Columbia in the US, at the same time as they were complaining about 'taping piracy', enabled by the, mainly, Japanese manufacturers of cassette decks, sold themselves lock, stock and barrel to Sony, who re-branded them as Sony International: classic case of, if not poacher turning gamekeeper, poacher and gamekeeper becoming one.

The most magnificent example of a Music Biz industry being at the top of their game came in 1982 with their 'Let's sell coals to Newcastle' innovation: the compact disc. As the Beatles led the way into a new gigantic market for LPs from 67 onwards, record buyers who had previously a few dozen singles and a handful of albums to place on their auto-changer, now increasingly possessed collections of LPs that ran into hundreds, if not thousands, and stereo systems that looked like the flight deck of the Starship Enterprise on which to play them. No coincidence this would be the year my Bournemouth record shop opened.

The record industry then expanded into a multi-billion dollar funfair to rival Hollywood and the movie industry. Add into this the tango they were now dancing with simpatico chums on the tech hardware side of the dance, and these music masters of the universe were now laughing all the way to the bank: a bank in all probability they now owned! After 15 years of this financial fun what could be better than to do it all over again? Enter the CD and the invitation for many, but emphatically not all, to junk their correctly prized record collections and turntables, and repurchase much of it, expensively, all over again on CD. Plus of course new equipment to play it on. Brilliant!

Initially sold on the premise of a superior frequency range to old analogue vinyl, not quite true, only better than budget to mid range stereo systems, high-end Linn and Quad products could match and surpass brittle and over bright sounding CDs, particularly the record companies' original offerings, frequently digitalised without re-mastering: just ask Stones and Zeppelin fans who repurchased their collections in the early 80s at up to £16 a disc.

But by the dawn of a new millennium the record companies collectively lost the plot. Like rabbits in the proverbial headlights shining fiercely at them from, at first Napster and then Mr. Job's Apple they did too little, too late.

Ten years on from 1967's launch of the LP market, at a moment close to the format's peak, my pal Al hit the upper echelons of the world's Hit Parades with his *Year of the Cat* album, by then a long way from a garden hut in Canford Bottom. Twenty five years on from its original release in 1976 (my, my doesn't time fly!) EMI Records issued a 'Twenty Fifth Anniversary Edition' on CD: this indicated the UK company had made plenty of loot from the record over the years and were continuing to do so. They threw a celebration launch party for Al at Abbey Road in 2001. He arrived at the famous St. Johns Wood studios with the writer of these words and my son Daniel.

In passing I should mention the reason my name appears in the re-issued anniversary edition Cat CD small print – of course small print, we're talking the absurd mini-fonts utilised by most CD booklets – is my assisting EMI reassemble the original *Hipgnosis* artwork.

As Daniel, by then in his early twenties and interested in sound production, took in the atmosphere of Studio 2 where the bash was held, and the Beatles had created the soundtrack to our lives, I chatted with Mike Heatley, an EMI director in charge of the company's worldwide back catalogue. Later, after my son had been shown round the studio control room by Andrew Powell, who'd produced Kate Bush's debut album *The Kick Inside* right there back in 78 and arranged *Year of the Cat* two years earlier, and I'd enjoyed reminiscing with Move vocalist Carl Wayne about 'Blackberry Way' and the Move's original manager/svengali Tony Secunda, I shared some more chit-chat with Mike.

Specifically we talked of the, even then, non-royalty paying download threat from the internet. I expressed an opinion that as the maturing CD market entered its inevitable cyclic decline, EMI, along with the other major manufacturer/distributors would soon find a way to monetize the cyber world and balance the loss from CD sales with further gains from their copyright assets. If I'd paused for a moment and considered EMI's past follies: nearly missing out on the Beatles; totally and unnecessarily missing out on owning a majority share in Lennon & McCartney's song publishing (not once, but twice!) and enduring an out of touch seventies period when the music biz joke – 'What's the difference between EMI and the Titanic?' Answer: 'The Titanic had a good band', was spot on, I should have realised this historic music corporation was quite capable of screwing it up. And, along with the world's other giant record label conglomerates, did just that.

Californian Apple, who long ago reached a seemingly amicable deal with Beatles Apple, the one staying with computing hardware and the other the software of recorded music (an arrangement that required frequent revisiting as fast moving digital times fused everything together), now, with a slight of hand that appeared to baffle and bemuse the record industry, Steve Jobs' Apple morphed from a computer tech organisation into a consumer orientated company with a market capitalisation as big as Exxon oil!

Prescient and smart, the informed Mike Heatley said he was not so sure. Indicating Daniel, who'd been contributing to the conversation, EMI Mike suggested that my son's generation would take a very different view to the long-standing existing patterns of collecting recorded music. My son confirmed this view, and they were both soon proved to be right.

By 2011, iTunes and Spotify aside, an estimated 90%+ of downloaded, supposedly copyright-protected music would be accessed for zilch. By then the once mighty EMI was a financial basket case, the plaything of investment banks and hedge funds.

The current state of affairs can be traced back to summer 67, and the beginning of the modern world's amalgamation of music, art, technology, and big, very, very, big business.

That same month of June, not content with bringing the fabled riches of Sgt. Pepper to a grateful and slightly stunned sixties' populace, presented the world with another music/tech breakthrough: *Our World*. Following on from sci-fi guru Arthur C. Clarke's 1940's prophesy that geo-stationary satellites would one day exist and allow instantaneous world-wide telecommunication, and the launch of Telstar and friends, the very first trans-global, satellite linkup was now possible. The future with GPS, Sat Nav, Skype, and One World TV availability was about to begin.

Sitting alongside Al in my parents' Branksome Park flat we tuned the, still black and white, TV to the obvious channel, the one hundreds of millions of viewers from Bournemouth to Bangkok, Bermuda to Brazil, would be watching in real-time. Basically a 2 hour documentary style travelogue, with each participating country putting forward a representative example of their nation.

Only Great Britain chose, splendidly, to use their allotted slot for music: the Beatles live in Abbey Road studios, surrounded by friends such as Jagger and Faithfull, and supposedly glimpsed in the creative act of producing with George Martin a new single. Long believed to be a song commissioned for the *Our World* broadcast the John Lennon led 'All You Need Is Love' was according to Paul McCartney based on an idea the song-writing partners had already begun. Whatever its genesis this Beatle song and record remains the audio emblem of the *Summer of Love*.

June 67 completed a hat trick of significant music moments that would give pop culture's kaleidoscope a significant and influential shake, this time a few time zones away from Bournemouth, in Monterey, California.

A hundred miles or so south of San Francisco, Monterey's Jazz Festival was already well established and esteemed by the time Lou Adler and John Phillips decided now was the time for a Pop festival. At this point the '*British Invasion of 64*', shell-shocked US PopRock establishment had, while being delighted and informed by the Beatles and Stones, already begun to join the post solo-singer (Bob Dylan aside), contemporary world of groups.

First to join the party had been, the already well-known Beach Boys. By 65/66 New York's Lovin' Spoonful and L.A.'s Byrds, plus the West Coast based Mamas and Papas were contributing to the mid-sixties cornucopia of golden pop music. *Monterey Pop Festival*, however, would prove to be the launch pad for America's re-engagement with the transatlantic battle for Rock music's crown. And yes, although the first Monterey festival not to focus on jazz or folk, was proclaiming pop music in its heading, these 3 days became popular music's atom splitting moment: now there would be pop groups and rock bands. Sure, not quite an instantaneous clean cut divide, but just as it had become obvious the Beatles were no longer Moptops, and the Stones and Who, shared little, if any, DNA with Herman and his Hermits, so a new differentiating descriptive generic term was essential.

From a standing start at the end of April, record producer Adler and Mamas and Papas leader Phillips, assisted by ex-Nems publicist Derek Taylor, with added input from Andrew Oldham, put together in 7 weeks an event that would be copied and extended from then to a seemingly ongoing now. Two years later in upstate New York: *Woodstock*, a year on in England – *Glastonbury*. And so on, and on, and on.

A 50,000 strong congregation of pop pilgrims assembled for three days to form the vanguard of festival crowds of the near and far future: by 1969 and *Woodstock* their numbers had surged to half a million and Joni Mitchell's 'Golden and Stardust' generation became worldwide headlines.

From time to time a glance at Pop 'n' Rock's back pages reveals names some way distant from the frontlines, but hugely significant nonetheless. In England during the late 50s and early 60s innovative TV producer Jack Good would spring to mind. In the 70s, US music mogul David Geffen. And for American rock of the late 60s we need look no further than one astute member of the June 67 Monterey multitudes, CBS Records legal eagle, Clive Davis.

The monolithic US entertainment company, while appreciating the opportunity, thanks to John Hammond, to print the name Bob Dylan on their labels, and thanks to Bob Dylan to enjoy a hip hits association with the Byrds, was still principally in the mainstream album market provided by Barbra Streisand and Tony Bennett.

As the San Andreas Fault Line stayed still, but Oldham's UK bookings, Hendrix and Who, erupted Clive Davis reached for his corporate cheque book and started to sign up any other available *popquake* causing act. San Francisco's Haight Ashbury combo Big Brother and the Holding Company did not interest the soon to be president of a grateful CBS; but their singer Janis Joplin did. You can see where this is going, so could Clive D. In his case Santana and Chicago, creating cross-market synergies for Simon & Garfunkel with Mike Nichol's *Graduate* movie, and eventually his very own major imprint, Arista Records.

In case all of this seems remote from Bournemouth's *Swinging Sixties*, the shared generalities of these rapid mid-sixties musical and cultural changes aside, without *Monterey* it would be highly unlikely a small island named Wight, anchored close by our town, would have invited Bob Dylan to headline 1969's historic festival. Nor would Clive Davis and ex Bournemouth beat band guitarist Al Stewart have joined up for Al's 1978, double platinum LP, *Time Passages.*

The last high day of summer in England is usually taken to be around the weekend of August Bank Holiday. In 1967 hindsight might also show this one to be the high-water mark of the nineteen-sixties. The Beatles had just met an Indian guru, who along with Yoko Ono, would unknowingly facilitate the groups eventual, and inevitable, separation into solo identities once again.

On the 27th August, in the London house, where only three months before he had displayed the extraordinary *Lonely Hearts Club Band* for the first time, the lonely heart that was Brian Epstein said a tragic goodbye to a world, that thanks to his confident, adoring, estimation of the Beatles magical talent, now looked and sounded very different from the one revolving on its axis the day he first visited the Cavern. He was 32.

To give further credence to the suggestion that this month presented a key turning point for the exciting decade that had been running with gleeful exhilaration for 5 years, Andrew Loog Oldham and his rock music innovating experiment, the Rolling Stones, parted company for ever.

Oldham had a few years earlier brought *Vogue*'s star photographer David Bailey into the Stones orbit to shoot the cover for *The Rolling Stones No.2*, released in January 65. Cinema screens of the late summer of 67 displayed a roman à clef Bailey, acted by David Hemmings, in *Blow Up.* If you caught his movie as I did in one of Westover Road's picture palaces, perhaps we shared a feeling that the 60's silvery moonlight was beginning to be obscured by clouds.

Director Michelangelo Antonioni having decamped from the fading significance of Rome's supposed Dolce Vita decadence to visit London's vibrant and relevant scene, brought with him a downbeat, melancholic, sense of emptiness. Perhaps a harbinger of a darker sixties' flipside: no longer just a fun-filled hedonistic decade fuelled by fabulous pop songs and Quant mini-dressed, pill-contracepted girls.

Hemmings' lead role, originally envisioned as a perfect fit for Terence Stamp the then partner of Bailey's superstar model, muse and previous girlfriend, Jean Shrimpton, presented a blank character seemingly existing in a moral vacuum. As a cipher for the Italian outsider's perception of *Swinging England* in 66 it felt bleak. Even the appearance of the Yardbirds – the Who having declined Antonioni's offer to reprise Pete Townshend's auto-destruction art rock – failed to spark the by then expected 60's pop pleasure. Amusing though it was to watch Jimmy Page's sideways glance at Jeff Beck as, following direction to imitate Townshend, he faithfully smashed a borrowed guitar against his annoyingly feedback plagued amplifier, the overall effect was despair and unfocused anger.

Beside this fascinating cameo, *Blow Up* was filled with trivia treats, from the first sighting on screen of 17 year old Jane Birkin, about to marry England's premier soundtrack composer John Barry, frolicking with Gillian Hills, the female star of Adam Faith's 1960 movie *Beat Girl*, to the drophead Rolls Silver Cloud coupe leased to the production by owner Jimmy Savile.

Another indication, that while on the surface the decade's at times jolly detachment from reality was struggling to hold down a simmering uncertainty, beamed into our homes in late September, courtesy of TV's *Danger Man.*

While filming an episode of this hugely successful series the previous year in North Wales, Patrick McGoohan became aware of Clough Williams-Ellis' Portmeirion. This Italianate style fantasy famously became the base for outside location scenes in co-creator, occasional director, leading actor McGoohan's cult production *The Prisoner.*

Even after visiting a fortunately *Rover,* the sinister bouncing weather balloon, free Portmeirion in the mid 70s, I still could not shake off an ongoing empathy with the central character. OK a little exposition is called for. The series ran for 17 inconclusive episodes: perhaps mirroring real life's frequent loose ends. A key event in my real-life occurred the day following the, critics bemusing, broadcast of *The Prisoner's* first episode: I opened a shop in Westbourne, soon to become popularly known as *Jon's.* And although popular with me too, surrounded by guitars & records, it felt like my '*Village*'.

No longer a teenager, having turned 20 a few months before, I still identified with that uniquely 60's mindset, assuming and accepting quick changing, short-term, ideas and events. The Beatles and Stones have just released yet another great single? Well 12 weeks later along would come the next one! Similarly fashion in male and female attire would frequently have a remarkably short shelf-life by the standards of previous decades, with Carnaby Street initiating the now accepted vogue for fast changes in style.

And so, with *Sgt. Pepper* atop the LP charts, and a window offering a bunch of guitars, backed up with a selection of recently released counter-culture albums, my bright yellow retailing opportunity debuted. From day one, with no advertising, and little promotion, customers appeared, seemed pleased, bought stuff, and told their friends. No, a fortune was not to be made from such a relatively small-ticket business; but the timing was right and word of mouth delivered the shop's existence to a, mainly young, demographic from Swanage to Christchurch.

How long, taking in to account that ever changing sixties ambience, had I envisioned owning such an emporium? Not sure – 6 months perhaps, maybe a year or two: then do something else. Forty two years later, that same lifetime, the *Bournemouth Echo* devoted a full page to the passing of "A landmark shop!"

Re-branded twice, painted red once, relocated a few steps to the east in the early 90s, stocking only recorded music and eventually movies, with or without my direct day by day involvement, Bus Stop Records survived.

Not sure that I would have, if I'd not found a way to enjoy the records and chat as much as so many customers apparently did over the years. This to a degree was achieved by a loose, trust-based, collective of frequently changing regulars who, spending increasingly large amounts of time in the shop's 'club like' atmosphere, progressed to the status of 'assistants'. Gordon, Ellis, Barry and most of all QPR Tony (eventually to be known as Chelsea Tony!) allowed me for a sizable percentage of those many years to separate 'doing' from 'being'. Not to put too faux a philosophical slant on this, but the value of what we do for an occupation is often used as a short-hand description for who we are. For example the common place conversational gambit "What do you do?" The implication being, that if not defining a person, once established it tends to go someway towards doing so. I believe that 'being' shares a least top billing with 'doing': after all we are all known as Human Beings – not Human Doings!

As McGoohan's, creation, No. 6, from time to time sought to escape from the supposed pleasure-dome attractions of his geographical and psychological '*Village*', so I too would make my absence from Bus Stop

Records a reality.

One alternative reality that continued to invite my participation was undergoing an overdue expansion a hundred miles north-west in London Town. Just as Richard Whittington Esq. had failed to locate streets paved with gold, so too had Al Stewart yet to make the career jump from Soho cellar club singer-songwriter, with one Decca single to his name, to a concert hall performer in possession of an LP recording contact. By November 1967 this changed and stayed changed.

That month *Bedsitter Images*, Al's first album, was released on CBS and he played a solo concert at the Royal Festival Hall with the Sinfonia of London as a backing band.

'Bed Sitter Images' Al's first LP 1967

The previous year back in Bournemouth, semi-surrounded by familiar record booth peg-boarding, Al and I listened to Judy Collins. Al spent a lot of 1966 in Bournemouth as the slow progress he was encountering in London indicated the support and friendly encouragement his old home town presented was preferable. The years that had rolled by since 62 had not dimmed my conviction that my buddy was a 'Star'; just one the world at large was yet to recognise.

That day he was keen to draw my attention to a new contemporary songwriter, a Canadian poet, as yet to record his songs, and receiving an initial airing via Judy Collins. It would not be till the following year, encouraged by friend Judy, his debut album, *Songs of Leonard Cohen*, was released.

Reflecting on the obvious qualities of 'Suzanne' and 'Dress Rehearsal Rag' we had no way of knowing either the direct and positive effect the American singer's *In My Life* LP would generate for Laughing Lenny's career, or how the confusing example set by the album's lush orchestration would negatively impact on Al's first LP the following year.

During 67's famous summer Al recorded a bunch of original words and music; songs that described love: sought and found, lost and lingered over in bed-sitter land. They set a direction and image that would prevail for the next few years and 3 more albums. Fortunately by LP number two, 1969's *Love Chronicles*, he managed to escape the false start *Bedsitter Images'* stifling symphonic strings had needlessly brought to its production party.

Ostensibly produced by manager Roy Guest, who, entranced by the Collins' record, decided that singer, plus songs, plus symphony orchestra was the way to go. It wasn't. Three years after the LP's original release, Al supervised a slightly remixed reissue, with reduced string arrangements and lightened by the removal of three tracks.

If Al's *Bedsitter Images* debut LP had been recorded 6 months earlier his songs would have been performed by a solo singer backed by his acoustic Epiphone guitar: 6 months later would have delivered an electric folk-rock album, closer to *Love Chronicles.*

Although at the time the sheer delight he and I felt that, at last, he was represented in music's market place with an album of self-composed songs, released on a major label, overwhelmed our standard levels of taste and judgement.

Another managerial misstep compounded matters: booking the Royal Festival Hall, plus Alexander Farris's Sinfonia of London musicians, supposedly to launch Al Stewart on to the concert hall circuit and generate sufficient publicity to catapult the 'Bedsitter Images' single into the Top 20.

The concert turned out to be a critical success and a commercial failure: costing more to promote than ticket sales could recoup and not boosting either LP or single into shifting the required units to chart.

Complimentary ticket for Al's first major concert

However on the third of November 67, following a pre-concert dinner party in the RFH restaurant over looking the Thames and a uniquely special performance attended by my parents and his, Al and I stood on the Royal Festival Hall stage looking out at the empty concert hall and felt this is it, the long anticipated breakthrough was now here. Well not quite!

A memorable evening that would have been even more interesting if the comp seats next to mine hadn't remained empty. Unfortunately, but not surprisingly, a slightly erratic, some would say eccentric, artist friend of my friend, missed the gig.

Yoko Ono has been quoted on more than one occasion that, having relocated to London from New York, one of her very few British friends was Al Stewart. Some time before her famous first meeting with John Lennon, Fluxus movement innovator Yoko and her then husband Tony Cox had met up with Al on the scene centred around Tottenham Court Road's UFO club. Al, having turned 21 and come into a little trust fund cash, even invested in the semi-notorious Yoko Ono, Warholesque, movie *Film No.4*, featuring a succession of naked posteriors retreating from her camera lens! A couple of years later he received a cheque from her new partner, Beatle John, refunding his cash.

I'd first heard of Yoko when Al recorded her avant-garde music on his portable, reel-to-reel, B & O tape deck, capturing for the first time the artist's evolution from conceptual art to soundscapes, in a reprise of three years earlier when I'd captured his songs on my Telefunken.

Yoko aside, that Festival Hall evening, did give me the opportunity to make the Green Room acquaintance of playwright Troy Kennedy Martin, then best known for his TV creation *Z Cars*, and author of another mid 60's TV miniseries, a favourite of mine at the time, *Diary of a Young Man.* Also a pre Curved Air, Sonja Kristina.

Once upon a time in the late 1950s, on through the mid 1960s, the sound still resonating through stunned ears as you left a pop package tour performance would be at least 70% down to screams of female teenage ecstasy. By the late 60s as pop groups matured into rock bands and the scream age faded away, 100% of that exciting volume would be generated from the stage, via increasingly powerful amplification: frequently provided by Jim Marshall.

As Al and I exited the Winter Gardens 12 days after his Festival Hall extravaganza, a combination of hunger and temporarily diminished hearing, led us to make, what, in retrospect appears to be, a strange choice. "Want to go back stage?" – "Not sure I can be bothered tonight; let's go eat." Whichever of us said whatever is neither here nor there: the fact is we headed for Holdenhurst Road and our favoured Italian restaurant, The Continental.

There we no doubt continued with Part 547 of our continuing conversation; the one started back in 1962. This night we'd just been entertained by a promotion that signalled the demise of package tours, already in transition to a new standard rock show format of headliner plus support act, and two bands, stating loud and clear that PopRock's '*Tomorrows World*' was here, now, today.

Looking back to that far distant Bournemouth evening in November 67, we really should have taken the opportunity to say hello to Jimi Hendrix and Pink Floyd!

Openers Eire Apparent, a Track Records' band, whose main claim to your attention would probably be centred on their producer, Jimi Hendrix, were to be followed on the W. Gardens stage by a sequence of state of the art PsychPopRock musicians.

Andy Fairweather-Low's Amen Corner, preceded the Move, and as the Carl Wayne/Roy Wood project disappeared, a fortunate Bournemouth audience were enabled to tell future Floyd fans: 'I saw the original Syd Barrett Pink Floyd, complete with prototype psychedelic light-show.' At this point I'm sure any reasonable person would have been quite content to end the event there and then; considering their ticket money well spent. But wait! What could be better as time flowed by then to casually tell any one who had a scintilla of interest in such things that, yes, one late-sixties night in Bournemouth, you caught Pink Floyd and they were supporting Jimi Hendrix! Well I would contend that, pop-package tourwise, you'd win; game, set & match.

Six weeks earlier BBC Radio 1 had set sail on the UK's airwaves with a pic 'n' mix of disc jocks, including several press ganged from the recently banned pirate radio ships. Among the new intake that included the most significant music broadcaster of the next few decades, John Peel, was Bournemouth's one time Pavilion Ballrooms' Cliff impersonator, Tony Blackburn. Following George Martin's 'Theme One', commissioned by the BBC to launch their new youth-oriented station, it fell to ex-matelot Tony B. to spin the inaugural chart record: The Move's 'Flowers in the Rain'.

By the time the tour had reached Bournemouth this had provided the group with their third chart hit of 67. Performing it, along with its predecessors, 'Night of Fear' and 'I Can Hear the Grass Grow', the Move comfortably established their credentials as one of England's top ten sixties pop groups.

Well produced by Denny Cordell, and excitingly managed by Tony Secunda in the style of Andrew Oldham, the Who's Kit Lambert, and Yardbirds' svengali Simon Napier-Bell, the only slight let down of the group's appearance that night was the relative absence of their ersatz auto-destruction club act: a Secunda directed, Who inspired, Carl Wayne delivered frenzy of TV set smashing.

Pink Floyd, having recently dropped the definitive article 'the' from their name, took to the Winter Garden's stage that night with a unique look, sound, and presentation. To add to this outstandingly original band's strangeness and charm was the asset of two fey Syd Barrett songs: 'Arnold Layne' and 'See Emily Play', plus 'Interstellar Overdrive' from Floyd's debut album, released that summer, *The Piper at the Gates of Dawn.*

As the liquid-light wheel projections battled with relatively simple stroboscopic effects, Pink Floyd brought a successful facsimile of their UFO club psychedelic set to Bournemouth. The scene-changing visual and aural dynamic was completed by Roger Water's occasional mallet attacks on a large, centre stage, suspended gong.

Significant and frequent changes through 1967 would limit the chances to catch this first iteration of the seminal and long lasting rock band. From first producer, UFO promoter Joe Boyd, and managers Pete Jenner and Andrew King of Blackhill Enterprises, they were now managed by Bryan Morrison and produced for EMI by ex engineer Norman Smith.

The stand out reason to value being in the audience on November 15th had to be the inclusion of Syd Barrett in the line-up: by December the troubled band leader had gone: replaced by David Gilmour.

Now the stage is briefly empty. Sometimes you can be both aware in the moment and further informed by retrospection enhanced by historical perspective. Looking back over the years since then, and reflecting on a rock-legend time-line inaugurated by Presley and Buddy Holly, perfected by Lennon & McCartney, Bob Dylan, and Mick Jagger; the headlining star of that extraordinary musical event was probably the last of the true giants of the era, before its brief flowering was to, perhaps inevitably, give way to the commercial imperatives and arch-knowingness of the next decades' rock 'n' pop superstars. From protean Bowie, to sex-siren Madonna; a stadium-filling, multi-platinum, record company accountant thrilling, RockStar, could never again lay claim to the genuine and natural force of nature presented by a very small number of 60's iconic originals.

Experiencing the Jimi Hendrix Experience could in essence be distilled into two words: 'Purple Haze'. From the primordial thump, thump of the trio's rhythm section to the overlaying jagged answer from Hendrix's Stratocaster, the intro – once heard, never forgotten – intimated a sexual tension, with a hint of danger, commanding attention for his beat-generation cool psych lyric that followed.

Imported into the U.K. from the U.S. of A. the previous year by ex-Animal Chas Chandler, Hendrix took to the stage that evening resplendent in big, wild-man hair, *I Was Lord Kitchener's Valet* finery, and two, similarly attired, English side-men: Noel Redding and Mitch Mitchell. The impressive 'Purple Haze' aside, the power trio had a rock solid set list drawn from *Are You Experienced* the band's summer of 67 debut album, plus hits, 'Hey Joe' and 'The Wind Cries Mary'.

The total overall impression though of being in relatively close, concert hall, proximity to the great Hendrix, was certainly more than the sum of its parts. Although the pyrotechnics of his Monterey Festival performance back in June were not on display, the rest of Little Richard's ex-lead guitarist's box of tricks certainly could be seen, heard, and enjoyed to full effect.

The impact of this electric guitar wizard's mélange of feedback, wah-wah, and sustain, frequently reaching a level of sensory overload climaxed, for me, when, before departing the Winter Garden's stage he swung his Fender Strat away from his shoulder, over his head, and, back to the audience, hurled it towards the amplification stack. The resulting howl of feedback buried itself in the lingering remains of the maestro's last chord. As the Experience exited the stage, the flickering strobe lights gave the impression of three figures moving through an old-time *Chaplinesque* movie, and as, at gravity's insistence, the temporarily abandoned electric guitar fell to the stage floor, an after-image remained amidst the diminishing sonic thunder, almost suggesting the musical theatrics had taken place in slow-motion.

As Hendrix, Floyd and Move began their journey into Bournemouth sixties' gig folk-lore, Al and I chatted, drank and ate in the Continental. Almost certainly we would have mused on the recent rise of the guitar-hero led, rhythm guitar-less, rock trio: the Experience having arrived soon after Eric Clapton's post Yardbirds and Bluesbreaker's adventure with Cream.

Possibly we recalled some Fortes, Westover Road, chit-chat from three years back, when the topic had then also been trios. That day ex-G-Man Al suggested to two other local names, Unit 4 guitarist Greg Lake and Planet's drummer Lee Kerslake, that they form a trio. Lake declined the invitation, perhaps having a flash forward moment visualising a future trio with less 'Lakes' in its name. I guess Emerson, Lake and Palmer sounds a bit punchier then Stewart, Lake and Kerslake!

Nineteen sixty seven firmly established with *Bedsitter Images* that my amigo was not destined to be a beat band guitarist, toping the pops, with a group introduced on *Ready Steady Go!* by Cathy McGowan as being "All the way from Bournemouth"; but instead a singer-songwriter whose career-long need would be for words and melodies, rather then riffs.

Previous chapters have, here and there, referenced some of Al's songs: in the next one I'd like to reflect on those and a few more; especially lyrics and associations connecting with Bournemouth.

The Songs Of El Stuart

No, not a typing error or a delinquent spell-checker, but rather a Minns Music mistake, circa 1969. I'm sure I spoke clearly phoning in my request for a recently published book of sheet music; the ears at the other end of the line obviously disagreeing!

With two LPs of self-penned songs on sale, Gwyneth Music, decided to publish a song-book: *The Songs of Al Stewart.* His song publisher was co-owned by the Beatles' Northern Songs co-owner Dick James and Al's manager Roy Guest. Even though I knew Al would have a copy for me the next time we met up, I was keen to see at long last some of the songs I'd been enthusiastically encouraging him to write over the past seven years actually in print.

Minns Music retailed musical instruments, sheet music and records, and had two outlets at the time, one in the town centre, the other a short distance from my shop in Westbourne.

A few days after placing my order I strolled along Poole Road, entered Minns, and was informed by an assistant, flourishing a letter of 'proof', that Gwyneth Music did not publish *The Songs of El Stuart*! When I stopped laughing we decided they should try again.

Over the next few decades Al would write and record hundreds of songs; though perhaps not surprisingly those early ones would always retain a special 'something' for me. I'd like to focus now on his songs that have either Bournemouth references or connections. Some personal, others not. And one, his biggest hit, that had its roots in a first draft of a song about one of Bournemouth's, and England's, greatest 20th century stars, Tony Hancock.

I know that you'd remember 'cause I know that you were there

The above line from 'Millie Brown', a song from Al's *Down In The Cellar* album, released in 2000, is, along with the rest of the lyric, not specific, but rather representing a general reminiscence from days we shared in mid-sixties Bournemouth.

Do you have the photograph we took with Millie Brown
It's such a lovely picture of a night out on the town
She was dressed in purple and we took her to the fair

I know that you'd remember 'cause I know that you were there
You got out your camera we were standing on the beach
Millie wore her yellow hat and seemed just out of reach

Al looked back in a similar way with these lines from the title song of his 1975, American Top 30, LP *Modern Times*:

Chasing skinny blue jean girls across the building-site
Checking out the dance floor while the band played 'Hold Me Tight'
See the blonde one over there - I bet she'd be alright
It all comes back like yesterday
It almost seems like yesterday

The dance floor would have primarily been the Pavilion's – occasionally the Arcade Ballroom's – that we would have been surveying on nights when, as colourfully described in Al's *Love Chronicles* saga, he wasn't performing and:

Playing electric guitar in a beat group, we set the ballrooms alight
Acting it up for the dyed blonde receptionists who told us we were alright.

While future stars of the Police and King Crimson, the then unknown local musicians Andy Summers and Robert Fripp, sent amplified waves of electric pop 'n' rock across those teen-scene hunting grounds, we enjoined with Bournemouth's young male populace to chance our luck.

The daytime beach scenario indicated by 'Millie Brown' was less likely to figure in our quest for female company; night time and clubs held greater appeal. One sunny afternoon in 64 I noticed Zoot Money on the East Cliff beach, just along from the pier, and removed from his natural late-night habitat he seemed, to me, a fish out of water.

Although in those days being enthusiasts for the *yin* of the great indoors rather than the *yang* of the great outdoors, the town's wide open spaces did have a part to play as another glance at *Love Chronicle's* revealing lyrics declaim: '*the first girl I made love to was in Bournemouth's Lower Pleasure Gardens*'. In the circumstances the town centre's mini-parkland possessed a pleasingly accurate name!

'Life and Life Only', another song from Al's second LP in 69, describes a cast of characters, unknown to each other, sharing a moment on Bournemouth beach:

Smithy Smithers-Bell; clerk from Clerkenwell on the beach at Bournemouth
Thinks he may very well be next year in France
Inspired for a while, he decides to risk a smile at Mr. Willoughby who passes,
Polishing his glasses, studiously averting his glance
Renée, several deckchairs away, wonders if they would be better
While Maurice is with the kids out in the sea

These printed words can't quite capture the reflective uncertainties delivered by a recording imbued with the metallic, snagging, insistence of Fairport Convention's Richard Thompson playing an electric guitar obbligato to Al's seaside story.

Here and there Al would appropriate a person's name to identify a fictitious entity in one of his third person tales: Renee, in the above verse, being an example originating with Renée Sandstrom, a Swedish girl who enlivened the summer of 1965 for me.

Sometimes a song's subject would acquire background provided by a real person e.g. 'Delia's Gone', when Al sings of Delia, a painter, on his *Indian Summer* album, apparently he had my artist wife Abi in mind.

Abi and I first met on a hot August day in 1973 while I was staying as a guest in Al's north London house. She arrived for a dinner-date with Al, his girlfriend, and me, a few moments after Al and I had finished listening to the final mix of 'Roads to Moscow'; a seminal song for him. This stand-out track from his 5th LP, *Past, Present & Future*, besides remaining a personal favourite for me, was to point the way forward, away from first person bed-sitter-land love songs, to a unique, long running, niche career as a creator of historical folk-rock music.

Along with 'Nostradamus' it also provided Al with his first substantial coast to-coast American FM radio play, a necessary precursor to 1976 and huge success with *Year of the Cat*; both album and single.

This brings us to 'Year of the Cat' and Bournemouth. 'Year of the Cat' and Bournemouth? Well perhaps surprisingly – yes. I guess it all began one day back at the start of the sixties when Tony Hancock invited Ray Galton and Alan Simpson, his long-standing simpatico script-writers, to a meeting at the Dorchester Hotel in Park Lane.

In October 1961 England's greatest comedy actor was at the summit of more than half a decade of BBC radio and TV triumphs with *Hancock's Half Hour*. Early that year a six episode series, *Hancock*, had justifiably been lauded by both the public and critics, as the self-delusional everyman created by Hancock, Galton and Simpson delivered gold-standard, timeless comedy, including *The Blood Donor*, *The Radio Ham*, and *The Lift*.

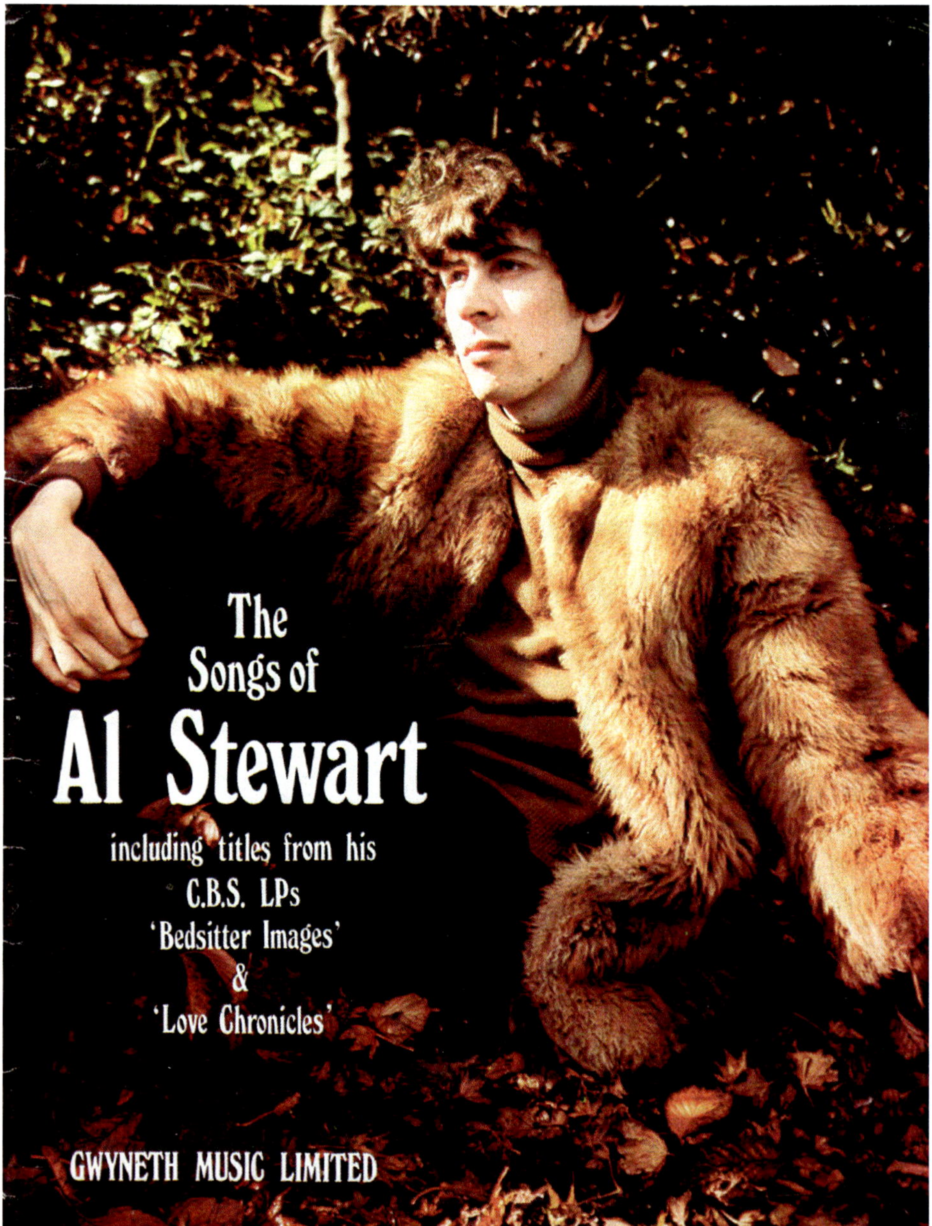
The
Songs of
Al Stewart
including titles from his
C.B.S. LPs
'Bedsitter Images'
&
'Love Chronicles'
GWYNETH MUSIC LIMITED

Incredibly at that moment this great star, who, over 40 years later in a 2002 BBC poll would be voted Britain's favourite comedian, decided to break with his script-writing partners at their hotel showdown, throwing over his splendid success as a No.1 UK entertainer in favour of a quixotic tilt at international stardom via movies, a character realignment and different writers. This failed, and following seven years of decline and confusion Tony Hancock ended his search for another comic persona, and self-enlightenment, in 1968, far from his Bournemouth childhood home, half way round the world in Australia.

Decades before his sad demise, one of the first sights to greet 1930's visitors to Bournemouth, arriving as many did in those days by train, would be the Station Hotel in Holdenhurst Road. It was here, followed by his next home in Gervis Road, that the man destined to hold a unique place in this country's comedy psyche, spent his childhood. Later, in his teens, Tony H studied at Bournemouth College based at the Lansdowne, and Hancock biographies detail these and many more local connections. But for the focus of this book one evening in 1966 holds most significance.

As I've mentioned before, Al Stewart spent many months, on and off, in Bournemouth during 1966, especially the summer. Late in the season and far from his comedic peak, Tony Hancock performed at the Winter Gardens, attempting once more to rediscover a 'Tony Hancock' entity that would reconnect with a still hopeful fan base, while allowing himself to be at one with the 'real' Hancock. Al sat in the audience that night and watched, as a man whose comic acting brilliance required the conduit of close-up TV cameras capturing his subtly revealing facial mannerisms, struggled to play the alien part of a 'stand up' comedian. Not helped by a hotchpotch of sub-standard, old and new, material, it seemed to my friend that life itself appeared to be draining away from the man on the stage; flowing away in a stream of a past lost and a looked-for future that hadn't arrived. Perhaps Tony Hancock believed a return to his old hometown, where his career began and inspiration for his 1962 film, *The Punch and Judy Man*, had been found, would enable an escape from the decline set in motion that October day in 61. Unfortunately this was not to be.

Several years later, with a strong melody in mind, Al set about writing a new song; one that would explore the emotions generated by Tony Hancock that night: it was entitled '*Foot of the Stage*'.

Al wasn't completely happy with the song and, not unusually as part of his writing process, decided to park it for a while. Just before a decision to record the song was needed, fate intervened and the 'Ballad of Tony Hancock' never made it to the airwaves or vinyl grooves. However, a similarly scanning four words having caught Al's attention in a book on Vietnamese astrology, and coupled with a new set of lyrics, plus the 'Foot of the Stage' tune, did reach the world's ears: 'Year of the Cat'.

A few million people may never have heard of a romantic interlude in a timeless country spot lit by Humphrey Bogart style cinematography, and instead a few thousand British fans would have possibly collected a minor cult classic on England's premier tragic clown.

A world-wide hit, most significantly in the USA, 'YOTC' ironically didn't achieve its deserved chart-topping status in Al's homeland. Although to this day, through sustained radio-play, his 70's classic is believed by many people to have been as big a UK seller as in almost every other major record buying country.

The key deciding moment that flipped its domestic chart progression from huge No.1 generating sales, condensed necessarily into a few weeks, to a slow-burn, steady seller, over months and years, involved *Top of the Pops*. By then based in America and on frequent career boosting US tours, he was unavailable to appear 'live' on the essential record-plugging TV show, instead an Al Stewart Band video was provided for the pivotal, momentum building week and not used by the BBC; in part due to a surplus of new chart entries that week. So that was the way, as they say, the cookie crumbled.

In England back then the narrow TV time slot provided by *TOTP* was important if you were looking for a hit, even more significant than radio play, due to its influence on single sales in 'chart return' shops. This relatively small number of designated record retailers provided the data for the BBC's 'official' Top 30 chart.

In GB the charts were, supposedly, based on units sold the previous week, whereas in the USA *Billboard* and *Cashbox* Hot 100 listings combined sales, shipping orders, and radio play statistics to determine a record's commercial status. The obvious need to build rapport with, and support from, hundreds of coast-to-coast FM radio stations, required frequent live gigs and P.R. work.

To capitalise on the escalating success engendered by the Top 30 *Modern Times* album, Al had relocated to America's west coast and, with his band, did just that. The result: by the spring of 77 virtually the only impediment to my number one friend having an American number one LP was provided by the gigantic Eagles' hit *Hotel California*.

Over twenty years later the enduring popularity of 'Year of the Cat' was highlighted by a survey revealing it to be one of the hundred most played records of all time on American radio! The most played? The Righteous

Brothers, 'You've Lost That Lovin' Feeling'.

The following vignette may capture something of the experience of enjoying ownership of a record receiving hit-making 'heavy rotation plays' at least once every hour on US FM radio in the seventies.

March 1977: a rented limo cruises through a wet and shinny Los Angeles in the aftermath of a severe rainstorm. During its journey from L.A. International Airport to West Hollywood four occupants, two having recently landed after a ten hour flight from London, exchange celebratory champagne toasts. The reason Al Stewart, his girlfriend Marion Driscoll, Abi and I had convened in California was to share Al's American success at the moment *Year of the Cat* reached its millionth happy punter and went 'Gold'.

The previous year at the beginning of December Al headlined a London gig at the New Victoria, briefly absenting himself from the US, and *YOTC's* steady ascent of the Hot 100. Between the soundcheck and performance Al, Abi and I had a meal in nearby Overton's sea food restaurant. As we scanned the menu, replete with delightful Edward Ardizzone illustrations, two topics occupied our chit-chat. First an early evening TV 'event' that had caught many peoples' attention that day: the Sex Pistols' notorious run-in with presenter Bill Grundy; and then of more personal significance, an Al idea regarding 'Year of the Cat' and its snow-balling US record sales.

"If the album hits the US Top 10 in the New Year come to California and share the moment with me; I want you both to be my guests, I'll pay for the flights, you should be there."

A millisecond later, as the three of us beamed in anticipation of 'party-time' in the then capitol city of the 70's music biz, I said, "O.K."

Over the next few weeks Al, having returned to touring in the States, would phone me every week with an ongoing update of the *YOTC* LP's various chart positions in *Billboard* and *Cashbox*. We'd analyse the record's progress in three areas, all key to continued progression to Gold (and eventually Platinum) sales. First, obviously next week's chart position and had it retained the necessary 'bullet' symbol indicating sustained momentum; second being added to major FM radio stations AOR (Adult Oriented Rock) play lists, and also importantly, unit ship-out figures. As all these signs remained on track for a huge hit Al arranged the TWA tickets and Abi and I made our plans to spend a month on the West Coast where we hung out with Cheap Trick, The Tubes, Genesis and Thin Lizzy; mainly round the hotel pool.

Before reaching our immediate destination of a suite in the Sunset Marquis Hotel, a rock-central LA base for bands, our host excitedly pushed the buttons on the limo's stereo system, making instantly available the sounds of Los Angeles dozens of rock radio stations. As the frequencies rolled by, brief bursts of current hits came and went: suddenly 'Year of the cat' boomed out – yippee, smiles all round. A few seconds later another station: 'Year of the Cat'. Another spin of the dial, another station, simultaneously playing 'Year of the Cat'!

The trip into town took hardly any time at all. The journey from Bournemouth's Disque a Go Go to Sunset Strip's Whiskey a Go Go had taken 15 years.

Jon and Al Stewart

Al Stewart and Abi
West Hollywood 1977

Cheap Trick's Rick Nielsen with Jon
Sunset Marquis, Los Angeles 1977

Movietime

Do you remember that strangely evocative, but transient, feeling which accompanied you as the final reel of a film had reached fin, and leaving the cinema foyer behind rejoined the *real world*? For a moment or two, as the staccato twang of John Barry's lead guitarist Vic Flick seemed to continue playing the Bond theme for your own private soundtrack, the strangers walking Bournemouth's streets appeared to be merely extras and in an instant Sean Connery might teleport from the Bahamas, or wherever, and continue the *Goldfinger* story.

For a James Bond movie substitute any other sixties movie drama of fantasy and fiction and such was the power of big screen images that, just for a while as a reacclimatising gear-change took place, another world stayed with you.

This movie magic having begun decades before, as far back as the fan-mania inspiring Valentino in the pre-talkies 1920s, certainly continued beyond the 1960s; but the beginning of its diminution and absorption into multiple modern media alternatives, began with the seventies: slowly at first, and not with the films, but rather the cinemas.

The architecture, fascias and interiors of most picture-palaces had remained essentially unchanged from the 1930s. This environment can be seen in retrospect to have contributed to the celluloid entertainment's effect. Viewing a film from either the stalls, or circle, in a smoky, theatre-like setting, with usherettes and intermission ice cream girls cruising the aisles, was more than somewhat removed from the multiplex experience that was to come. Leaving aside for a moment the changes in form, content and technology of mainstream post seventies films, the somehow less immersive interaction provided by a one level, pop-corned multiplex leaves, if not a void, at least a quantifiable disconnect between viewer and viewed.

An even bigger contribution to the change from the 60's movie time to the contemporary scene is presented by the sound and images beaming out from the various size screens on offer today. Starting with 1977's *Star Wars* an ongoing journey commenced from character and plot driven scenarios to CGI laden extravaganzas delivered with speedy jump-cuts to stay in synch with a generation or two attuned to the swiftly shifting images of Nintendos, Playstations and X-Boxes. This era-defining changeover can also be seen by comparing sixties TV programmes and adverts with their equivalents during the last 20 years.

As the 60s ended so in a way did Bournemouth's ABC cinema. In 1970 as a harbinger of things to come, this large, classic format movie theatre transformed into a multi-screen, able to offer three different programmes at the same time. The revamped triple cinema was still something of a novelty at the time and being the first in town had a fanfare opening night followed by an invitation only black-tie dinner at the nearby Royal Bath Hotel hosted by owners of the ABC cinema chain ABPC. Associated British Picture Corporation had been purchased the previous year by EMI and was soon to be re-branded EMI Films. As the film company was headed by Bryan Forbes, husband of the delectable actress Nanette Newman, and he would be present that day, I accepted an invitation to the opening night bash believing this would be a pleasing opportunity to say "Hello," especially to Mrs. F.

My entrée to the event came via Gay Pirrie-Weir and Fanny Charles. Gay and Fanny (yes, real names – real people!) were friends and both *Bournemouth Times* journalists and enthusiastic record buyers when visiting my shop. Did Bryan Forbes make an after dinner speech in praise of all things cinematic? Yes. Any sign of Nannette Newman? No. Oh, well. Instead I wound up knocking back cocktails with TV's infamous Alf Garnett beside the hotel's swimming pool. Fortunately the talented actor Warren Mitchell, who'd enjoined with writer Johnny Speight to create the *Till Death Do Us Part* character, turned out to be the polar opposite of his television persona.

At the other end of the decade two, slightly theatrical, movies illuminated fledgling pop culture's uncertain potential: *Expresso Bongo* and *Beat Girl.* Seen today both of these UK films would appear period pieces of limited appeal but in 1960 they were for teenage Britain 'hot' cinema items.

The *Expresso Bongo* film, released the previous year and based on a hit stage show from 1958, provided a second shot at screen acting for Cliff Richard. Directed by Val Guest and written by Wolf Mankowitz the film was to indirectly affect and influence a major sixties player and scene-shaper courtesy of a lead character called Johnny Jackson. Laurence Harvey starred as the agent/manager of the pop idol played by C.R. and with fast talking Soho street-smart style caught the attention of a 15 year old cinema goer who decided that image was for him. So three years later Andrew Loog Oldham invented himself as a manager/producer, discovered the Rolling Stones, and contributed hugely to the sixties sounds and sensations. For a detailed account of how such a significant pop-rock timeline commenced it would be worthwhile checking out Oldham's fascinating autobiographies, *Stoned* and *2Stoned.*

The X-rated *Beat Girl* introduced 20 year old chart-topper Adam Faith to movie audiences in his first film. Another first: the accompanying soundtrack album featured the music of John Barry, initiating his illustrious career as a composer of movie music. The leading role of the 'Beat Girl' featured sixteen year old Gillian Hills, who subsequently acted alongside John Barry's wife Jane Birkin in a memorable *Blow Up* scene later in the 60s.

In 1960, as the number of X-rated certification films released were subject to a limiting quota; *Beat Girl*, the story of a supposed 'wild child' going wrong in Soho, waited for most of the year before reaching cinemas. By then Adam Faith had rapidly progressed, with a distinctive sound generated by John Barry's pizzicato, 'Buddy Holly' style string arrangements, from semi-unknown, to one of the top three record-sellers in the country. With the iconic 'What Do You Want', the Londoner with the pronunciation of the word 'baby', a gift to impersonators, had achieved the first No.1 record of the famous decade.

By the year's end Faith had added several more Top 5 hits, been acclaimed by an *NME* chart survey, along with Anthony Newley and Cliff Richard, in June, as one of the country's three most popular pop stars, and significantly survived an intense 30 minute *Face To Face* BBC TV interview with John Freeman. The famously probing and psychoanalytical Freeman had earlier in that year conducted a similar session with Bournemouth's Tony Hancock and in the retrospective opinion of many kick-started, or at least considerably contributed to, Hancock's psychological decline.

For a pop singer to be accorded the acceptance and approval of involvement in a 'serious' programme as represented by *Face To Face*, along with the top pop performers in the UK being, for the first time since Rock 'n' Roll's original roar, indigenous home-grown products, indicated early signs of the sixties eventual 'Swinging England' pop culture domination by Beatles and Stones.

Viewing *It's Trad, Dad!* a 1963 pop-exploitation flick from the back row of Bournemouth's Odeon I might have noticed a clue to the fab 60's movies that lay ahead. Nothing to report from the, even by then, slightly passed their sale-by date, featured pop 'stars': Helen Shapiro, Craig Douglas and John Leyton. Just as you would expect from a low budget, so-so, UK film of the early sixties; with an incongruous Gene Vincent lip-synching a ludicrous lyric expressing his desire to 'Get you on a rocket-ship to Mars'. The only noteworthy aspect of *It's Trad, Dad!* could be glimpsed in the credits, with the director listed as: Richard Lester.

Within a year or two Richard Lester would bring innovation and style to a handful of movies, which whether viewed from Bournemouth or Timbuktu, were essential elements of the sixties' long lasting and influential image.

The most significant late fifties/early sixties UK films had arrived on screen at your local cinemas, not via the colour of pop music à la *The Young Ones* and *Summer Holiday*, but theatre and literature in B and W scenarios devolved from the pens of the Johns, Osborne and Braine, with *Look Back In Anger* and *Room At The Top*. To complete the picture add in *Saturday Night and Sunday Morning, The Small World of Sammy Lee, The Loneliness of the Long Distance Runner, A Kind of Loving* and *A Taste of Honey*. But prior to Lester, with screen writer Alun Owen, and the Fabs, the 60's music and movie art forms had remained separate, non-homogeneous, and waiting. Waiting for *A Hard Day's Night.*

By the time this energising imagining of a day or two in the life of Beatlemania Beatles had debuted in July 64, the group had already won the contest to be the world's No.1 Pop phenomenon. Added to this the Lennon and McCartney song writing partnership had made the jump from unprecedented success as the originators of spectacular Pop hits for a mainly under 25 demographic to purveyors of great songs for anyone, of any age, anywhere. A notable contribution to the depth and width of their appeal arrived with the release of Ella Fitzgerald's cover of a standout from *A Hard Days Night's* soundtrack: 'Can't Buy Me Love'.

Appropriating a Ringo neologism John Lennon, still then the group's leader as he had been since the Quarrymen, had the title for the Beatles first film, seventh Parlophone single, and a line in his soon to be published, first book, John Lennon *In His Own Write*. An indication that in 64 he was still first among equals with Paul McCartney can be seen in the *Hard Day's Night* LP track listing: the majority of songs originating with Lennon.

The Beatles' movie was such a smash that screening times in Bournemouth that summer required an unprecedented extension to accommodate the Westover Road cinema queues. Instead of the usual options to view from early afternoon to mid late evening, *A Hard Day's Night* was on offer from mid morning to late evening. Yet another sign that the Beatles' Sixties were rewriting the rules as they rocked along their way.

In 1965 Richard Lester completed his mission to entertain us with Phase 2 of his celluloid take on an imaginary Beatles World with *Help!* The movie's working title, *Eight Arms To Hold You,* apparently failed to find favour with Lennon and McCartney as the basis for a song.

On hearing the rumour indicating the mighty Fabs had yet to come up with a song for the film's work in progress title, Al Stewart decided to write an ersatz 'Beatle Song'. In late Spring 65 as the spools of my reel-to-reel tape deck revolved in tandem, whilst strumming enthusiastically he burst into song: *If I told you that I had, eight arms to hold you, would it really make you glad, eight arms to hold you by my side.* A similar verse or two later, complete with a couple of McCartney style 'Oooos' and the impromptu effort collapsed into genuine Lennon/McCartney with 'Eight Days A Week' and he and I collapsed into laughter.

Along with Westover Road's ABC and Gaumont cinemas, plus another Rank Organisation screen with an Odeon at the Lansdowne, Bournemouth's town centre provided a fourth option in the sixties with the splendidly named Electric Cinema. Long gone, along with Bealesons department store, it was situated on Commercial Road, and if you viewed *Help!* locally in the summer of 65 the Electric's box office would have been the recipient of your three shillings and nine pence.

In the same year *Catch Us If You Can* provided above average cinema exposure for the Dave Clark 5, thanks to the fledgling talent of an ex Southern TV news editor. The north London group having sold considerable quantities of 45s either called 'Glad All Over' or retreads sounding like 'Glad All Over', now, with John Boorman's directorial debut, added a movie to their Pop C.V.

The next step for Boorman in a considerable and varied career produced in 1967 a movie somewhat ahead of its time – the low key, high style, cool San Francisco film *Point Blank*. A few years later he attempted to recruit the support of Branksome Park resident J.R.R. Tolkien in a quest to acquire the film rights to *Lord of the Rings*, three decades before Tolkien's epic eventually reached the screen. Some of the themes he envisioned for Rings can be seen in the director's 1981 retelling of Arthurian legend in *Excalibur*.

Pop Quiz question: what's the connection between the Dave Clark 5 and Bournemouth? Yes, that's right – as the 60s ended tenor saxophonist Denny Payton left the group, moved to the south coast, and became an estate agent.

Talking of agents; agents of the secret variety rather then real estate, synonymous with the high ground of British 60's movies James Bond remained unequalled throughout the decade. Alongside the Beatles in the Autumn of 1962 *Dr. No* gave this special era its slightly late, but nonetheless genuine, real beginning. By the time movie No.2, in what would become the most successful, long running film franchise in cinema history, reached Bournemouth's Odeon a substantial wait in a lengthy queue could be expected prior to hearing Lionel Bart's 'From Russia With Love' and enjoying 007's continuing triumph over cinematic cold war warriors. The next year brought the supreme *Goldfinger*, replete with a theme song composed by John Barry, Anthony Newley and Leslie Bricusse.

Music and movies came together nicely as the Bond title songs became events in their own right, reaching a memorable fusion of Bond and Beatles with Paul McCartney's *Live And Let Die*.

By the time the series reached *Diamonds Are Forever* Blofeld had been established as Bond's nemesis: this time the role of Sean Connery's opposition was played by Charles Gray. Hopefully the image of a major movie villain remains undiminished with the knowledge the actor's career had begun in Bournemouth theatre productions following Charles Gray's education at Bournemouth School. A forerunner of another local schoolboy's eventual trip to Hollywood when Christian Bale became the modern era Batman.

An antidote to the terrific Bond fantasies was provided by screenplays based on the literature of Len Deighton and John le Carré. Personally I have always been a huge fan of one in particular: the film that made Michael Caine a star: *The Ipcress File*. Great sixties British cool.

Added to the Beatles' films Richard Lester also directed *How I Won The War*. Released in 67, darkly comic, anti-war, and featuring John Lennon. In keeping with films deemed less than commercial for the mainstream market this one did not receive a full general release on the country's cinema circuit of Odeons, Gaumonts and ABCs, but surfaced here and there in smaller chains and independents. One such being the Grand, located alongside my Westbourne shop. Just before *How I Won The War* opened in Bournemouth I attended a late night private screening in the Grand with a handful of local press reviewers and a couple of entertainers currently appearing in the town.

Preview of John Lennon's 1967 movie at the Grand

One, a familiar face from TV soap opera, I failed to put a name to but called 'Miss Crossroads' instead: Sue Nicholls seemed quite pleased. Then in her early twenties, she later became a 'resident' of *Coronation Street*, where she still resides. Not sure what she made of the quirky flick; it was probably of more interest to Bob Monkhouse, a serious collector of original film prints and student of cinema history. Attired in a black leather jacket, he conversed in a measured and straightforward manner, with not a hint of his well known, rapid-fire, jokes.

For me the only interesting element of *How I Won The War* occurs with the eerie prognostication delivered by John Lennon as he momentarily appears to step out of character and deliver his penultimate lines of script directly to you, the viewer. Private Gripweed has been fatally shot. Looking directly at the camera he issues a rhetorical question: "I knew this would happen. You knew this would happen, didn't you?" Such a strange future echo of December 1980.

Not long before its days as a cinema were over Bournemouth's Grand Cinema featured as an interior location for Southampton born Ken Russell's 1977 movie *Valentino*. Two years on from huge commercial success with the Who's *Tommy* film, the controversial director had chosen to shoot a substantial amount of footage for his take on the life of silent era sensation Rudolph Valentino, in Bournemouth: principally at the Russell-Cotes Art Gallery and Museum on the East Overcliff.

With an unconventional cast including Rudolph Nureyev in the title role, Felicity Kendal, and ex Mama and Papa Michelle Phillips, the production spent a few days shooting scenes in the Russell-Cotes to replicate Valentino's Hollywood home from the 1920s. One day was devoted to capturing a relatively brief scene featuring *The Good Life's* Ms Kendal, ostensibly part of an audience in New York and watching a Valentino film.

As the cinema adjoining my Bus Stop Records shop closed for the duration of the filming and busily filled up with a 'fake' 20's audience and a spasmodically hectic film crew I wandered around chatting and watching. Many of the locally recruited extras were students from Bournemouth College attired in suitable period clothes. Remaining seated between takes they were joined for a while by another student: one I was showing around the movie action, and of course dressed in contemporary clothing. My wife Abi, currently studying Environmental Art, knew several of the 'audience'.

With Felicity Kendal once again about to express overwhelming emotion on viewing Valentino, prior to running down the aisle and exiting the theatre, just a moment before the cameras rolled Ken Russell's second unit assistant director spotted Abi and avoided a print of the movie existing with the anachronism of one 1920's New York Valentino fan being dressed for 1970's Bournemouth!

Talking of laughs, in the unlikely event of you catching this film on TV, the Valentino film the audience appear to be watching did not exist on the screen that day. To keep everyone consistently staring in the right direction and correct angle the Grand had been requested to project something. They did: that week's movie. Kendal and co. were actually watching a sub Bruce Lee Kung Fu flick.

Perhaps the most significant 'local' film of the decade came at the end, when a short boat trip away from Bournemouth, Murray Lerner's cameras filmed the 1970 *Isle of Wight Pop Festival.* The man who recorded the influential mid-sixties Newport Folk Festivals, documented the third, and biggest, I o W festival, and captured the last major public performance by Jimi Hendrix. Not, as some people believe his very last appearance with Stratocaster in hand, but a last hurrah, even if not a golden one, in front of a gigantic crowd, appropriately saluting a unique guitarist and Rock Star.

As time ran out for both Hendrix and the 60s, taking a closer look at a nearby island called Wight and its three remarkable festivals, may indicate how very different the last years of the decade felt compared with its earlier shining optimism and go! go! middle years.

Which Way Did The Sixties Go?

'The Sixties': the buzz word decade of the 20th century, a universally recognised shorthand for so many events, ideas, changes, and misconceptions. The first, and hopefully most obvious, of the potential confusions wrought by referring to the famous/infamous sixties' years as a singular, monolithic, block of time, is caused by ignoring the decade being a game of two halves.

Surely the 'Sixties' from 68 to the decade's calendar conclusion recall a darker toned, semi-politicised, heavier time, than the sparkling 62-67 'Sixties' years of roller-coasting enthusiasm for a seemingly ever brighter tomorrow.

A microcosm of the 60's split-personality could be acquired from the Isle of Wight's festival atmosphere during three days at the end of 1970's August. The vast size alone of the assembled multitude paying tribute to the preceding years' achievements in rapidly altering England and the West's cultural paradigm. Over land and sea came hundreds of thousands of travellers to reach a small island just across the water from Bournemouth. How many? No one knows for sure: most estimates record at least half a million. Why had they come?

In Paul Simon's classic song 'America' the people he viewed from a Greyhound bus had '*All come to look for America*'. What, I wonder, had the *Third Isle of Wight Festival* gatherers come to look for. O.K. – Jimi Hendrix, The Doors, The Who, Leonard Cohen, Miles Davis, Joni Mitchell, Procol Harum, plus, amongst a long list of late sixties festival favourites, Bournemouth musician Greg Lake making an early appearance in tandem with Emerson and Palmer.

But surely, as indicated by America's *Woodstock* gathering the previous year, something else; something more than even a tip-top line-up of contemporary singer-songwriters and rock bands could provide. And here lay the 60's paradox, combined with the essence of the division between the decade's launch-pad years and, slightly anti-climatic, splashdown finale.

First the paradox. Choose one word to represent the gift bestowed by the 1960s and it may well be *individuality*. Looking backwards to the black and white 1950s and preceding decades reveals a sense of individuality curtailed; restricted by deference to institutions of state and education, social and sexual behaviour, modes of dress, and limited opportunities for self-expression through musical taste. As the sixties progressed a demographic emerged populated by bright and breezy individuals displaying an aura of freedom.

Freedom from relinquishing 2 years of teenage male life to Queen and country via military conscription as National Service ended in 1960. Freedom to laugh at Parliament and authority in general, and by doing so substantially reduce the institutions' influence on individual expression, thanks to contemporary satire delivered by *Beyond The Fringe* and *That Was The Week That Was*. Freedom to listen to, watch, and possibly perform, exciting, original British pop music from 1962, i.e. *Before Beatles* and *Onwards* from *Love Me Do*. Freedom to dress in colourful, fast changing, clothes designs for both sexes; coupled with release from the sexual tyranny experienced by previous generations, courtesy of the contraceptive pill.

By the late sixties this newly enfranchised opportunity to stand out from the crowd appeared to have run out of steam. How individual can a person be in a crowd of 5 or 6 hundred thousand? A scene from George Harrison's HandMade Films, *Life of Brian* Python movie, easily comes to mind: '*You are all individuals*', the response: '*Yes! We are all individuals*'.

Paradoxically, within a relatively brief timeframe, a key element of the decade's genuine claim to a new take on individual freedom of expression, allowing a fresh, and often rapidly evolving, identity, free from all but the slightest of peer pressure, had declined into a stylistically limiting accommodation with an everyman ex-hippie Tom, Dick and Harry.

A cursory assessment of the 1970 *Isle of Wight Festival* ambience and audience would give even Dr. Watson, let alone Sherlock Holmes, sufficient data to deduce England's Nineteen Sixties Part 2 differed substantially from Part 1.

A very different vibe had evolved since the end of 67. Gone were the Kings Road and Carnaby Street attired parades of individuals looking primarily to be entertained, stoned or sober, by favourite bands and singers: replaced by a vast number of t-shirted, desert booted, denim clad, frequently drug enabled, noticeably more downbeat, seekers of moments beyond 'mere' entertainment.

As locally-based Fiery Creations struggled to contain an invasion of their unfortunate choice, logistically hard to secure, festival site from a horde of radicalised, post hippie, 'Festivals should be free, man', interlopers camped on an overlooking hillside, the paying punters also struggled. Poor facilities for food, drink and sanitation coupled with an, at times, shambolic organisational relationship between promoters and performers, led to a 'curate's egg' of an experience. The good parts, where a favoured band's sound system successfully won a battle with the windswept open arena, have probably been enhanced by the passage of time and a suitable pair of rose-tinted spectacles.

Hendrix and the Doors delivered sets far from their best and many of the booked artists were not suited to entertaining in the great outdoors. From a long list of both first rate and second rate names, Miles Davis and the Who triumphed, the latter reprising their success from the IoW's 2nd festival, the previous year.

By the decade's fading days over two years of a desperate, dispiriting and seemingly unending conflict in far away Southeast Asia, had disappointingly shown a generation of, initially American students and conscripts, followed by UK and European students, that, sometimes, 'Love' is not all you need. Anti-Vietnam war protests had erupted during 1968 in Washington, London and Paris: the earlier sixties 'freedom' to disrespect, and on occasion dismiss, the views of University authorities had transmuted into an understandable urge to confront and obstruct.

Following on from the Isle of Wight's first, relatively small, one day festival, and a further year on, in 69, the famous 'public reappearance' of Bob Dylan event, by 1970 that 3rd festival, identity subsuming, crowd, reached out for a sense of belonging. A presence within a community of like-minded, rock music enthralled, politically concerned outsiders. Outsiders not willing to be a part of a seemingly slow to change, essentially conformist, mid-range of society: for a few days at least.

The late sixties festivals presented an, apparently needed, validation merely by being amongst a gigantic 'comfort blanket' of compadres. Although understandable in a fast growing secular society, this late sixties 'belonging' was perhaps acquired at a cost: the reduction of an earlier individual, buoyant style, coupled with a progressive spirit.

As I stood to one side of the Pavilion stage one night in 68, a Fender guitar signalled to me the changing times from the *Big Beat Night* days of 63. Where just a few years before its hard-shell plastic surface would have gleamed in red or white, now the Strat in Mick Taylor's hands was almost unrecognisable; stripped down to a wood base and decorated with semi-psych swirls and motifs.

Following in the illustrious lead-guitar footsteps of Eric Clapton and Peter Green, prior to replacing Brian Jones as a Rolling Stone, Taylor more than competently led the R 'n' B line that day for John Mayall's Blues-beakers.

John Peel had joined them for the gig, ostensibly to spin a few counter-culture records from his collection. A 'live' sampling of his – nothing whatsoever to do with Jeremy Clarkson(!) – *Top Gear* radio programme.

Around that time Al Stewart was a frequent guest on Peel's show and knowing the laconic Liverpudlian was heading for Bournemouth enthused me to stop by and say hello. That first time we met he was predictably low-key, and appeared a little uncertain as to just what function his role as a 'performer' was achieving. The next time we met, a year or so later, he was animated, relatively intense, and far more voluble.

This dramatic, temporary, persona adjustment accompanied his reaction to a problem he'd inadvertently initiated during a recent BBC broadcast. For personal reasons of tone and taste John Peel did not like The Move. Information readily available to anyone listening to *Top Gear* at the time. This was clearly indicated by his on air statement that he had no intention of ever playing the group's records. Unfortunately the then still prevailing, slightly utopian, umbrella of *Love, Peace and Understanding*, did not encompass the Move's vocalist. In an era slowly emerging from the *flowers in your hair* daydream of 67's summer, Carl Wayne, like the Who's Roger Daltry, presented a more pugnacious, old school, personality. Wayne's publicly stated response was to inform Peel that at the first opportunity he, Peel, could expect fisticuffs! Or words to that effect.

Nothing, as far as I am aware, came of this storm in a rock 'n' pop teacup, but as I sat chatting one evening in 1969 with Al, JP, and Fairport Convention's Sandy Denny and Simon Nichol, in the Royal Festival Hall, in-between a soundcheck and that evening's concert, the outcome was far from certain. We all empathised with Peel's concerned incomprehension at an attitude that seemed far removed from the prevailing late-sixties ethos.

Fast forward 32 years to 2001 and another conversation; this one in Abbey Road with Carl Wayne. Quoting John Peel's reaction to him from all those years ago, the relaxed, by now mature, Hollies vocalist – the Move being long gone, remembered his hot-headed, youthful outburst, with rueful amusement. I think we could all agree that 'Blackberry Way' was a great record, one that anyone would be pleased to broadcast.

'Way Back in the 1960s', a track on the Incredible String Band's second album, was however a recording Peel was delighted to play on the radio in 67.

Slightly strange to be referencing a song, here, in the 21st century, recorded in the sixties, written from an imagined future perspective, looking back humorously to the 1960s! Also strange is the eventual destination of a photograph, taken in Bournemouth during 67, of Al and me holding a copy of the recently released *5.000 Spirits* LP. The colourful album sleeve is echoed by a bright yellow, briefly in vogue, satin shirt, worn by me, and hectically patterned surroundings. In the 90s, *To Whom It May Concern*, a retrospective CD set of early recordings by Al, included this snap in its accompanying booklet: enigmatically captioned – 'Al and Jonny Kremer, Bournemouth 1967', and facing an illustration of his first LP *Bedsitter Images*. Perhaps an appropriate location for it as the album's title song lyrics make passing reference to me in the couplet: *The friends I've left back home all write / with laughing words that warm my sight.*

More strangeness occurred for me when Marc Almond released his *Stardom Road* album and included a cover of Al's *Bedsitter Images*: a neat version that closely followed the original's arrangement, with my personal connection to the *'friends'* lyric now transposed to a mythical Marc memory.

'I'm just sitting here reminiscing' sang Buddy Holly on his aptly titled recording 'Reminiscing'. Released in 1963, four years after the original modern pop singer/song-writer/guitarist, had fatefully chartered a small airplane in America's mid-west to reach the next date on his tour. Sadly this hugely talented young man never reached either the gig or the nineteen-sixties – a decade whose greatest stars, the Beatles and Stones, have always paid testament to his influence. If Buddy Holly had received a more fortunate shake of the celestial dice and been able to reminisce about the 60s, I wonder if the man who played a Fender Stratocaster at the London Palladium in 1958, would have preferred the earlier sixties of Hank B. Marvin Stratocasting or the Strat dynamics of late sixties Hendrix. Who knows?

For me, from great nights at Bournemouth's Winter Gardens in 61/62, Rock 'n' Popping with Del Shannon, Johnny Burnette, Dion, Gary Bonds, Eden Kane and John Leyton, to the PsychDrama of 67's Floyd/Hendrix performances on the same stage, it certainly felt like *'a mighty long way down rock 'n' roll'* had been travelled in just a few years. At the time, and looking back from now, both halves of the decade excited, energised and entertained; but the former possessed an uncomplicated innocence no longer available to the heavier later years.

In 1980 BBC Radio Solent broadcast *Baked on the Premises* a series revisiting the south coast's 1960's music scene. The episode covering Bournemouth circa 1963 included interviews with Robert Fripp and me. King Crimson Robert recalled tales of his League of Gentleman group and I referenced many of the names that have populated the pages of this volume: Al Stewart, Andy Summers, Zoot Money, Greg Lake, Gordon Haskell, Tony Blackburn, Lee Kerslake and, of course, Robert Fripp.

Programme presenter Oliver Gray introduced me as – Jon Kremer of Bus Stop Records, indicating how well known the shop had become by then.

An internationally published IPC magazine, popular in the mid-eighties, called *Mizz*, nominated Bus Stop Records, in a two page feature on Bournemouth, as a local attraction: the place to find reasonably priced vinyl rarities. Selling collector items was the easy bit; obtaining them slightly trickier.

One source provided, for a while, a stack of mint condition records from the 50s and 60s: BBC radio producer Jimmy Grant, originator of Brian Matthew's *Saturday Club* programme. Local newspaper reviewers, and eventually 2CR Radio could be relied on for a constant stream of current LPs. All of these, and more, were required for adding to the collections of customers like local collecting legend Pete McConnell.

Pete, whose enthusiasm for, primarily American, music had begun back in the early sixties with visits to my dad's shop, accumulated a vast collection of quality recordings. By the time I'd decided another re-branding of Bus Stop Discs, from Bus Stop Records, on to Bus Stop Downloads(!) was not feasible, Backtrack Pete owned many thousands of 45s and LPs. The appellation Backtrack dating to a brief period when he owned a vintage record shop in Southbourne, before realising his true calling was collecting, not dealing.

As an avid organiser of his vinyl treasures he collated the date and provider of each purchase. Not long after saying my farewell to real-time, high street, record retailing, Pete showed me a list of nationwide record outlets, charting how many LP's he'd acquired from each: pleasingly No.1 of the Bournemouth area shops was Bus Stop Records.

In the years that followed the sixties I'd occasionally connect with Robert Fripp, here and there, usually with Al, or sometimes through art, and my wife Abi. Sometimes he would be accompanied by his wife Toyah Wilcox, though frequently their busy careers, split between England and America, precluded this. An example of this occurred in 1991 when Robert was a guest at Al's wedding to Kris, in a small 12th century church, near Chalbury in Dorset. The Fripps had just arrived from the USA, but as a probably jet-lagged Robert said at the time, this was not an occasion he wanted to miss.

I had accepted Al's invitation to be his best man, reversing the roles from my wedding to Abi in 1974, when Al had been mine. A small guest list of close family and friends included Abi, our son Daniel, and my parents Blanche and Monty. Also Tori Amos and her then partner Eric Rosse. Besides enjoying a dance or two with Tori, I appreciated reassuring comments from Eric following my best man speech, as along with producing her *Little Earthquakes* album, he had recently appeared as an actor in the hit US TV show *Thirtysomething*. In common with possibly every best man, before or since, I felt my effort could have been better; so compliments from a professional actor worked for me.

One Abi/Fripp art connection occurred in the mid-nineties when DGM, a record label owned by Robert, released *The Starving Moon*, a CD by The Europa String Choir, featuring artwork based on an original painting by Abi. The Europas were led by Poole based musicians, violinist Cathy Stevens and guitar player Udo Dzierzanowski. In a moment of serendipity I booked Cathy and Udo to perform 'Year of the Cat' with Al at a 'mini/semi-secret' Bournemouth club date in 2001. As I mentioned in an earlier chapter I arranged this gig primarily as an opportunity for Al and beat band musicians from the 60's Bournemouth scene to meet up and play together again. The size of the deliberately chosen small venue, Mr. Smiths, necessarily restricting the audience numbers gave the event an unusually intimate scale. Thanks to the internet, ticket enquiries came from as far away from this town as America.

A, perhaps surprisingly, larger audience had awaited an Al 'performance' as he delivered an amusing, but sincere, speech at my wedding. Our reception of over 200 guests received the expected best man remarks, but enhanced by his years of experience talking to concert goers from stages around the world. One line that meant a lot to me stated his fondness for my mum and dad, recalling that at times they had seemed like 'second parents' to him.

One night earlier that year, at a Winter Gardens' Stéphane Grappelli performance, I would have been surprised to be told that in the near future, Grappelli's sidemen, bass player Lenny Bush and pianist Alan Clare, would play at our wedding. Even more extraordinary to have known that the small combo would be organised, and led, by one of the UK's first R 'n' R exponents from the 2i's coffee bar, back in the 50s: Tony Crombie.

Jazz drummer par excellence Crombie's brief excursion into Rock 'n' Roll via recordings with his group the Rockets on Decca and Columbia labels included a contender for the first home-grown R 'n' R hit single with 'Teach You to Rock' in 1956. By 1974, long established on the international jazz scene, and closely associated with Ronnie Scott and Tubby Hayes, he brought together a small group of musicians to give our wedding dancers a somewhat above average band to twist the night away. This musical bonus to our day, yet another thread to my life's musical tapestry, resulted from Abi's parents, Martin and Margot, being near neighbours of Tony Crombie in north London.

Backstage at that early 70's gig, Django Reinhardt's violinist partner

Stéphane Grappelli, while answering my enquiry as to the value of his violin, gave me a déjà vu moment recalling another Bournemouth night when John Lennon handed me his guitar. As if to confirm his reply that the instrument was not of any significant value he casually proffered the violin to me. I held it for a moment before returning it to its virtuoso owner; this time not having to risk embarrassment by any attempt to play it!

Not all time spent backstage at the Winter Gardens produced memorable conversations. In the summer of 67 I met Tom Jones, who as a performer has never been less than dynamite, and 'Its Not Unusual' a sixties classic, but for some reason, while noting he was not quite as tall as I had expected, there appeared to be little to talk about; probably down to me.

At another post gig Winter Gardens opportunity in 1973, however, I did find plenty to talk about with Paul McCartney.

Jon Kremer and Paul McCartney backstage Bournemouth Winter Gardens 1973

No longer a Beatle, in his mind at least; but a Beatle forever for the rest of the planet's population, he was touring *Red Rose Speedway*, a post Beatles stepping stone from initial solo album *McCartney* to gigantic *Band on the Run* success, and an ongoing further batch of solo records. The month of May that found the famous bass guitarist, the possessor of an unparalleled ability to compose and sing the most popular of pop songs, in Bournemouth, held probably more significance for him at the time then any since the Fabs parted ways.

Along with the release of his Wings' LP, *Red Rose Speedway*, that month also encompassed the premiere of the eighth instalment of the James Bond movie franchise, *Live and Let Die*, with a title song written and recorded by Paul, plus *James Paul McCartney*, a one hour TV spectacular for ITV.

All in all this made for an interesting moment for me to fill in the gap on my 'Meet the Beatles' CV, outstanding from 1963.

The SRO audience that night had not bought tickets to see a Wing, or Mr. and Mrs. McCartney, the simple, obvious, fact; everyone was there for a live show by the next best thing to the Beatles. Three years on from the split-up John Lennon remained a semi-recluse, three thousand miles away, in New York City, and George Harrison was more likely to be quietly meditating with a sitar close by, than to be rocking-up a UK concert tour. So, Ringo aside, it had to be Paul. Did they get what they wanted? Yes, no, and of course not.

Yes, from the moment he ran onto the Winter Gardens' stage to join Linda, Denny Laine, Henry McCullough and Denny Seiwell, pausing briefly to smile and hoist aloft an early version of the soon to be 'trademark' Macca thumbs-up greeting, he was Beatle Paul McCartney, about to perform on a Bournemouth stage for the first time since the sixties.

No. Unlike the worldwide mega tours of recent years, when having reached a personal, and totally correct, rapprochement between his awesome 60's back catalogue and post-Beatles music, there were to be no *I Want To Hold Your Hand's* that day. And of course not: it had not been possible to buy a ticket to see the Beatles since 1966.

Back then a McCartney performance of 'Maybe I'm Amazed' presented you with the nearest song to the Beatles. A song for Linda – just as 'Here There and Everywhere' had been for Jane Asher – 'Maybe I'm Amazed' written pre Beatles' break-up in 1969 and recorded with composer/vocalist Paul playing all the instruments plus drums, in Abbey Road's '*Beatles*' studio 2, would have been a cert for the next Beatles album: the one that never was.

Sitting next to him in his dressing room after the show, talking about 'Amazed' was also as close to referring to the fabulous Fabs the day's conversation allowed. Nineteen seventy three was definitely not a year to talk Beatles with the future Sir Paul. Expressing my pleasure with the amazing 'Amazed', I believe he revealed that even then the song was one of those *special* ones for him, by telling me he didn't think much of Rod Stewart's version. If you'd like to compare his opinion with yours, check-out the Faces prosaically titled LP: *Long Player.*

Prior to being introduced to Paul by Denny Laine, I'd enjoyed a chat with the ex Moody Blue backstage in an area close by the McCartneys' dressing room, in the company of Gay, Fanny and Sherry (and please remember these are real names!). The Moody Blues superb 1964 No.1 'Go Now' had featured a lead vocal by Denny; he then followed his Moody days with a group of his own: The Electric String Band. We fell into conversation about 'Say you don't Mind', a song written and recorded by him in 67, and a big hit in 72 for Colin Blunstone. Ex-Zombie Colin was an acquaintance of Al Stewart, someone I'd occasionally come across while staying with Al in his London house.

Following an exchange of music biz trivia I optimistically enquired "Is Paul around?" The charming Mr. Laine replied, "Oh yeah, he's with Linda. Follow me." That seemed an excellent idea, so I did.

He opened the door to a medium size, relatively lo-tech room, typical of Winter Gardens type venues back then. There were half a dozen or so people chatting, including Paul and Linda.

Paul McCartney had been sitting alongside the far wall to the left of the door and as we entered I was slightly surprised to hear Denny Laine say, 'There's someone here to meet you." Paul responding by standing up, crossing to the middle of the dressing room, extending his hand and saying hello. Well, well, well: game on! No security, no minders, just a couple of local journalists, a photographer and band members.

As he returned to his seat, and Gay and Fanny chatted with their colleagues from the *Bournemouth Echo*, I turned to Linda and began a conversation about Suzy and the Red Stripes. The Red Stripes were basically Wings, and Suzy was Linda. As she happily chatted with me, responding to my questions about 'Seaside Woman', a light reggae song, written by her, and recorded during the *Red Rose Speedway* sessions the previous year, a flashbulb erupted enabling the nearby photographer to freeze a moment of animated chatter.

You probably know this already, but a sound basis for talking to almost anyone, be they famed or anonymous, initially is to reference an idea or topic known to be of interest to them. Here, as Mr. and Mrs. Macca both loved reggae, I was on safe, quicksand-free ground. Also highlighting what would be her only lead vocal, single record release, with the aptly named in view of our Bournemouth location 'Seaside Woman', provided another conversational plus.

At the time Linda continued to endure the pointless, unfair criticism of her musical value to a keyboard playing presence in Wings: a position regarded by some people, mainly rock journalists, as nepotism. Personally I thought, so what? Paul and Linda hardly ever spent more than a day or so apart during the decades they shared together, and true love is one of the greatest things this world has to offer, so given the chance – take it.

Linda McCartney and Jon Kremer backstage Bournemouth Winter Gardens 1973

By now Paul had joined in our chat, so I took my chance and asked about James Bond. It appeared to many a new direction for *Beatle* Paul: writing and recording a movie title song; the dramatic, still a key element in his current live shows, 'Live and Let Die'. But remembering his original engagement with film soundtracks predated this one by several years by way of a mid-sixties Hayley Mills movie, *The Family Way*, gave me the synergy required to link the two films and enquire if he intended to write more soundtracks. The 1966, Boulting Brothers film had music composed by McCartney and arranged by George Martin. Yes, he ventured, he probably would; indicating that coming up with music for this, that or whatever, was what he did, by inference suggesting, to me at least, that the then Wing, 'ex' Beatle, regarded his musical gifts in a holistic way: all part of an interconnected whole.

Fizz. Pop. Another flashbulb. I made a mental note: really, really must get copies of these photographs!

Before talking about 'Maybe I'm Amazed' and that night's show, a moment of equilibrium tilting uncertainty arrived, due to Sir Walter Raleigh's 'gift' to England: tobacco. Tobacco in the form of a king-size, filtered, cigarette.

Accepting a proffered Rembrandt International before setting fire to it in the usual way McCartney ripped the filter off, discarded it, and continued to chat. I'd not seen such a casually displayed craving for a maximum nicotine hit before, and found myself entertaining a bizarre thought regarding Beatle *etiquette*: when next offering him a cigarette should you detach the filter first? What would you do?

Talking briefly about his *James Paul McCartney* TV special – broadcast just 5 days earlier – almost provided an opening for Beatle chat, but not quite.

During the one hour show three acoustic versions of sixties songs surfaced: *Blackbird*, *Michelle* and *Yesterday*, but I failed to engage Paul's attention for long enough to focus on them.

Then 'road management' entered the room suggesting it was time to go. As Paul and Linda made their way to the exit they continued to chat and appeared unconcerned that the small entourage accompanying them still included me.

Before reaching the fans gathered outside the Winter Gardens stage door they were handed two masks, each fashioned in the style of a Kabuki face. The first glimpse the waiting crowd that night caught of Mr. & Mrs. Macca was of the two famous faces obscured by these oriental visages. I'd naturally dropped backed a few paces behind them, but still gained a momentary flash of that unique look of slightly amazed joy projected by Beatle fans, as Paul and Linda stepped out from behind their temporary 'disguise' and began signing autographs en route to their getaway vehicle.

Soon after their departure Sherry and I exited the stage door car park in my white Volvo P1800; known as the 'Saint' car. Due to the TV show's enduring popularity it usually generated friendly glances. In that far off day, when filling the tank didn't require an overdraft facility, petrol stations were still manned by attendants and the P1800 was frequently greeted with a smile, and an occasional whistled rendition of the Simon Templar theme tune.

Driving along the East Undercliff Drive between Bournemouth and Boscombe's piers with the waves continuing their ages old advance and retreat on England's shore line, I reflected that something seemed to have reached completion with time spent in the company of Paul adding to the go! go! Bournemouth Beatlemania days with John, George and Ringo.

Bournemouth beach: easy to take it and all the other nearby stretches of sand and sea for granted when you live by the coast. But I guess this geographical amenity is still most likely to be the first identifying image that comes to mind when thinking of the town. It entered the thoughts of the late, great, Douglas Adams when he pictured a 100 foot tall robot lying on Bournemouth Beach! In a scene from *So Long, and Thanks for All the Fish*, an instalment of *The Hitch-Hiker's Guide to the Galaxy*, the gigantic automaton is encountered by a journalist from the *Echo*, who, for the sake of the implicit joke, tries to come up with a 'local angle' that might make for an interesting story! Hopefully we all agree that the Sixties provided us with an interesting story.

In 1997 Bob Dylan encountered a serious health problem, one that restricted his standard heavy touring schedule to just a few dates that year. On the first of October, a couple of days after singing three songs at a special Vatican gig, he performed the first of two concerts at Bournemouth's International Centre. Abi and I caught one of them. Notoriously unapproachable in his completely understandable desire for privacy, he was spotted one evening near the pier, quietly looking out across the sea towards the Isle of Wight; perhaps contemplating 1969 and the festival that brought him back to the stage. I wonder if Bob Dylan was thinking, "Which way did the sixties go?"

Outro

The rhetorical question posed back in chapter two regarding how the 60's decade can be measured, appears to have been answered, at least by this memoir, with the parameters: 1955-1973. As these are music based Bournemouth memories hopefully it has been appropriate to roam around the days from the contemporary world's pop culture origins in the mid-fifties Rock 'n' Roll explosion through to that early 70's pause for breath in the pre-punk, heyday of singer-song writing.

My thoughts have from time to time extended beyond the geographical boundaries of Bournemouth and Poole, but the links seemed to possess natural synergies as they reached the page in front of me.

In the unlikely event of being offered the chance to choose a favoured castaway book for *Desert Island Discs*, I'd probably go with Absolute Beginners. Colin MacInnes' novel first published, and set, at the end of the 1950s, captured in print an atmosphere brilliantly exploring, and pre-dating, the sixties teenager and his or her elevating instincts to reshape a black and white landscape into the kaleidoscope excitement of the 1960s.

By the calendar end of the sixties the fun-filled friendship between Al Stewart and myself that has permeated these pages had a neat encapsulation when, in 1970, a sleeve note list of acknowledgements for his third album, *Zero She Flies*, thanked me for being his friend. It is my pleasure to now return the sentiment.

Bing Crosby called his autobiography *Call Me Lucky*; sometimes you do need to be lucky. As far as the sixties go I nearly missed the whole thing.

In the spring of 61, as a Mark 3 Standard Vanguard approached the end of a 100 mile journey from Bournemouth to London conveying me and my parents to our first family visit following our recent relocation to the south coast, it crashed. In an attempt to avoid the misadventure of a young cyclist, inexplicably traversing an inner-city dual carriageway, my dad braked, swerved, and saved the situation at the cost of rolling the car. Fortunately as mum and I occupied the back seat that day we all survived with minor bumps, slight concussion, and one broken collar bone. On most trips I would have been seated alongside my father in the front. The nearside front of the vehicle's roof had taken the first impact, resulting in the wrecked metal ultimately residing a few inches above the front passenger seat. Call me lucky? I guess so.

And now, echoing down the years, which Bournemouth musical moment would be my personal No.1? It would have to be John Lennon handing me his black Rickenbacker guitar and saying: "Here, try this."

Soundtrack to Bournemouth A Go! Go!

This chronology follows the text and suggests some of the records you might like to play from time to time to enhance these musical memories.

Singles

'Johnny Remember Me' JOHN LEYTON
'Why Should We Not' MANFRED MANN
'Night Has a Thousand Eyes' BOBBY VEE
'End of the World' SKEETER DAVIS
'How Do You Do It' GERRY AND THE PACEMAKERS
'Let's Dance' CHRIS MONTEZ
'One Night' ELVIS PRESLEY
'Love Chronicles' AL STEWART
'I've Got My Mojo Working' MUDDY WATERS
'Hoochie Coochie Man' MUDDY WATERS
'Do Wah Diddy Diddy' MANFRED MANN
'Sack o' Woe' CANNONBALL ADDERLEY
'Rollin' Stone' MUDDY WATERS
'Brother Jack' MANFRED MANN
'Take Five' DAVE BRUBECK
'Nostradamus' AL STEWART / MANFRED MANN'S EARTHBAND
'Cock – A – Hoop' MANFRED MANN
'Now You're Needing Me' MANFRED MANN
'5-4-3-2-1' MANFRED MANN
'I Advanced Masked' ANDY SUMMERS AND ROBERT FRIPP
'My Generation' THE WHO
'Good Vibrations' THE BEACH BOYS
'Genevieve' LARRY ADLER
'Rock Around the Clock' BILL HALEY AND THE COMETS
'Shake, Rattle and Roll' BILL HALEY AND THE COMETS
'Sleepwalk' SANTO AND JOHNNY
'Flamingo' EARL BOSTIC
'Hoover Factory' ELVIS COSTELLO
'Love Me Do' THE BEATLES
'Apache' THE SHADOWS
'F.B.I.' THE SAHADOWS

'Man of Mystery' THE SHADOWS
'In the Hall of the Mountain King' NERO AND THE GLADIATORS
'Frightened City' THE SHADOWS
'Willie and the Hand Jive' CLIFF RICHARD AND THE SHADOWS
'Quartermaster's Stores' THE SHADOWS
'Please Don't Tease, CLIFF RICHARD AND THE SHADOWS
'The Young Ones' CLIFF RICHARD AND THE SHADOWS
'Diamonds' JET HARRIS AND TONY MEEHAN
'Wonderful Land' THE SHADOWS
'Post World War 2 Blues' AL STEWART
'Return to Sender' ELVIS PRESLEY
'The Uncle Willie' ZOOT MONEY
'Zoot's Suite' ZOOT MONEY
'So Long Little Girl' THE DICTATORS WITH TONY AND HOWARD
'If You Gotta Make a Fool of Somebody' JAMES RAY
'Elvaston Place' AL STEWART
'The News from Spain' AL STEWART
'In the Court of the Crimson King' KING CRIMSON
'Telstar' THE TORNADOS
'Little Sue' DOWLAND BROTHERS
'Big Big Fella' DOWLAND BROTHERS
'Breakups' DOWLAND BROTHERS
'All My Loving' THE BEATLES/DOWLAND BROTHERS
'She Loves You' THE BEATLES
'I Want To Hold Your Hand' THE BEATLES
'Bye Bye Love' EVERLY BROTHERS
'All I Have To Do Is Dream EVERLY BROTHERS
'Cathy's Clown' EVERLY BROTHERS
'House of the Rising Sun' ANIMALS/BOB DYLAN
'Come On' THE ROLLING STONES
'I Wanna Be Your Man' THE BEATLES/THE ROLLING STONES
'What Kind of Fool Am I' ANTHONY NEWLEY
'Bring it to Jerome' BO DIDDLEY
'Till I Kissed You' EVERLY BROTHERS
'Good Timin'' JIMMY JONES
'Wipe Out' THE SURFARIS
'Pretty Golden Hair' AL STEWART
'How Wonderful You Are' GORDON HASKELL
'Roll Over Beethoven' THE BEATLES
'From Me To You' THE BEATLES

'Thank You Girl' THE BEATLES
'Chains' THE BEATLES
'A Taste of Honey' THE BEATLES
'I Saw Her Standing There' THE BEATLES
'Baby It's You' THE BEATLES
'Boys' THE BEATLES
'Will You Still Love Me Tomorrow' THE SHIRELLES
'Twist and Shout' THE BEATLES
'P.S. I Love You' THE BEATLES
'Hey! Baby' BRUCE CHANNEL
'Shazam' DUANE EDDY
'The Cruel Sea' THE DAKOTAS
'Peggy Sue' BUDDY HOLLY
'Norwegian Wood' THE BEATLES
'Funny Old World' JOHN ROSTILL
'Don't Bother Me' THE BEATLES
'Something' THE BEATLES
'Here Comes The Sun' THE BEATLES
'While My Guitar Gently Weeps' THE BEATLES
'It Won't Be Long' THE BEATLES
'Blowin' in the Wind' BOB DYLAN
'Masters of War' BOB DYLAN
'Chimes of Freedom' BOB DYLAN
'Gates of Eden' BOB DYLAN
'Baby Let Me Take You Home' ANIMALS
'Baby Let Me Follow You Down' BOB DYLAN
'Freight Train Blues' BOB DYLAN
'I'm a Hog for You Baby' THE COASTERS
'Don't Think Twice, It's All Right' BOB DYLAN
'Walk on the Wild Side' JIMMY SMITH
'Can't Buy Me Love' THE BEATLES
'Walking the Dog' RUFUS THOMAS
'Do the Dog' GEORGIE FAME
'I Can't Explain' THE WHO
'Whatca Gonna Do About It' THE SMALL FACES
'Land of a Thousand Dances' THE ACTION
'Lonely Doll' ANN SIDNEY
'The Times They Are A-Changin'' BOB DYLAN
'The Wizard' MARC BOLAN
'Language School' TOURS

'We Gotta Get Out Of This Place' THE ANIMALS
'The Elf' AL STEWART
'Yeh Yeh' GEORGIE FAME
'Go Now' THE MOODY BLUES
'Satisfaction' THE ROLLING STONES
'The Last Time' THE ROLLING STONES
'Little Red Rooster' THE ROLLING STONES
'It's All Over Now' THE ROLLING STONES
'Around and Around' CHUCK BERRY
'It's Alright, Ma' BOB DYLAN
'Flowers Never Bend With The Rainfall' PAUL SIMON
'Homeward Bound' PAUL SIMON
'Shakin' All Over' JOHNNY KIDD AND THE PIRATES
'Move It' CLIFF RICHARD AND THE DRIFTERS
'Blues Run The Game' JACKSON C. FRANK
'Angie' DAVY GRAHAM/BERT JANSCH
'Help' THE BEATLES
'Yesterday' THE BEATLES
'Ticket To Ride' THE BEATLES
'Michelle' THE BEATLES
'In My Life' THE BEATLES
'Nowhere Man' THE BEATLES
'Sunny Afternoon' THE KINKS
'Daydream' THE LOVIN' SPOONFUL
'Summer in the City' THE LOVIN' SPOONFUL
'Monday, Monday' MAMAS AND PAPAS
'Wild Thing' THE TROGGS
'Paint It Black' THE ROLLING STONES
'Paperback Writer' THE BEATLES
'Eleanor Rigby' THE BEATLES
'Yellow Submarine' THE BEATLES
'River Deep and Mountain High' IKE AND TINA TURNER
'Bus Stop' THE HOLLIES
'God Only Knows' THE BEACH BOYS
'Here, There and Everywhere' THE BEATLES
'For No One' THE BEATLES
'Tomorrow Never Knows' THE BEATLES
'America' THE NICE
'Albatross' FLEETWOOD MAC
'Reach Out I'll Be There' FOUR TOPS

'Strawberry Fields Forever' THE BEATLES
'Penny Lane' THE BEATLES
'Blackberry Way' THE MOVE
'All You Need Is Love' THE BEATLES
'Arnold Layne' PINK FLOYD
'See Emily Play' PINK FLOYD
'Interstellar Overdrive' PINK FLOYD
'Purple Haze' JIMI HENDRIX
'Hey Joe' JIMI HENDRIX
'The Wind Cries Mary' JIMI HENDRIX
'Millie Brown' AL STEWART
'Modern Times' AL STEWART
'Life and Life Only' AL STEWART
'Delia's Gone' AL STEWART
'Roads to Moscow' AL STEWART
'Year of the Cat' AL STEWART
'You've Lost That Lovin' Feelin'' THE RIGHTEOUS BROTHERS
'James Bond Theme' JOHN BARRY
'What Do You Want' ADAM FAITH
'Eight Days A Week' THE BEATLES
'Glad All Over' DAVE CLARK 5
'From Russia With Love' MATT MONRO
'Live and Let Die' WINGS
'Way Back in the 1960's' INCREDIBLE STRING BAND
'Bedsitter Images' AL STEWART/MARC ALMOND
'Reminiscing' BUDDY HOLLY
'Teach You To Rock' TONY CROMBIE
'It's Not Unusual' TOM JONES
'Maybe I'm Amazed' PAUL McCARTNEY
'Say You Don't Mind' COLIN BLUNSTONE
'Seaside Woman' SUZI AND THE REDSTRIPES

In *2Stoned* Andrew Loog Oldham described 'The Last Time' by the Rolling Stones as a 'Forever' record. I thought you might like to know in an email to me a year or two ago he also called Al's 'Year of the Cat' a 'Forever' record.

LPs

It Should've Been Me ZOOT MONEY'S BIG ROLL BAND
Love Chronicles AL STEWART
I Advanced Masked ANDY SUMMERS AND ROBERT FRIPP
Taking Liberties ELVIS COSTELLO
Sgt. Pepper's Lonely Hearts Club Band THE BEATLES
The Beatles ('The White Album') THE BEATLES
Little Earthquakes TORI AMOS
Last Days of the Century AL STEWART
In the Court of the Crimson King KING CRIMSON
The Cheerful Insanity of Giles, Giles and Fripp GILES, GILES AND FRIPP
With The Beatles THE BEATLES
Stop The World I Want To Get Off ANTHONY NEWLEY
Year of the Cat AL STEWART
Bedsitter Images AL STEWART
Harry's Bar GORDON HASKELL
Sail In My Boat GORDON HASKELL
Please Please Me THE BEATLES
Revolver THE BEATLES
Abbey Road THE BEATLES
Rubber Soul THE BEATLES
Hard Day's Night THE BEATLES
The Freewheelin' Bob Dylan BOB DYLAN
Quadrophenia THE WHO
Parallel Lines BLONDIE
Bringing It All Back Home BOB DYLAN
Highway 61 Revisited BOB DYLAN
Another Side of Bob Dylan BOB DYLAN
The Paul Simon Songbook PAUL SIMON
Jackson C. Frank JACKSON C. FRANK
Help! THE BEATLES
PM THE NITE PEOPLE
The Huge World of Emily Small THE PICADILLY LINE
The Kick Inside KATE BUSH
The Rolling Stones No.2 THE ROLLING STONES
Songs of Leonard Cohen LEONARD COHEN
In My Life JUDY COLLINS
The Piper at the Gates of Dawn PINK FLOYD
Are You Experienced THE JIMI HENDRIX EXPERIENCE

Down in the Cellar AL STEWART
Modern Times AL STEWART
Past, Present and Future AL STEWART
Beat Girl JOHN BARRY WITH ADAM FAITH
5,000 Spirits or the Layers of the Onion THE INCREDIBLE STRING BAND
To Whom It May Concern AL STEWART
Stardom Road MARC ALMOND
The Starving Moon THE EUROPA STRING CHOIR
McCartney PAUL McCARTNEY
Zero She Flies AL STEWART

Acknowledgements

I would like to thank all the many people who, directly or indirectly, informed, encouraged, and/or inhabited *Bournemouth A Go! Go!*

Abi Kremer – for never forgetting to remind me to write this book

Daniel Kremer – for allowing his Dad to tell him so many, many times of those 60s days when I met the Beatles

Al Stewart – for always being an echo to these memories

John, Paul, George and Ringo – for sharing a few moments of Beatles magic with me

Nev Judd – who first met me long ago when taking the first steps to writing his book and whose sustained friendship includes videoing my 1980s

Martin Morris – for support and understanding, here, there and everywhere

Martin Bloomberg – for always saying yes on days obscured by clouds

Andrew Loog Oldham – for making the 60s the 60s and writing his memoirs

Brian Epstein – for saying goodbye to RADA and hello to the Cavern

George Martin – for saying "Yes Mr. Epstein, I do like your boys" (or words to that effect)

Jack Good –*Oh Boy* indeed

Manfred Mann – for the Mann-Hugg Blues Brothers (featuring Paul Jones)

Alan Azern – for Le Disque a Go Go

Anthony Newley – for being an idol on parade

Robert Freeman – for bringing his camera to the Palace Court Hotel

The Shadows – who, along with Sammy 'Move It' Samwell, proved all those years ago that England was not Pop World's 51st state of America

Les Paul and Leo Fender – without whom the electrifying sounds of the sixties would have had no electricity

Nick Churchill – for sharing the belief that the Beatles' Bournemouth stories should be told

Mark Lewisohn – for allowing me to quote him from our correspondence and using his encyclopaedic Beatles knowledge to write the history they deserve

Peter Davies – who, when not writing his own books, enjoys a John Lennon story almost as much as seeing Arsenal score goals

Jane Martin – for enthusiastically shaping the words of this book

Mark Paytress – for making the journey from schoolboy Bus Stop Records customer to respected Rock writer and reviewer

Bus Stop Records customers – for buying a record, taking it home, placing it on a turntable, then finding their day had become a little better

John Ralph – whose deep appreciation of music led him to my shop long ago, and who then patiently waited for me to respond to his perennial suggestion: "You should write a book about the Bournemouth 60s scene"

Although not directly imported into this book the thoughts and words of many writers read by me either in the sixties, or in more recent years looking back to that time, have, at least subconsciously, played their part in my sixties recollections. So, if you feel so inclined may I recommend you try the following:

Anything by Mark Lewisohn, *Revolt Into Style* by George Melly, *Love Me Do* by Michael Braun, *Revolution in the Head* by Ian MacDonald, *Big Beat Scene* by Royston Ellis, *You Don't Have To Say You Love Me* by Simon Napier-Bell, *Shout!* and *John Lennon: The Life* by Philip Norman, and of course *Stoned* and *2Stoned* by Andrew Loog Oldham.

Photographs copyright

Manfred Mann with the Crystals © Colin Saunders
Dowland Brothers © Dowland Brothers
Dave La Kaz and the G-Men © Neville Judd
Pavilion crowd scene photos (2) © Dave Robinson
Other photographs © Jon Kremer

Song lyrics copyright

Lyrics quoted in part from the following songs;

'Love Chronicles' © Gwyneth Music
'Cock-A-Hoop' © Francis, Day and Hunter
'Post World War Two Blues' © Gwyneth Music
'Millie Brown' © Al Stewart/Miramar Recordings
'Modern Times' © Gwyneth Music/Dick James Music
'Life and Life Only' © Gwyneth Music

Beatles Monthly cover © Beat Publications Limited

Book cover:
Design: A&D Design
Photo: Monty Kremer

Contact email address: bournemouthagogo@gmail.com

About the Author

Born in London. Jon has lived in the Bournemouth area since his teenage years began, coinciding with the start of the Sixties. For over 40 years he owned Bus Stop Records, Bournemouth's original vintage vinyl shop and experienced many aspects of the music industry through a long-standing friendship with the singer-songwriter Al Stewart.

Married to artist Abi Kremer, with a son, Daniel, who along with Abi shares his love of 60s music.

Photo: Richard Jeffery

Index

A

B

C

D

E

F

G

H

I

J

K

L

M

N

O

P

Q

R

S

T

V

W

Y

Z

Jon Kremer and Al Stewart in the shadow of the 1960s